To Terry
Hope you enjoy it.

Best wishes
o
FuNKY Si
X

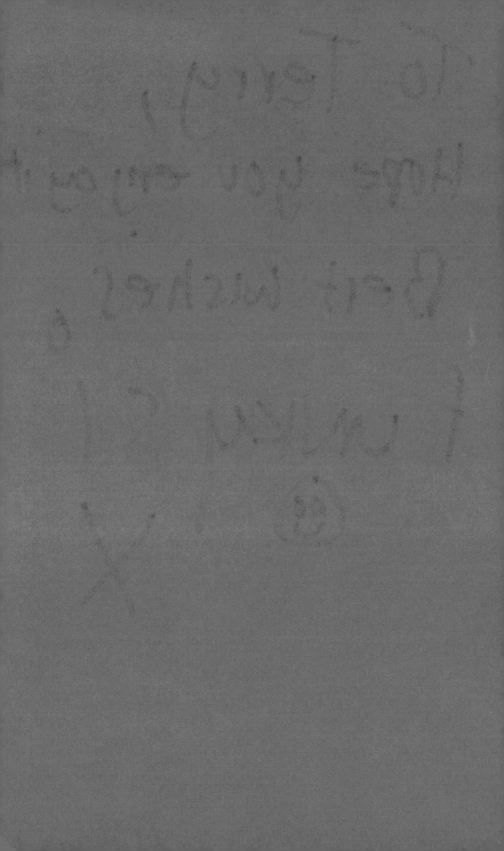

YOU CAN DRUM BUT YOU CAN'T HIDE

SIMON WOLSTENCROFT

strata books

A catalogue record for this book is available from the British Library.

ISBN 978 0 9573690 7 8 (PB)
ISBN 978 0 9573690 6 1 (EB)

Printed and bound in the UK by TJ International, Padstow, Cornwall.

Cover design by Gavin Wallace
gavinwallacephotography.co.uk

Cover photo by Steve Devine 2014

Strata Entertainment Ltd
Anwoth House, 41 Cockhill,
Trowbridge, BA14 9BG.

www.stratabooks co.uk

Contents

ACT II

ACT III

Acknowledgements

Prologue

In a quiet suburban bar he begins to open up.

Perhaps two dozen people have watched the covers band we play in, most invited by band members.

We break down the equipment and drink the lager we believe we deserve as friends wander over.

He is from these parts, and at ease with the patrons. He is, in truth, at ease with most. Congenial, low-key, with an infectious grin and a gentle drawl that suggests time served in the Republic of Mancunia.

His playing is, of course, exemplary. Tight and distinctive without being showy - as true to the original as he can be.

Funky Si.

'Great drumming,' someone says. 'Class.'

They pull up stools and I introduce Si, mentioning that he was a professional drummer for fifteen years.

'What's the biggest gig you ever played?' one asks.

I think, for a moment, that this is a touch unfair - a challenge. Is this how to judge the man? But I quieten the cynic, convinced that the question is innocent, reflexive.

Si tilts his head as his eyes wander up and to the left, as if retrieving an old film from a dusty box in the attic.

When he answers, it is matter of factly.

'Hundred thousand people?' he offers. 'Fuji Festival.'

We want to know more.

How the man got to that place ... and to this place.

Quietly, he mentions drumming with Ian Brown and how he had been in a band with Ian and John Squire at school. People laugh and say

Prologue

What? You could have been in The Stone Roses?

He smiles, and adds that he once turned down The Smiths.

We shake our heads and laugh some more. The banter flies: some say slitting wrists, some say dodging bullets, the old Pete-Best-of-Manchester chestnut.

Si has heard it all before. A grin crosses his face anew. Contagious. We all grin too. He laughs. We all laugh. There is more. Highs and lows and hi-jinx … we ask for an encore.

Years later, he tells me he wants to get it all down. Write a memoir. Before he forgets. Put it down for posterity before drugs, and time, catch up and cloud his brain in a cacophony of drums and crashing cymbals, and it becomes harder and harder to make out.

So, from that embryo, this is his story. Amusing and cautionary. Tackling the extraordinary and the day-to-day.

A shrug, over what might have been and what was.

From the beginning, through a century half-lived.

Simon Wolstencroft.

Stuart Bisson-Foster
2014

For Emily

ACT I

1

The Doctor's Son

I was born at home in my parents' bedroom during the coldest month of the twentieth century - January 1963 - in the parish of Ringway, three miles from Manchester Airport. It was the swinging sixties and the beginning of the jet age.

My dad, Peter, who was a GP, bought our four-bed detached with my mother, Pat, who he had met at a medical dance in Sheffield, where my mum qualified as a state registered nurse.

Simon Wolstencroft: the doctor's son.

I suppose, though I didn't know it at the time, my elder sister Jane and I were lucky to have had a lot of advantages in life, as we grew up happily in the affluent commuter belt.

Jane now has a successful career in HR after going down the university route. Me, well, the music got in my blood, and though it wasn't as rewarding financially, I did what I loved - I travelled the world playing drums.

Anyway, back to the beginning...

My earliest memory of Three Gates, as our house was known - my earliest memory of anything, actually - was of peering down through the slats of the landing balcony as my dad's patients sat in the hallway, waiting to be called into his surgery. Who were these people in the house? As the practice grew in the early seventies, he moved to a health centre in Sale Moor.

As part of his surgery, Dad was often on duty as an emergency doctor at the weekend. He used to take me in his Vauxhall Victor on his rounds in Sale and Wythenshawe. While he tended to his patients I would sit in the Vauxhall and tune in to pop stations and the Sunday evening chart show, dialling in the frequency on the crackling wireless when glam rock was king.

I really got my love of music from Mum who was always playing vinyl records on a wooden radiogram the size of a bathtub. The thing looked like it was made of teak and sat in the dining room at the front of the house and Mum played tunes whilst she was doing housework or cooking. Once, when I got home from school I found my mum and her sister, Catherine, both dancing to Nancy Sinatra's 'These Boots Are Made for Walkin' *on the dining room table!*

This generally stopped before Dad got back from work at about six thirty in the evening ready for his tea. Although he had a mischievous streak, Dad was a man of his time and didn't want any part of the swinging sixties or pop music.

The first thing he would do when he got in was pour himself a large whisky, then plonk himself down in his favourite armchair in front of the TV in the lounge, worn out from his efforts. Unless it was summer - then he seemed to mow the lawn almost constantly.

Jane would be at her homework while mum cleared up and got ready for the next day.

Meanwhile, I'd be in the dining room in front of the record player listening to Motown, Northern soul, and Rolling Stones 7-inch singles. I used to have the tone knob turned right down to ensure maximum bass sound as I learned the drum parts.

Our family was fortunate enough to go on foreign holidays to sunnier climes. We would often board a Dan-Air Comet jetliner from Ringway Airport to Spain or Portugal.

It was on one such holiday that I first sat on a drum kit - in a hotel bar in Estoril before the cabaret band started up one Saturday night in 1971.

I just loved the look of the silver sparkle kit that the drummer was using and the tight crack of the snare drum that cut through everything - the cheesy keyboards, the approximated bass lines. That was it. Eight years old - I was hooked.

When I got home, I started playing biscuit tins and paint pots with Mum's thickest knitting needles along to the new bands on the scene like T.Rex and David Bowie, and my favourite at the time, glam rock band, Sweet. I had all the Sweet singles and was made up when my mum bought me my first ever album: *Sweet Fanny Adams*. The single 'Wig-Wam Bam' was a particular favourite of mine as was their number one smash

'Blockbuster' with its air raid siren intro and kettledrum driven middle eight.

I would copy all the drummers who played on Thursday night's *Top of the Pops*. They were miming, but though you'd get the odd joker messing around, they generally played faithfully to the record. I would practise twizzling the drum sticks in my fingers. Sweet seemed to be on the show nearly every week along with T.Rex, Wizzard, and Slade. It was essential viewing all through my childhood.

It was all we talked about in the school playground the next morning. There were only three channels to talk about to be fair.

My first foray into a 'band' was when I started a little group with my next door neighbours, Keith and Stuart Murray, who were my age and owned an old acoustic guitar. We used to thrash out half a dozen ditties stood on top of their bunk bed with me playing on the old biscuit tins. I filled one of them with gravel to get a snare type sound. We didn't get any gigs.

We were calling ourselves the 'BG Boys' after The Bee Gees who were massive back then. This, along with the music from some of the TV shows, like *Starsky and Hutch* or the film *Shaft*, instilled my love of the 'funk sound' which later came through in my playing and led to the nickname 'Funky Si'.

Funk is a feeling, it's about what you don't play, not what you do play. About the space in-between the beat.

One January, all the family went to the sales in town where I stared at a little drum kit in the window of the Lewis's department store for ages, thinking, it's my birthday soon. But no amount of hinting and puppy dog eyes got the message across. I got a remote control Stuka dive-bomber instead, and my dad nearly took the top of someone's head off with it, in Melrose Park as he lost control of the plane.

I got my first experience of show business at the circus in Wythenshawe Park aged ten. A clown act was in full farce when they announced, 'We're looking for a skinhead to help us with our next trick.' I mean, I had short hair and a denim jacket but I was only ten. They made a beeline for me, probably because I was right near the front. I was petrified as they dragged me up and made a show of putting out a safety net flat on the sawdust floor. I was thrown from clown to clown, balancing on their shoulders, feeling less than safe above their comedy health and safety show. They wouldn't be the last clowns I worked with.

While I was still bashing away on the biscuit tins, at some point, my dad bought a baby grand piano which stood proudly in the lounge. He could read sheet music and occasionally played classical pieces, which was his idea of music. Proper music.

Jane started to have lessons once a week and reached a respectable grade a few years later. Meanwhile, I would bang out bass lines on the lower end of the piano, especially the black keys, whilst pressing down on the sustain pedal. Sometimes at the same time as Jane was practising a piece. This really annoyed her, as you can imagine. We did generally get on well, though.

We had a great upbringing, some real luxuries, especially in that era. My mum kept a couple of horses in a field near the hospital, though I soon gave up riding after her palomino, Dominique, bolted and threw me off into a barbed wire fence. My dad bought me a little rowing boat that I named *Neptune (Ruler of the Sea)*, which Jane and I would row sedately, up and down the canal, by Ye Olde No. 3 in Lymm. We also had two cars, took regular trips abroad, and we often ate in restaurants.

Mainly though, I led a normal happy life playing football with my mates from the estate at the back of our house. I played football for Bowdon Rangers and started to watch Altrincham Football Club on Monday nights. Later, after starting secondary school I would get the bus on my own and pay my three quid to watch Manchester United in the Stretford End paddock.

But that was later. Before then I had unknowingly made a significant decision.

After passing the eleven-plus exam, I decided to go to Altrincham Grammar School rather than North Cestrian. My decision was based on two things: my mate Dan Weaver from junior school was going, and, according to the bumph, AGS had better sporting facilities.

The school was only a fifteen-minute bike ride away so I cycled off, drowning in my new green blazer to start a new chapter in my life.

2

Red Boots, Red Arses, Red Alert

During the first few months of first year I hung around with Dan Weaver most of the time. He was the only person I knew. His mum was a journalist and anchorwoman on Granada TV. They lived in a beautiful house overlooking Springbank Park just near the school. Dan had two brothers and a sister, and I remember his elder brother Gavin was particularly musical. I used to go back for tea. We'd sit in the attic room talking about girls and music.

I soon become aware of one Ian George Brown, who was also in my form. Ian would become well known in our year in fact, as he had an uncanny ability to mimic the teachers' voices and mannerisms that got the whole class roaring with laughter before the start of each lesson. Even at that age, I found him engaging.

We had the same haircut, spiky on top and longer on the sides. Ian had a bit of the rebel in him. I think I connected with that. I would often spot him practising karate stances and moves, which impressed me as I had recently watched the film *Enter the Dragon* starring Bruce Lee. Perhaps inspired by this, I ended up learning judo, though I only got to yellow belt.

Ian asked me where I had got my cherry red Doc Martens from, as he wanted some too. That was the fashion: Dr Martens, brogues, Oxford bags with three or five button waistbands, depending on how cool you were. Blakey's segs (metal sole protectors) banged into the heels, with your dad's hammer, making a racket down the corridor.

I liked Ian's impressions and his karate. He liked my boots. I guess when you're a kid that will do. We were mates.

As a couple of would-be martial artists, Ian and I both got involved in a few scraps in the playground during our time in school. Whilst it was mainly messing about, I do remember him using his training once on a guy who was winding him up in the chemistry lab. He suddenly unleashed a surprisingly adept flurry of punches and high kicks. We were all a bit startled. Shit. We hadn't really expected anything expert. What was *that*? Ian got detention anyway.

Most of us younger lads began getting into the kung fu films. I remember going to watch another violent film *Rollerball*, starring James Caan, at Altrincham pictures. It seems strange looking back but it particularly made an impression on me. I spent many an hour during lessons sketching scenes from the film when I should have been studying hard, like my sister.

It was a violent time. Football hooligans on the terraces knocking ten bells of crap out of each other. Labour relations were confrontational. The recipe for riots was brewing.

Still, we were out in the suburbs, and for a bit of cash Ian and I did some caddying on a Saturday morning at Dunham Forest Golf Club. They paid £1.80 for a round. You used to have to turn up and wait outside a stable building that functioned as a greenkeeper's shed. Eventually, an old guy with a flat cap who reminded me of Steptoe wandered out and looked you up and down and made his choices from the line-up. If you didn't get picked, you had to go home disappointed and tell your mum you weren't earning anything that morning. I think, unfortunately, it was a matter of whether your face fitted.

Ian used to laugh about carrying clubs for a retired army major whose drivers had characters from *The Muppets* for covers.

'Pass me Miss Piggy,' he would demand in clipped tones, or 'let's see what Animal can do today shall we?'

We'd knock off for the day caddying, head down to the tip on Sinderland Road, salvaging pram wheels and bits of wood to make go-karts and race them down the hill next to Three Gates. I painted mine red and named it 'Caroline' after a stable lass I had taken a shine to.

John Squire was a quieter lad who Ian seemed to know, and while we were in the same class, I didn't immediately get to know him. He was the opposite of Ian. While we knocked about a fair bit, and we became good mates, I suppose I still don't know him.

Our first shared experience was when my black Adidas holdall went missing from our classroom one day. The teacher came in in his black gown, very thick glasses, and interrogated every one of my fellow class-mates individually before the start of the school day.

'Was it you Astley?'

'No sir!'

'Was it you Critchley?'

'No sir!'

Down the line this went, twenty odd times, and because our teacher hadn't had time to put his false teeth in, the lads were struggling to control themselves at his spitting, gurning drawl.

By the time the teacher asked a bemused Squire, 'Was it you Squire?' John just exploded with laughter - I think it was Ian's impressions too - and the whole class followed before order was finally restored. I knew John well enough by then to know he'd not nicked it - it wasn't his style - but I never did find out who the culprit was.

At the end of the year, John and I found ourselves stood waiting together outside the deputy head's office to each receive six of the best with a split bamboo cane for drawing on our desks with Magic Marker pens. We didn't have to pull our kecks down thank God, but it did hurt I can tell you that.

This was probably the start of my friendship with John, chatting as we had to stay behind after school and get to work with some sandpaper.

John excelled in art class after being allowed to drop sports. He and I were in the Latin set (Ian did woodwork). We both found Latin very tedious and spent most of the lesson sat at the back drawing cartoons in our exercise books.

Some of his drawings looked like Leonardo da Vinci's futuristic designs for helicopters. I drew a lot of drum kits and different types of aircraft which always held a fascination with me.

Ian's mimicking continued, more and more confident, marching into the classroom pretending to be the teacher, writing on the board saying, right, homework assignment, make sure you watch the Pistols on *Top of the Pops* tonight seven thirty or some such. He could send up all the staff, including Fred Talbot (later a TV weatherman) who taught us biology and Mr Black our English teacher. Me and Ian went on a camping trip in Scotland with Fred one year, with about 10 other lads. We walked for miles in the freezing cold, snow pelting down, and the main thing I remember was sitting by a roaring log fire in a remote pub and having the best burger and chips I ever tasted. Or the most gratefully received anyway.

One of Ian's stand-up routines got a bit out of hand, just before a French lesson, when he got most of the class stamping their feet to a 4/4 beat on the room's parquet floor for what seemed like ages. Even the swots. It sounded like the marching intro on the Pistols' track 'Holidays in the Sun'. The French teacher, who was a very timid kind of person, finally entered the classroom to a wave of jeering and a hail of scrunched up balls of paper. He nearly had a breakdown as he tried meekly to control us. He fled, in tears, while we congratulated ourselves on riling him, before our form tutor, who we nicknamed 'Killer,' burst into the room after hearing the disorder, which was at odds with a polite grammar school.

There was no investigation. He made straight for Ian and dragged him out of the classroom. I looked out and saw Killer backing Ian against the tiled wall, digging him in the stomach as he tried to force a confession from Ian for starting the commotion.

'It was you Brown, admit it. It was you, wasn't it?'

Ian denied it.

I didn't like Killer. Despite him being my form tutor, the only time he talked to me was the night after my appearance (TV debut!) on BBC2's *The Money Programme*. My dentist had been filmed by a TV crew working on my teeth whilst he talked to the camera about NHS charges. Killer slid up to me the next morning and said 'I saw you on telly last night,' to which I just sort of smiled and replied 'Oh.' I couldn't think of anything to say. I'd never spoken to him before and perhaps I thought of him as the enemy. While he never treated me particularly badly I thought his idea of justice was well over-the-top.

When it came to corporal punishment, however, our geography teacher was in a different league. He had dead eyes, reminded me of a shark, and kept a broken desk at the front, which, when you lifted the lid up, had a hole in it. He would make unruly pupils stick their heads through, to humiliate them, like medieval stocks. This punishment could sometimes last for the whole hour lesson if you misbehaved early enough. He used to use a filthy white plimsoll to maximum effect on your arse, depending on what mood he was in, and was a dead shot throwing blackboard dusters from his desk on the raised plinth.

He only ever caught me out once. In a classic bit of schoolboy tomfoolery, I was using an empty Bic biro as a pea-shooter, firing bits of chewed up paper balls into a neat grouping on the ceiling above my desk. Spotting this, he stormed over and grabbed the whole set of brand new felt-tip pens my mum had bought and snapped them one by one until the last pen was destroyed. I was a bit freaked out as he cracked them, leaving shards of splintered plastic all over me and the desk.

He was sacked a few years later for smashing a chair over a pupil's back in a rage too far.

Whilst I can't condone some of the disciplining that went on back then - it would be unheard of today - I suppose, like a lot of schoolboys, we were a bit anarchic.

Ian and I used to go down to the Altrincham Ice Rink where gangs from all over Manchester would come down to cop off, skate to David Bowie's 'Sound and Vision' and kick someone's head in.

There was a new music feeding this rebelliousness that Ian, John and I would bond over: punk rock. It exploded into our lives after the Sex Pistols' notorious interview on Bill Grundy's TV show, *Today*.

While Ian was more of a Pistols fan, John and I favoured The Clash. We picked up the first Clash album on its release and buzzed about each track. It was so fresh and energetic. It swept aside all the glam rock and dull prog rock in my mind. There were basically two camps: punk and prog, and you were either one or the other.

Although we used to live about three miles apart, John and I began to meet up to cycle to school together in the mornings on our matching Carlton racing bikes. We would hang out at his mum's place or in Ian's house listening to the Sex Pistols album, *Nevermind the Bollocks*. The three of us made a special trip into Manchester on the 263 bus to purchase it on the day of its release.

A big musical influence closer to home in those days was a classmate named Andy Wake who brought to our attention the latest punk releases and new bands. As a matter of fact, he was the first person to introduce me to Mark E Smith and his band The Fall who by that time had released a clutch of well-received singles.

Wake listened to John Peel on Radio 1 fanatically and turned us on to Manchester punk band Buzzcocks whose EP *Spiral Scratch* I thought was superb. He would bring the latest 7-inch singles he had bought to school, just to show them off to us but we could only look, not touch, as he had a Gollumesque fervour about guarding his precious singles. Andy lived just opposite the Bowdon Vale Club, a village hall that would become locally famous as a venue where Joy Division played one of their early gigs. I didn't go as the fact is I wasn't really a fan.

But the whole DIY ethic that the punk movement was preaching appealed to our sensibilities. You could feel something big happening and we wanted to be part of it.

John's dad Tom was an engineer in Trafford Park and in his spare time had built his son a tiny little amplifier so he could practise playing on his new electric guitar in his box room on Sylvan Avenue in Timperley, a few doors down from Ian's. He took a couple of guitar lessons from an elderly man called Mr Morley, after spotting a postcard in the post office offering his services. I went with John once with a bass guitar, from Woolworth's. Mr Morley had wild hair, high-waisted trousers, and lived in a house that didn't look like it had been decorated since the fifties. John quit after a few lessons because he was sick of playing 'Hickory Dickory Dock' as Mr Morley accompanied on piano. John didn't want to learn nursery rhymes. He wanted to be in a punk band. So he taught himself. He started to learn all the guitar parts on The Clash's first album as well as tracks by the Pistols, Generation X, and Slaughter & the Dogs.

Ian started to learn the bass guitar after I had sold him mine. I got bored of playing it on my own. I got back on the drums and stuck with it thereafter (give or take a bit of keyboard noodling now and again). For me, I always felt a lot more comfortable playing with other musicians. It's much more fun and you learn the vital art of timing. When you get that moment when you're all on the same wavelength, you look around grinning at each other, I know it sounds a bit hippyish, but it's the closest thing I know to a spiritual experience.

I began saving my wages from my part-time job at a greengrocer in Altrincham. I had lost interest in playing football by now as punk and hanging around with mates were my new pastimes. I would work in the shop on Railway Street at every available opportunity saving for a decent set of cymbals.

I'm not proud to admit that I acquired the basis of my first drum kit by less earnest means. I nicked it.

In 1979, I asked the music teacher if I could take the dust covered Olympic three-piece drum kit home for summer holidays. It had been sitting neglected, on top of a load of storage cupboards in the Portakabin that housed the music room, untouched for two years at least. My request was refused.

10

So, after waiting a few days, I roped John into helping me liberate the little jazz kit. We put it in black bin liners and moved the kit in two trips to the top of the school playing fields to an out of bounds area known as The Swamp where I hid it in some thickets. I waited a while to see if there was any furore about the missing kit. Nothing seemed to be said.

I waited a bit more.

With no hunt for the kit under way at the school we moved it to my house. I can't remember what story I concocted to justify the kit's existence at home, but nobody at the school seemed to know or care what had happened to it. This was the kit I would use in the early days of The Patrol, until my mum bought me a blue Beverley, that she had spotted advertised for sale on a postcard in a post office window.

We bought a cheap microphone from electronic shop Tandy and Ian plugged his bass into the ancient TVM amplifier we had acquired, in what seemed a great stroke of fortune, from another school. That summer, me and John were mooching around on our bikes one evening when we noticed a smashed window in the school's gym, just big enough to climb through. It looked like someone had thrown a medicine ball through it. We had a nosey and couldn't believe our luck when we saw a PA set up on the gym floor below. I carefully climbed in and passed the thing out to John - there was still jagged glass in the window. And the amp was heavy, 30 kilos I'd say. It was hard work. We couldn't carry it back to my mum and dad's so we stashed it in the school grounds under a manhole covering a storm drain. The speakers were too big and screwed to the walls so we left them.

We weren't naturally thieves but with the window being already smashed in, it didn't seem to make the crime as serious in our minds, and we reasoned that if we didn't take the amp, someone else would. Also, I suppose we thought it was cool because the Pistols had nicked a lot of their equipment when they started out and we weren't able to afford a PA or a drum kit. Well, my dad probably could have, but he wasn't likely to buy one for me - he wanted me to knuckle down, stop messing around.

That served us well for a couple of years before finally exploding after we started plugging more and more stuff into it once Andy Couzens had joined the line-up. It ended up being ceremoniously thrown into the Bridgewater Canal at the back of Ian and John's houses and sank to the bottom, where it probably lies to this day.

In the back bedroom of my house on Grove Lane, where on a clear summer evening you could see Winter Hill twenty odd miles in the distance, the three of us began to work as a group for the first time using The Clash as a template. We were together after school a lot by now, listening to as much new music as we could. Bands like The Slits, Siouxsie and the Banshees, and Ramones. For a couple of rehearsals we called ourselves Red Alert. Me on drums, John on guitar, Ian playing bass and singing. Thursday night at my house became practice night as my dad was out playing snooker and my mum had gone back to work as a night nurse at Wythenshawe hospital. We practised until my dad came home after the snooker.

I don't think he was too pleased about the noise we were making even though the house was detached and he wanted to know where the red glitter drum kit had come from (the amplifier was less conspicuous). As a result, we relocated to Ian's garage until one day as he was thrashing about on the three-piece, he saw the outline of a helmet-wearing copper through the frosted glass in the door on the side of the garage. He was told to stop immediately as there had been a few complaints from his neighbours. That summer we started to rehearse above a pub called the Unicorn in Altrincham.

My dad was happy to have us rehearsing elsewhere. He only liked classical music and would constantly air his negative comments about most of the bands on *Top of the Pops* as I was trying to watch. It was the usual stuff: 'I can't hear a word he's singing' or, 'Just look at that ridiculous hair cut the singer's got.' Or the classic, 'It's much too loud.' That was the gist of his feedback when he saw me play live for the first time with The Fall about 10 years later, 'It's much too loud.'

Back in the last couple of years at Altrincham Grammar, my dad was seriously worried about my academic future because I always went straight out after school before he returned from work and he never saw me doing any homework, unlike my sister. In fact, I would go as far to say he was horrified.

John, Ian and I only ended up with a handful of O levels. I'll tell you why.

3

You Won't Be Told

Starting sometime in 1977, but in earnest during 78/79, I began going out more and more, and studying less and less. And to be honest there wasn't a time when I could have been described as a keen student.

I remember my dad shaking his head a lot in those days at the road I seemed to be headed down, going, 'Simon. You won't be told. You *just won't* be told.'

We started dating girls from Delahays Road School and would walk the streets at night during the weekends, going from one house party to another in the Sale and Brooklands area.

We started going to pubs. Back then you could get into a lot of places at 15 or 16 - there were no IDs and bouncers and all of that. We started hanging out in a pub in Brooklands called The Vine. I remember Ian got barred from there for something or other and, ludicrously, tried to come back in wearing a balaclava. It didn't prove an effective disguise.

The landlord spotted him straight away.

'YOU! OUT!'

A weird thing happened one night en route to The Vine: me, John and Ian were strolling along next to Brooklands Road train station when a black Jaguar pulled up next to us. Three middle-aged heavily built blokes all wearing Crombies jumped out of the Jag and gripped Ian by his lapels. Meanwhile, John and I had legged it down the canal towpath, shitting it. They had cockney accents, Ian said later. They wanted to know what his name was before satisfying themselves that he wasn't the man they were looking for and driving off.

We'd jib the train into Manchester to have a look in Virgin Records or Paperchase or the latest punk fashions down in the Underground Market next to the Arndale Centre.

And we started to check out bands in Manchester, often at Cavendish Hall or 'The Poly' as it was known, just along from The Salutation pub in Hulme in the student area of town. We went with friend and future Stone Roses member Pete Garner. Garner knows all there is to know about music. He lived at his mum's over the bridge from the Sylvan pub in Timperley, where John would later collect glasses, and he turned us on to lots of new bands.

We saw bands such as Generation X, The Ruts, and 999 at The Poly and lied to our parents about where we were going to sleep. We lied because 'abandoned clinic' was probably not the answer they were looking for.

After the gigs had finished we would board the all-night 263 to Altrincham. The top deck of the 263 could be a dangerous place to be if some pissed-up psycho was up there. We saw a lot of needless violence erupt just because someone had stared at a nutjob the wrong way.

We'd get off near South Trafford College then walk up Park Road for about a mile to a disused children's clinic that had stood empty for a good few years. We had some stinking sleeping bags in the attic room that we slept on and kept bottles of lager up there for our return in the dead of night. We entered the clinic from the rear after peeling back a wooden door panel and all climbed in on our hands and knees through the kitchen area hoping not to meet anyone else inside. By then we had all watched our mate Steve Pugh's dodgy VHS cassette of *A Clockwork Orange* and didn't fancy getting set upon by a gang of tramps inside the building. The former clinic still had a few eerie medical fixtures about, weird clamps and pulleys, and was beginning to decay. With the cold and the creaking all night and probably a bit of fear too, we didn't get much sleep before having to go home at dawn pretending we'd slept at each other's houses.

We started following The Clash as much as we could.

After John and I had seen The Clash for the first time together (I saw them with my mate Adam Tarsh in 77) at the Apollo in July 1978 on the *Out on Parole* tour, our desire to make a go of our own band was increased overnight. (As a footnote, supporting The Clash that night was The Special AKA, whose singer, Terry Hall, I would cross paths with later on).

In November, John and I bought Clash tickets for the *Sort It Out* Tour and bunked off school early and made our way to the Apollo Theatre again.

We stood near the stage door hoping to get the band's autographs as they arrived for the soundcheck. This was before all the health and safety rules we have today, so we were allowed to help the local Apollo crew push flight cases from the trucks and onto the stage. John and I got to know a huge bloke, Mike Henley, who looked like a Native American and worked for a big rock promoter of the day, Straight Music. He wore two watches, one with New York time and one with UK time, which I thought was pretty cool. He said he could get me a job at The Who's studio once, and stay at his place in Battersea. Over the next year he gave us quite a lot more backstage passes, not just for the Clash but any band he was looking after as their tour hit Manchester, and would invite us for a drink in his fancy hotel bar after the gig was wrapped up. Me and John did have a drink with him in a couple of hotels when The Clash were in Manchester in case we got to meet the band.

We would have to wait another year for that. The Clash relocated to the USA to begin work on the *London Calling* album, whilst simultaneously touring the country with the *Pearl Harbour* tour for most of 1979.

As ever, the musical landscape was changing in 1979. It was our last year at school and we were getting into Two Tone Records and the whole ska revival as it was known back then. Our trio would spend many hours together in John's box room huddled around his Dansette turntable listening to songs like The Special AKA's 'Gangsters' and 'The Prince' by Madness. Admittedly it was The Clash who turned me on to dub and reggae. Whenever Two Tone acts were playing in Manchester, we would go along. It was a really exciting time, musically - it seemed every year the music scene was shifting and you'd discover whole new genres. Completely different. Not like today where people split hairs over sub-categories of electronica.

A couple of times, we travelled to London on the National Express just to get a feel of the place. We wanted to visit some of the landmarks we'd heard about. We went to World's End in Chelsea where Malcolm McLaren and Vivienne Westwood first opened their boutique, Sex, in the mid-seventies and where the Sex Pistols had formed and hung out. We went into a shop called Johnsons and the next time we were in London, John and I bought some black jeans with red piping down the seam. We visited a few other places, walking around all day soaking it up and blistering our feet. We hadn't realised how big the place was. We went around Notting Hill Gate. The Clash's social commentary on the 1976 riots, standing up against police brutality and racism made a big impression on us. We went checking out a few clothes shops and a record shop called Dub Vendor, which specialised in top quality Dub imported from Jamaica. I bought myself a copy of *Prince Jammy Presents*, which I've still got.

On another London trip, Ian and I bought a Two Tone tonic suit each at the Camden Market. Fishtail parkas were also purchased, but not by me, as I wasn't into scooters that much. I promised my mum I'd never get one as she saw motorbike casualties wheeled into the hospital every night. Ian and John were well into it though. Ian bought an old Vespa 150 and John a stylish Lambretta Jet 125, though the engine was forever pissing oil over his spark plugs. You'd go round his house and see him on the drive with the panels off and oil all over the shop.

'Plugs oiled up again John?'

This was also the year I flew to America for the first time on holiday with my parents and Jane for two weeks in May. We went to visit our ex-neighbours Pam and David Murray whose sons Keith and Stuart had been my bandmates in the BG Boys. David, who had grown up with nothing in the Gorbals district of Glasgow, was now the chief accountant at the oil company Occidental, in Houston, Texas.

After touching down in Houston in the British Caledonian DC 10, I walked past a news stand in the arrivals area and straight away spotted a picture of The Clash on the front cover of that month's Rolling Stone magazine and realised just how massive the band were becoming.

We had one of the best holidays our family ever took together, touring the southern states of Louisiana, Mississippi, Alabama, Georgia and Florida in a huge GMC motorhome. My dad and David took turns to drive it. Dad was scared to death of driving the behemoth through unfamiliar territory. We stayed in a different motel every night while the Murrays stayed in the camper. This was great: living out of a suitcase, travelling the country. I felt like I could get used to touring.

In Mobile, Alabama, the motorhome broke down one night on one of the quieter federal roads where there had been a spate of murders over the last week or so and the mechanic from the AAA asked the police to take us to safety in two black and white police cruisers to the nearest hotel - a little Holiday Inn - where we bolted our doors and flicked through all the TV channels available. Bear in mind, back in England we still only had three channels so this was a revelation to me. Between all these channels and discovering a drink called Welch's Grape Soda I was unconcerned about our safety situation.

By the next afternoon the motorhome was fixed and we were on our way to finish our last holiday together as a family before Jane went off to the University of Leeds and I started to go on holiday with friends.

I continued to do the bare minimum amount of work required to get me through my O level exams and would end up passing a respectable six of them at grade C or above, which was about the same number Ian and John gained. The three of us decided to further our education at South Trafford College just a mile or so up the road from Altrincham town centre.

4

The Patrol

We started at South Trafford in September 1979, where I was studying geology and biology A levels and wanted to be a marine biologist. This may seem a lofty aspiration for someone who did no school work but I guess I felt I had the intelligence and could pull it off. I was drawn to the idea after watching a TV documentary series with Jacques Cousteau. John was doing art and Ian politics so we only met up during break times or after college.

By now we were calling the band The Patrol, but there was something missing. Up until now Ian was doing all the vocals at the practice sessions but had stated that he just wanted to play bass. We were actively seeking a new singer and Ian had spotted a guy he thought might fit the bill: Andy Couzens. Andy had a spiky haircut, wore a Crombie and had a pair of American-style biker boots which The Clash had been wearing as they blazed across the States.

One lunchtime, John and Ian took me to meet Andy in the canteen and pointed him out. He was beating up another student. Like I say, it was a violent time, so this seemed about par for the course.

When we found out Andy owned the mustard-coloured MG Midget in the car park, we decided he was the new singer before we had even heard him sing.

We started rehearsing at the Walton Park Scout Hut in Sale after picking up the keys for the place off a woman called Mrs Slaughter who treated us with utter contempt after taking one look at us. We hammered out half a dozen or so songs at Walton Park, including 'Jail of the Assassins', 'You're Laughing Now', and 'A Right Charlie', an early anti-royalist number which Ian had written after watching a news report about Prince

Charles being heckled by striking miners shouting 'Here comes the bastard' to the approaching entourage.

The four of us squeezed into Andy's tiny sports car or his dad Colin's new white Jaguar and rode between Timperley, Manchester and Andy's parents' mansion in Poynton. Andy had a CB radio and Ian liked winding up the local CB enthusiasts as we went, going 'get a life you saddos', and so on.

We thought it was hilarious, except Andy, who seemed a bit embarrassed.

We would listen in as infuriated CB breakers would try to pinpoint our exact whereabouts, threatening to teach us a lesson. 'I've got a really strong signal here,' one would say, while we pissed ourselves. 'They must be on the A538.'

A lot of time was spent at Andy's as there was space to rehearse. Andy had a company fuel card and didn't mind driving us all about. We watched videos like *The Texas Chain Saw Massacre*, *The Warriors* and horror flick *Carrie* in the TV lounge next to the games room with its full-size snooker table. We felt like a gang now. The four of us met in a cafe just along the road from South Trafford College and drank hot sweet tea on the red leatherette banquettes listening to The Specials and The Damned on the Rock-Ola jukebox watching the world go by through steamed-up windows.

Through Clash gigs we got to know a group of Stretford punks who looked a pretty mean lot but were alright. They were informally led by Gaz Wilkinson and briefly helped us create a bit of a local scene.

Gaz and the Stretford punks started to follow The Patrol round when we started to do gigs in the local area, the first one being in the refectory of South Trafford College in early March, supporting a heavy rock outfit called Fire Clown.

It was Gaz who first taught me to drive, whenever we went to gigs together. He would let me take his Mini Cooper home to my mum's after dropping him off at home, completely pissed after a session in The Vine or The Melville, in Stretford, then pick him up the next night to do it all again. He was really hard Gaz. That sounds trite to say, but the thing is, *he was*. He looked after us all, as did all his cohorts when we started to gig together.

As early as January or February 1980 I was dropping out of some of my classes, much to my dad's mortification, as The Clash went on the road to promote their best album yet, *London Calling*, on the *16 Tons* Tour.

Squire and I went to see the band first at Deeside Leisure Centre near Chester, where, with the aid of our backstage passes given to us by Mike Henley, we finally got to meet our heroes in the flesh.

We weren't disappointed. Even then, they had a reputation for looking after their young fans who followed them everywhere, sometimes even letting them stay on their own hotel bedroom floors.

I can't emphasise enough how much John and I were into The Clash back then. We went to great lengths to go the gigs. We'd go to London and come back on the 'milk train' in the early hours. Though I can't speak for the depth of everyone else's fandom, they had a massive influence on our band. At this time, The Patrol was basically a band trying to sound like The Clash.

We went to Liverpool, Derby and Stoke using the money earned from my job at the greengrocer. I drove to one of the gigs with Gaz at Bridlington Royal Spa, drunk. I know it's not clever but that's how it was - drink driving was almost the norm.

I travelled to Bristol, alone this time, on the train, to watch another show at Colston Hall, which was great until after the gig when walking back to my bed and breakfast, I was attacked by a middle-aged wino who pulled a blade out of his overcoat and demanded money. It shit me up a bit and I ran off as fast as I could to the safety of the main road.

At the soundcheck of one of the Manchester Apollo gigs on the same tour, I had one of the biggest buzzes I've had playing drums. Baker Glare, Topper Headon's drum roadie was late and I was asked to play Topper's custom made silver Pearl drum kit by the sound man Taff, as I was the only person stood around who could play or could be arsed. Topper was my hero at this point, he was a superb drummer, he could play punk, soul, funk, reggae, you name it. I'd been around The Clash so much that the crew were aware I was a drummer in a band. So, keen to get a sound level, Taff asked me if I'd play and I jumped straight up. I played along to 'Brand New Cadillac', a cut off *London Calling*, through the huge PA - I'd never experienced a full-on sound system and could feel the kick drum reverberating through my body. I finished the tune to a round of applause off all the road crew before Henley told me to get off as Topper had just pulled up outside. But the crew were happy with the sound and I felt like I'd somehow contributed to that night's show.

During another Clash soundcheck at the Apollo I was asked by film star Ray Winstone if I fancied going for a pint with him at the Apsley Cottage pub at the rear of the building. I gladly accepted as I had seen his performance in the film *Scum* - the gritty realism really opened my eyes. Ray was a big fan of The Clash. We spent an hour together chatting away about our favourite tunes, Ray getting the beer in, before we both went back inside to see the support band.

The last time we saw Henley, John and I stayed at his shared flat in London, to watch Strummer and the boys while Henley himself was doing another tour. He left the key under the mat and we snooped around the empty flat. We were shocked to uncover a stash of gay porn in one of the bedrooms. We then started questioning Henley's motives in being friendly towards us. As we didn't have anywhere to go, me and John slept in his bed anyway. Henley came in at dawn and we woke up startled. We couldn't get back to sleep after Henley climbed in the bed. We got up, made a brew. In the morning, Henley's flatmate, a chauffeur, was going mad as he noticed someone had been through his gear. Turned out it was his porn. We didn't say anything and another young lad, sharing the chauffeur's bed, ended up getting the blame.

'Who's been in my drawer - you've been looking through my drawer, haven't you?'

We hit the streets as fast as we could.

In March, The Patrol played at the Sale Annexe Youth club behind the old Town Hall to a crowd of fifty people, mostly the Stretford punks, along with Gaz's own band Corrosive Youth. They would support The Patrol on further dates at Lymm Youth Club, in the small village in Cheshire near the M6 motorway and at Dunham Massey village hall, where we did a rendition of 'Blockbuster' by Sweet with Ian on lead vocals. The horrified villagers looked on as pissed up teenagers rowdily traversed the canal across a narrow metal pipe. No one like us had ever booked the village hall before as it was usually used for WI meetings or the summer fete.

When we played at Lymm Youth Club, Gaz and his punk army went upstairs to pull the plug on the jukebox that was spewing out some terrible heavy metal music to a load of bikers who used the club as a meeting place and there was a scrap with the bikers having to back down before the police were called in.

Our gig went ahead as planned and we all had a top night with local support band, Suburban Chaos, who played a stormer.

We later played the Portland Bars under the old Piccadilly Hotel in central Manchester, playing support to The Alarm, who went on to have a hit with '68 Guns'.

Lostock Youth Club was next, followed by Lymm Grammar School.

Then we missed a bit of a break. I'm not sure how it came about, but Pete Garner, who was then our roadie, got a call from Adam and the Ants' people, who were on the verge of stardom then. They were due to play at the Osborne Club in North Manchester. They were stuck in the snow on the M1 somewhere down south and wouldn't be able to make the gig. Did The Patrol want the headline spot instead? Pete started phoning around frantically trying to get hold of the whole band but this wasn't easy and he just couldn't get hold of John so we had to turn the gig down. We were gutted because we would have an audience of more than fifty odd. It ends up that John was just sat in some field.

1981 was the year The Patrol made their first and only recording at Greenhouse Studio on Great Western Street in Rusholme just south of Manchester city centre, a cramped eight-track studio above a vegetarian restaurant that had seen better days. By this time, I had sold the stolen drum kit and was using a new one that my mum, looking after me as ever, had saved up for. The recording, which cost us £120 - a lot of money back then - yielded a cassette recording of 'Jail of the Assassins' and 'Too Many Tons', featuring both Ian and Andy on vocals. If you look hard enough, they can be found on the internet. I had a listen recently myself - it's better than I thought it would be...

5

Freak Party

I keep harking back to it but there just seemed to be violence everywhere you turned at the start of the eighties, not just on the football terraces on Saturday afternoon but all over the place. The mainstream clubs were full of beer monsters with curly perms and half-mast Farah slacks with white socks and hideous black slip-ons. If they didn't cop off, they'd roam the streets looking for trouble after chucking out time, hoping for someone to look at them the wrong way so they could start something.

As Margaret Thatcher's government were closing all the coal mines, picketing miners were fighting with riot police on the six o'clock news on an almost daily basis, or so it seemed.

Peter Sutcliffe, 'The Yorkshire Ripper', was well into his reign of terror by now. This worried my family as Jane was studying at the University of Leeds and staying in halls of residence in an area Sutcliffe, who was no longer just targeting prostitutes, had used as a stalking ground.

The summer of '81 saw the start of the Moss Side riots after Brixton and Toxteth had gone up in flames the night before. I was a regular visitor to Moss Side, to score weed or see mates and witnessed the aftermath of rioting, but I was still living out in the safety of the suburbs and it seemed a world away to me.

Large quantities of cheap Afghan heroin and locally produced speed flooded the streets of Manchester. I knew a couple of kids who overdosed and died, one of them being the brother of my girlfriend Gina. A lot of these drugs were being imported via Amsterdam or Stockholm by youths who were a similar age to us and had acquired a taste for expensive Lacoste knitwear and shoes called Pods that looked like bowling shoes. We called them 'casuals'. Many of them carried modelling knives about their person and they weren't scared of using them. They wore their hair with a long floppy fringe, a so-called wedge-style, similar to how John would wear his a couple of years down the line, though he was never violent, the complete opposite, he just got into the fashion side of it. You could say they were the modern equivalent of the Victorian street gangs known as 'Cloggers' who had roamed the streets of Ancoats a hundred years earlier, taxing anybody they could.

In February 1980, when the Clash were playing the Manchester Apollo yet again, John and I went for a mooch in the Underground Market near the Arndale Centre in our punk/Two Tone style mishmash with Donald, a mate of the band, who was doing merchandise for the group. He was an albino from London and wanted some new jeans so we headed for the Stolen from Ivor denim emporium, just along from a cool record shop that used to blast out all the latest hip sounds.

A gang of casuals or 'Perry Boys' as they were sometimes known (they often wore Fred Perry polo shirts) were hanging outside the record shop, soaking up the sounds when one of them shouted an insult over at Donald who told them to 'fuck off you Northern cunt' in his South London accent, whereupon the three of us were under attack by at least four or five of them. John and I just bolted up the stairs (we seemed to be good at this), three at a time to street level, while Blondie's 'Heart of Glass' pulsed through the subterranean market. We knew the gang might be tooled up and we weren't taking any chances. Donald also lived to fight another day, though he suffered a bloody nose which looked worse than it really was as he wore a white shirt under his Crombie. We all reconvened to the safety of the bar in the Grand Hotel where the band were billeted and thought how lucky we were to come away unscathed. But also, I found the whole thing a bit of a rush.

At the tail end of the year, Ian and Pete Garner were lucky enough to witness The Clash record their next single, 'Bank Robber', at Pluto Studios on Granby Row in central Manchester, during an all night session after playing at their regular Manchester home, the Apollo. I was gutted that I'd missed out.

We started frequenting Pips nightclub (*behind the Cathedral*, as the tagline went) where we mostly hung out in the Roxy/Bowie room listening to DJ Dave Booth who I would hire as DJ at my wedding to my first wife Mandy at Old Trafford Cricket Club in 1993.

Our band had started to experiment with soft drugs, namely poppers, which were openly on sale in the clubs, and cannabis oil, that Pete had procured from somewhere or other. We would make our way round to his mum's house in Brooklands, just over the little footbridge on the border with Timperley. We spent an awful lot of our youth hanging around on this bridge, chewing the fat, chatting up girls. At Pete's mum's, Pete would put a tune on - Tubeway Army's 'Are "Friends" Electric' say - and spread a small ampoule of oil over the paper of a normal cigarette and smoke it. I felt it straight away and liked it, but not the amyl nitrate (poppers) that I sniffed from a little bottle down in the whitewashed catacombs of Pips Disco. It made your brain thump like your heart. I imagine you would get the same effect in the final death throes of a hanging by rope. It was horrible.

In the summer of 1980, I went to Torquay on my first holiday with mates. There was a load of us from The Vine: John, Wilf, the Columb brothers, Windy, Gles, Nik Erritsos, and Steve Brown. We started drinking lager as soon as we boarded the train at Piccadilly and by the time we made a stop at Bristol Temple Meads, all of us were plastered. At some point, the British Transport Police boarded the train as a member of the public had spotted us all dropping our kecks and baring our arses to someone on the platform at the previous stop and called in the cops. We were all hauled off and herded into the police station on the platform and interviewed, but without any pictures they couldn't do a thing. We had to wait for hours for the next train down to Cornwall, but we just bought more beer and carried on regardless. I can't remember much of the holiday at all apart from the club we went to every night. I met a girl in there called Katy, but John was the only one of us who copped off.

On our return to The Vine, Dave Columb introduced me to a hotshot 17-year-old guitarist called Johnny Maher, who soon changed his name by deed poll to Johnny Marr to avoid confusion with Buzzcocks drummer John Maher. He cut a striking figure straight away with his flat-top haircut and his X Clothes threads, where he worked by day. His vocation said nothing about him though. He was a guitarist by night, and that was his true calling. Marr struck me as a bit of a gun for hire or at least a man on a mission. He had the gift of the gab. He was starting a new band and looking for a drummer. Did I want to join? Course I did.

It was that fast.

Johnny Marr had been in a few bands. One was called 'White Dice', which also included his St Augustine's schoolmate Andy Rourke, a classically trained guitarist from Ashton-on-Mersey, as well as guitarist Kevin Kennedy (AKA Curley Watts, the binman from *Coronation Street*).

Though John Squire was getting better and better, at this stage, he was not the guitarist he would become - he was still honing his sound, as we all were. When I heard Johnny Marr play for the first time at Andy Rourke's dad's house, he blew my mind straight away. He could play anything after hearing it just once and his knowledge of music was even greater than Pete Garner's.

Johnny asked me if I wanted to join a new group he was setting up with Andy and to come and hang out with the pair of them at Andy's dad's house at Hawthorn Lane. Andy's dad was away on business in Holland. He was away on business a lot - leaving his four sons to look after themselves. Over the next few years, this address would be synonymous with drug use amongst all the cabbies in Sale as a couple of dealers basically came round and used the house as their base. A fireman in The Vine told me that his engine would pull up and get their gear from there.

Johnny was very street compared to me, stylish and cocksure, even at that age. He had this sheer bloody-mindedness, which perhaps helped him get to where he is today. The main thing that impressed me though was his ability on the guitar. He's the best British guitarist from my generation in my opinion.

So. I was in this new band.

Ian had started to work at Andy Couzen's uncle's business by now, opposite The Rising Sun in Hazel Grove, selling caravans and accessories after a short stint working for the dole in Sale. He wore his Two Tone tonic suit and shiny black brogues. It wouldn't be long before he would move into his first flat in Charles Barry Crescent in Hulme, just south of the city centre, an area notorious as a hotbed of artistes, musicians and drugs.

By now I had abandoned the geology and biology A levels at South Trafford and my plans to be a marine biologist were dashed. Ian and John stayed the course a little longer than me. For the rest of the year, I was working full-time at the greengrocer in Altrincham for a bloke called Brian, so I could save up to buy my first car: a clapped out Triumph Toledo in purple for £100. It broke down all the time as a lot of Triumphs did. Still, I started to have more fun now I had my own wheels and I could go on holiday whenever I had time.

I went with Johnny and Andy and his brother Phil to Amsterdam for a long weekend. It felt like we were a bona fide band. We were walking round in our new-wave gear from Johnsons in London, like we were already rock stars. There we were on the continent, lounging about, sampling all the cannabis in the coffee houses. We bought American imports from the record shops, and had a mooch around the red light district, where the girls looked like they were in a zoo. While I had a laugh and a smoke with Johnny, it was Andy who I really bonded with on the trip. He was a laugh a minute and it was to be a friendship that endured.

For rest of the summer, after work, I'd drive down to Hawthorn Lane to indulge my new hobby: smoking a bong. We'd sit in the back lounge listening to Parliament Funkadelic, Grandmaster Flash, Chic, and Grace Jones on the top of the range hi-fi that belonged to Andy's brother, Chris. We didn't have a drum kit set up there but Andy would dazzle us all with his bass playing and, like Johnny, could play anything after hearing it just once. Even complicated stuff like on *The Early Tapes*, by jazz-funk band Level 42, Andy was straight in. They weren't a cool band, but I could appreciate some of the musicianship. Another record we constantly listened to was an album called *Sextet* by a Factory Records signing called A Certain Ratio, whose bass player/singer Jez Kerr I would later cross paths with.

So, yeah, the band.

We decided to name the band 'Freak Party' and set about looking for a singer after working on the music, which definitely had funk at its core. It was Johnny who gave me the moniker 'Funky Si' during those sessions. My drumming is heavily influenced by all the records we were listening to at Andy's. I certainly wasn't playing glam rock anymore. Freak Party sounded like a cross between Pigbag, Chic, and A Certain Ratio. After rehearsing the music in the basement of a carpet shop on Washway Road in Sale for a couple of nights a week, we rented a room at Decibelle Studios in Beehive Mill, on Jersey Street, Ancoats. It was owned by a Frenchman called Philippe who was often over in Paris looking after some other business interest.

We auditioned a couple of candidates for the singing job.

They were crap ...

So were the next couple.

One wanted to sing 'Flowers of Romance' by Public Image Ltd. He was called Wade and said his nickname was 'Donkey', which made the three of us explode with laughter and became an in-joke between us. *EeeOrr*! There was an eight-track mixing desk at Decibelle on which Freak Party recorded an instrumental, called 'Crak Therapy.' We had a few cassettes made up with a view to giving them out to potential singers.

Andy was working at a timber yard in Trafford Park and would cycle home, so I'd have to wait around at home before driving over. I would leave home well before my dad got back from his surgery at six thirty to avoid his disapproving looks. He had totally given up on me pursuing a proper career now that I had dropped out of South Trafford altogether. He also didn't like me hanging about with Andy because our neighbour was a teacher at St Augustine's and had told my dad about Andy being in trouble for drugs and whatever else.

I realise I've probably put quite a bit of a downer on my old man, so I should address that. Though I often felt I'd disappointed him, the fact was, he was just looking out for his son like any father would. He would prove that he always had my best interests at heart. Maybe he was right? Shit, this is all getting a bit heavy.

Back to this band.

Johnny Marr quit his job at X Clothes to spend more time playing guitar during the day and we would see him most nights round at Andy's. But now, a casual called Docker, with his piss-stained tracky bottoms and Pods, arrived on the scene. He was skinny and ferret-like and wore a houndstooth deerstalker hat that made him look ridiculous. It was the worst get-up I've ever seen. Totally out of place.

His arrival, however, would have repercussions for us all. He had just served time at Strangeways for dealing Class As. The experience had not rehabilitated him. He used the place for serving addicts who would call round in the daytime when Andy's brothers were often at home and be quickly dealt with in the hallway. There is a fairly big estate called 'The Racecourse' just up the road from Hawthorn Lane where, at the time, there were a lot of addicts searching for drugs and knew Docker would most likely be at the Rourkes' place.

What I'm trying to say is, I began to flirt with hard drugs.

Docker asked me for a lift to Cheetham Hill, in the north of the city, one night, to see a man about a dog. He paid me £10 for the lift and gave me a bit of heroin to smoke on some tin foil. It was a fateful decision.

Docker's cronies began to fill the Rourke household from lunchtime onwards. They got into baking their own crack cocaine using coke and ammonia. Rocks of crack were not widely available at that time - so they had to make their own. They cherished the process and beavered like scientists with the guarded formula they'd picked up from inside Strangeways. I did have crack on occasion, but mainly couldn't afford coke so stuck with the five-pound bag of the brown.

Anyway. The band.

On Thursday nights, we got in my latest car, a bronze coloured Ford Escort, and made our way to Legends nightclub on Princess Street in town where Ian, John and Pete Garner could also be found. Legends had the best sound system in town by a mile and the tunes were good too. A lot of my contemporaries also turned out to be there on a Thursday, I discovered years later.

What you have to remember about Manchester at this time was that there were only a few places to go where they were playing slightly left-field stuff. The few nightclubs there were in Manchester played chart music to girls in white stilettos. Consequently, a lot of people who were interested in music rather than just copping off were going to places like Legends, The Gallery on Deansgate, or Pips (*behind the cathedral*).

Stuff like 'Pull Up To The Bumper' by Grace Jones was massive in Legends as was Sylvester's 'You Make Me Feel (Mighty Real)'. I used to like 'Quiet Life' by Japan. The Human League also appealed to me as did the first offerings from the ashes of Joy Division, namely, New Order, whose singer Bernard Sumner gave us an invite to his bonfire party at a house in rural Macclesfield. We also saw the band play one of their early gigs at the leisure centre there. Admittedly not a fan of Joy Division, New Order was much more my kind of thing.

Sorry. About this band.

One night, whilst Freak Party was rehearsing in Ancoats, we heard someone knocking loudly through the thickly panelled front door of the studio. Whoever it was, they were persistent in their attempt to gain entry. Dale Hibbert, who had the keys for the studio, eventually realised it wasn't the owner, Philippe, and gingerly opened the door to the visitors. It was the serious crime squad.

Four coppers burst in in their Crombies and shiny black shoes looking for Johnny in connection with an original Lowry that had been stolen. Johnny's name had come up on their radar due to his association with a 'fence' called Kev the Smoke who operated out of a block of flats in Wythenshawe, where we often went to buy Moroccan hash. They had a tip off that he could be found on the premises.

'Which one of you is Johnny Marr?' one of the burly coppers asked. After Johnny had identified himself, the three of us were bundled into two unmarked Ford Granadas that were waiting outside on Jersey Street and whisked us back to Longsight police station for questioning overnight. Andy and I hadn't known anything about it until earlier that day, and even then the details were sketchy. We kept our mouths shut and were released early in the morning, but they kept Johnny until his court appearance the next day and charged him with handling stolen goods. After this, we saw less and less of Johnny at Andy's place and who could blame him? I think the conviction was an awakening for Johnny and made him think twice about who he was associating with. Probably best for him to keep his nose clean and lay low for a while. He moved well away from the drug scene.

He'd be here, there, and everywhere as I remember. He was sleeping at a flat in Brooklands for a time before lodging for a stint at my old schoolmate Dan Weaver's house in Bowdon. He must have decided by then that Morrissey was going to be the singer in his new band, but at this time he didn't have a name for it and I didn't know much about it. I saw him a fair bit out and about, especially at Discount Records in Altrincham. Discount was run by our mates Pete Hunt and a little guy called Steve who was really into the Stray Cats, like I was for a while. In fact, I went with Steve to see them at Manchester Apollo. There still wasn't a larger venue anywhere in the city at that point, which is why I saw so many gigs there. I love the Apollo. I still think it's the best venue in Manchester.

But anyway. This band. That seemed to be the end of it. Which was a shame, because I thought we could go places.

Such is life. We move on. I want to tell you about this party.

In July of 1981, my parents went on holiday abroad for a week and left me in charge of the house in Ringway as my sister Jane was away all the time at university.

What a mistake that was.

A party was arranged for the upcoming Saturday night that happened to be Gina's birthday and a general invite was issued to our mates from The Vine. I didn't think loads would attend as I reckoned it was too far for many of them to bother coming over from Sale.

I suppose I was expecting maybe a couple of dozen at the very most so not exactly a quiet evening but this turned into a prototype for one of these Facebook parties you hear about that gets out of hand.

When I finished work, bagging tomatoes, on the Saturday afternoon, I went home with Gina and hit the bottle before anyone arrived, whilst setting up the record deck in the front lounge of the house, where the baby grand piano was kept. Within an hour the house was already full and I had drunk way too much booze, soon losing control of the situation as taxi after taxi pulled up outside and more people crammed themselves inside.

The piano stool's legs broke off first then a massive scratch appeared on the piano's lid. I had to get that fixed before my parents returned in three days' time. I was like that guy from the Yellow Pages advert desperately trying to find an antique restorer.

Then, for reasons only intoxication can account for, someone opened all the cans of dog food in the kitchen and proceeded to stamp it all into the hallway carpet where my dad's waiting room had once been. I mean, I know I was running in some rum circles but why would you?

For good measure, the crystal chandelier hanging above had also been damaged and the large landing mirror cracked.

Gina, as well as a few mates - I think Andy and Johnny helped - did their best to regain control of the worsening situation, while I was flat out in bed, but there were just too many people there. Someone finally woke me up to see the mess downstairs, broken wine bottles, pools of vomit.

The thing I remember most about that night though was the arrival of Ian dressed up as Alex, the gang leader from *A Clockwork Orange*, complete with black bowler hat, white Sta Press kecks, cherry red Doc Martens, white shirt, braces and silver-topped cane. He even had the fake eyelash under one eye. Ian went on to gain an international reputation as a bit of a showman and I guess it was evident that night. Ian was the only one in the house who could get away with that, bearing in mind it wasn't a fancy dress party.

Freak party.

The party rocked to the sounds of Sly & Robbie, Grandmaster Flash and the Furious Five's *The Message* album, The Special AKA's 'Gangsters' (they scored a number one this year with 'Ghost Town') and, inevitably, The Clash's *Sandinista*. The Clash reached their commercial peak after releasing the album *Combat Rock* a year later, the last album Topper Headon played on before he was booted out for taking hard drugs too often.

I guess this was where my infatuation with The Clash ended. Maybe my own turn towards hard drugs, and the ensuing creative conflict, enabled me to recognise and sympathise with Topper. Anyway, without him, it seemed to me the chemistry had gone in the band. I bought the last album, *Cut The Crap*, but then sold it, in disgust.

6

How Not to be in Iconic
Manchester Band, Part One

Johnny Marr had fallen off my radar for a few months until one night in 1982, out of the blue, he phoned me at my parents' house.

With the drugs scene at Andy's house and the arrest, he was still keeping away from any trouble. Meanwhile, I hadn't been up to too much in the intervening months.

Not long after the bollocking I got off Mum and Dad for the mess that had been made while they were on holiday (I'd not been able to get the smell of booze out of the carpets before they got home), my job at the greengrocer's wound down as Brian was planning to open a chippy.

Brian was a bit of a wheeler-dealer and, in an unlikely business synergy, he got me selling Christmas trees out of the chip shop while they were getting the fryers ready. With Christmas done, Brian pointed me in the direction of his dad's shop in Wilmslow where there was a job going. It was called Pimlotts and it was on the main road opposite the Rex Theatre, before it was turned into a cinema. This time I was preparing high quality fish and game produce to sell to a more a discerning type of customer, in the more affluent Wilmslow, and so I took to the shop floor in my white coat and fishmonger's apron.

By now I was driving a little mustard coloured Mini 1275GT I had picked up at an auction. I was still living at home as I'd found no need to rent my own flat yet - I was never there, except when I returned late at night from Andy's place to sleep in my bedroom, stoned.

John Squire had asked me if I wanted to share a flat in the Chorlton/ Whalley Range area, a mile or so south of the city centre, but as I say, I was quite comfortable paying my £25 keep and I could entertain Gina in my bedroom whenever I liked, though she couldn't stay the night - my mother wouldn't allow it.

Back at the fishmonger's we'd get some locally famous custom.

Stuart Hall, the eloquently verbose presenter of *It's a Knockout* game show, was a regular in Pimlotts. He lived nearby in a mansion on Prestbury Road. He would come in, perhaps before a day's filming at the TV studios in Manchester, where he was now a broadcaster on a local BBC news show. He often wore a very expensive mink coat and had a leggy blonde PA in tow who would pay for whatever Stuart required and carry his bags of venison or grouse, depending on what was in season, back to the Rolls Royce parked in the middle of our car park at the back of the shop, where he had selfishly blocked everyone in. Little did I know, the jovial Hall would later be found guilty of abusing minors in his dressing room.

When Mollie Sugden, the actress who played the 'battleaxe' Mrs Slocombe on comedy classic *Are You Being Served?*, was working at the Rex Theatre opposite, she would come in the shop and ask for me by name because I could slice her smoked salmon as thin as a Rizla paper. She would always leave a couple of pound notes as a tip for me too. What a pleasant lady she was. Her most famous character still makes me laugh today.

A lot of the top footballers of the day would also stop by, especially at Christmas time, when the place was stuffed to the gills with food fit for kings. We had live lobsters coming in the back door in the early mornings and being sold and taken home by customers through the front door on the same day. Occasionally I would take one home for my mum as a surprise. Whisk it through the back door and into the boot of my Mini out back.

I tried to trade live lobsters and salmon fillets for drugs a couple of times. The dealers never went for it.

'Go on mate. It might be nice for your mum.'

'Are you having a laugh?'

Cash they liked.

Not the discerning types maybe.

Though a lot of money went on fuel, drugs, and watching gigs, the job enabled me to save for my next drum kit: a silver Tama Swingstar.

The other thing, though, about this job - I constantly stank of fish, which wasn't ideal.

So anyway, Johnny Marr had been hard at work in the months since

I'd seen him.

Firstly making contact with Stephen Patrick Morrissey, one time singer in punk band Ed Banger and the Nosebleeds and also at that time a regular letter writer in the weekly music press. I'd never heard of Stephen, but Johnny was really enthusiastic about him. I had heard of the Nosebleeds before but I was not a fan, I was more familiar with Slaughter & the Dogs - another Wythenshawe punk band.

Secondly, he had been co-writing The Smiths first few tunes.

'Si, will you be the drummer in my new band? We're called The Smiths,' Johnny asked me. I was standing in my parents' bedroom, on the upstairs phone. My first thought was: what a crap name.

The Smiths?

Johnny went on to explain who Morrissey was and how urgently he needed to get in the studio for real to record a number of newly crafted songs that the two of them had been working on. He seemed determined to make this band work at all costs from the moment he first mentioned it to me.

My second thought was: is this yet another new band with unrealistic hopes of making it to the big time?

It was late at night sometime around the start of summer 1982 when Johnny rang and told me that Morrissey and he were hiring the studio at Decibelle to record a demo tape of the new band. This band was quite different from what we'd been doing in Freak Party, Johnny said. It wasn't a funk band, he said, which was a bit disappointing for me as that was what I'd liked. Also, I had visions of my new wheels being nicked in the dead of night. The previous year, my last car had disappeared from Jersey Street and Johnny and I had to walk all the way home in the snow, after a brief stopover in a freezing flat in Chorlton.

So I wasn't too keen at all, but, due to Johnny's persistence, agreed to do the recording over one night the following week, after filleting fish all day. Before that though, I was giving Johnny a lift over to Morrissey's mum's house on Kings Road in Stretford so they could exchange cassette tapes of tracks they were working on. Morrissey seemed a lot older than me and Johnny and he didn't seem to have much charisma either, but then I guess I had just met the guy and he'd yet to convince the world of his abilities. Plus, he says himself he's very shy. We nodded at each other in the hallway of the semi in Stretford. The songwriters briefly discussed the plan of action over the next week before Johnny and I went back into the cold and back to Altrincham.

The next week, after driving home from work and doing my best to scrub away the smell of fish from my hands, I loaded my new Tama Swingstar kit into the motor and went to pick up Johnny from his lodgings in Bowdon.

An hour later Johnny was running through the songs: 'Suffer Little Children,' which had obvious references to the tragic case of the Moors Murders in 1963, and 'The Hand That Rocks the Cradle,' which was less depressing in the circumstances, I suppose. Dale Hibbert was playing bass. Dale had a set of keys, and the boss Philippe was away in Paris again, so he let me and Johnny in before the three of us went through the songs and waited for the arrival of Morrissey.

By the end of the first run through, I realised that Dale wasn't as good as Andy on bass and wished he was here with us. There was a knock on the door and Morrissey was let in. He had a long dog-eared tweed coat, winkle-picker shoes and a carrier bag full of lyrics. After greeting his new songwriting partner, he gave the briefest of a shy smile in my direction, where I waited behind the kit for him to begin singing. When Dale had a sound level in Morrissey's cans from the control room, he came back into the live room and we were ready to begin.

You can say what you want about The Smiths and Morrissey's singular streak of genius and what a fool I must have been, and anything like that, but here's the thing: *I didn't like Morrissey's voice.* Straight away, I didn't like it.

As soon as he came in on the first verse going, 'Over the moor. Take me to the moor,' it grated with me and it all went downhill for me from that point onwards in more ways than one. I've had a listen to the recordings of this session on the internet and it still sounds bad to me.

The sound was a million light years away from what was turning me on musically at the time. I missed the super-funk basslines from Andy and Johnny's Chic-style guitar moves. I just didn't get it, whatsoever. I was just thinking, this is *depressing.*

Morrissey looked like a member of the dirty raincoat brigade, as one *NME* hack had loosely pigeonholed this type of music. I didn't like the cut of his jib.

I wasn't to know that in under a year The Smiths would be signed to Rough Trade Records with a cannon of vastly superior songs that would be embraced by people all over the world. And, despite what I've said about Morrissey's voice, I did like some of the tracks they'd come out with and even liked some of his singing. 'Panic', for example, I loved. Morrissey would become much more confident and comical in his vocal delivery as the band developed.

The next day, I told Johnny the gig wasn't for me.

So that was that anyway.

I didn't really think about Johnny's band for a couple of months and went back to smoking at Hawthorn Lane, until unexpectedly, Johnny asked Andy to replace Dale on bass. This was about the same time the first Smiths' single 'Hand In Glove' had been released. It went under the radar at first.

It was a bit of a shock to me at the time as I was hoping to be in a new band with Andy as my musical muse. Morrissey and Marr had auditioned two or three drummers and had settled on Mike Joyce, known for his work with punk band, Victim. Now they wanted my mate Andy Rourke too. Johnny and Andy had grown up together whilst at St Augustine's, so I shouldn't have been too surprised at this turn of events.

I was, then, consigned to a footnote in that little story.

My part in what would become a historic night in Ancoats was brought back to me in full, years later, when a bloke from Scotland appeared on BBC TV Show *Mastermind* with The Smiths as his specialist subject. He was asked by presenter John Humphrys, 'who played drums on the first Smiths' recordings?'

'Simon Wolstencroft,' he replied.

Thank God he got it right. Not entirely forgotten.

7

Feeling Numb

But now I felt a bit left out. Especially when The Smiths re-released 'Hand in Glove' later in the year. I didn't care for the song myself, but it soon became evident that the band was only going one way, and that was up. Morrissey and Marr had been hard at work writing the bulk of the first album. I had been offered the job of drummer with The Smiths and turned it down. My reasons were the right ones - if you're not into it, you're not into it - but I definitely would have joined had I known what they would soon become. I'm not that much of a purist. And later, I grew to love the band.

For the moment, I kept myself busy, but it would be a few years before I got over that mistake.

Since I wasn't in The Smiths, I carried on working at the fishmonger in Wilmslow in the day, slicing fish like a fucking champion, and then getting stoned in the evenings. I'd still go round to the Rourkes' in Ashton-on-Mersey and watch a lot of footage of the Falklands War on *News at Ten* with Andy's brothers Chris, Phil, and John, while Andy was away gigging with his bandmates a lot.

Hamilton Bohannon's 'Let's Start The Dance' was always on the decks at the Rourke place, a 12-inch import I had bought on Freak Party's trip to Amsterdam the previous year, as was the Dazz Band's 'Let It All Blow' and Patrice Rushen's 'Forget Me Nots.' So basically I'd sit there listening, getting caned, thinking what could have been.

I smoked a lot of brown, which I bought from Docker and his sidekicks and spent my time spaced out on Andy's dad's sofa until about midnight most nights. I tried to avoid my parents - they both worked for the NHS and I thought it would only be a matter of time before I was questioned.

Shipments of drugs would come in via a dealer who would turn up on the hour, every hour, in a three-litre S Capri. A gaggle of junkies would hang about at the allotted meeting place, like a load of monkeys at the zoo, waiting for feeding time. This is how it was done without mobiles. There was no CCTV either to speak of.

'Here he is, he's here,' they would be saying excitedly as the Capri purred up to the pavement. Us skagheads forming a queue at the window.

'Keep your B's down, the cops are about,' the dealer would be going. They'd be on edge about us waving fivers in the air, emblazoned with Queen Elizabeth herself, despite the conspicuousness of the queue.

Occasionally, I smoked crack - a short intense hit of euphoria that made you feel invincible. Then you'd feel down. Then you'd have a smoke of heroin to bring you back level. It was the one time in my life I'd say I was addicted to anything. I think I have an addictive personality, but when it comes to drugs, aside from this point in my life, I would argue I've been able to take it or leave it. Looking back, it probably destroyed a few brain cells and I wasted a lot of time and money, to say the least.

'It's alright this, eh, Docker?'

'Well ream.'

I ended up parting ways with my Mini. I wrote it off one typically manic dinner hour in a collision with a cab on the Racecourse Estate with Andy in the passenger seat as we zipped about after one thing or another. Well. One thing.

Docker and I decided to go to Ibiza for a couple of weeks. Soak up some rays, have a bit of a laugh. We were getting a flight from Luton and for whatever reason we didn't travel together. My mum and dad dropped me off at Luton Airport and there was no sign of Docker. My mum was obviously a bit concerned about this.

'Where's this friend of yours, Simon?'

He was nowhere to be seen, but I got on the plane anyway - I'd paid for the holiday, so I went without Docker and hoped he'd get a later flight. I hired a pushbike and rode around aimlessly during the days, looking for Docker who was supposed to be sorting me out with some gear. On the third day, I finally ran into him tooling about on a moped. He'd booked into some plush hotel in San Antonio, holed up with a stash of skag he'd smuggled over. I was happy to see him after wandering around on my own and being unable to sleep, cold turkeying. We got high and two or three days later we both ran out of money with days and days left before we were due to fly home. Out of money and drugs, we pleaded with the airline to get us back home, saying there was a family emergency. They helpfully found us seats on a plane to Newcastle. It would have to do. Marooned again in Newcastle and desperate for a fix we arranged for some mates to lend us some money when we got back. On this promise, we took a taxi all the way home, picked up the ninety quid for the fare and got a fix.

I stopped going to the Rourke household as often, as Andy was there less and less. In hindsight, Andy's absence was a blessing in disguise as I was able to maintain a bit of distance from the scene. With a bit of spare money and a vehicle, and Andy around, I could easily have been sucked further into the drugs and associated criminality by Docker and his ilk.

I immersed myself in the Manchester nightlife, such as it was. In the early eighties Manchester was far from the buzzing city it would become. The nightlife seemed to still be a bit in the dark ages.

In May, the Haçienda opened its doors for the first time after huge sums of New Order's money, who were doing all right by now, had been spent converting the former the yacht showroom on Whitworth Street West into what would become the hippest club in Europe for a while. As has been well documented, the huge space was very difficult to fill in the beginning, even at the weekends and it got very cold in the winter as a result of this. It was Johnny Marr who first took me along to the club and one of the first people I met there was the late Rob Gretton, New Order's former manager, who had been involved with The Russell Club, another Factory Records club down the road in Hulme. Ian and I had been there a few times before to watch a mod band called Secret Affair and a few others.

The first thing Rob said to me was, 'Ohhh … so you're Funky Si!'

After that, Marr's nickname for me seemed to stick.

Some people thought that Factory was elitist at the start but I don't agree with that. Tony Wilson, Factory Records and thus the club supremo, may have been a Cambridge graduate, but that doesn't mean the club was elitist. For me, it was just good to get away from all the beer monsters in places like Rotters on Oxford Road, where if you just looked at somebody the wrong way, you could get battered quite easily.

A lot of the music in the Haçienda I had never heard before, such as the superb D-Train, from the US. This is when I first got into techno music. A lot of the records had shipped over from Chicago and Detroit and were being played for the first time in what was now the only club other than Legends that I would visit.

After a few years I was granted an honorary membership card with my passport photo on it which gave me free access to the club on any given night. I didn't ask for one, I was just given it. I wasn't the only one who was given a free pass - there were hundreds. No wonder they didn't make any money. The card came in useful during the mid-eighties, when the queue started getting longer and longer until it snaked right around the corner down Albion Street, and enabled me to bypass the line and walk straight in.

Like I say, I wasn't the only one.

During the week, the cafe inside the club opened for business early in the evenings and I would often call in just for burger and chips, and have a chat with catering girls. Then I'd drive home all the way back to Ringway before getting up early for work the next day. I would get to see at least one band a week in the Haçienda some of the most memorable being Defunkt, New Order, and Grandmaster Flash in the first year of business. I didn't see the Madonna gig.

In 1983 I saw The Gun Club and The Smiths after their first performance on *Top of the Pops*, when the stage was littered with gladioli. The staff were all really cool with me, especially Leroy, the bar manager, who made sure I always had a free drink in my hand, to ensure they were losing more money. Not that I was complaining. Howard 'Ginger' Jones was the manager then before he set up Thinline Records a couple of years later and recorded The Stone Roses.

Ian and John used to visit occasionally when the club first opened but not as much as I did. Ian didn't have far to come from Hulme where the bohemian lifestyle in the infamous concrete crescents seemed to appeal to him.

John was working full-time at famed animation studio, Cosgrove Hall, in Chorlton as a model maker (most notably on an award winning production of *The Wind in the Willows*).

John once got me some casual work at Cosgrove Hall. The job was for the cartoon series *Danger Mouse* and I had to paint the pink inner ears of Danger Mouse himself, on transparent cellophane cells, in a little workroom on my own, all day long. It wasn't a difficult job if you can stay in the lines when you do colouring in.

Though I was thankful for the job and liked the cartoon, I got bored very quickly and stuck with the fish mongering. But even if it was only two days or whatever it was, I was quite pleased with myself that I could say I worked on *Danger Mouse*.

By now, Ian and John had started to go on scooter runs at the weekends and bank holidays with various scooter clubs in and around Manchester, which wasn't my scene.

Back in Hulme, Ian kept his customised pink Lambretta Chopper, with its extended forks, in the kitchen at the front of the flat. It had a racing engine in it and Ian reckoned it could go 90 mph! With the scooter in the kitchen, there was very little room for anything else. It made me laugh that you had to carefully climb round it to get in the flat every time.

The crescents initially won awards for the 'streets in the sky' design that replaced the rows upon rows of Victorian terraces that had become slums. So, at first, they presented a vast improvement both socially and economically, however, by this time, the design flaws had become apparent. Though the structures were mostly concrete there was a lot of timber used that was already infested with cockroach eggs before it was even put up. Soon the flats, which were reached by concrete walkways high up in the air (ideal for mugging people in the dark), were crawling with huge reddish brown cockroaches that scurried under the cooker as soon as you turned the kitchen light on. It smelled of piss everywhere. The lifts never worked and the underfloor heating was far too expensive for the tenants, most of whom were on the dole.

By the early eighties, when I started to visit, Hulme was practically a no-go area for the police who just left the inhabitants to it. Numerous flats were declared unfit and squatters moved in, including many musicians and arty types as well as a high volume of students, and therefore earning it a bohemian reputation. It was a bleak looking place even in the summer months. The crescents looked like communist state run blocks, but there was always a party going on somewhere. Soul superstar Geno Washington famously attended one of them one night after a gig nearby. When he met Ian, he told him he was going to be a star.

Drugs were being sold openly by young lads on mountain bikes from Moss Side and surrounding areas. Moss Side was the only place I knew where you could get grass as opposed to resin. There was a Rasta on the ground floor of a nearby block of flats and you had to knock on his back gate and pass your money through a letterbox. The deals were shit though - you didn't get much for a fiver.

After the riots, the police were nowhere to be seen, but there was no doubt about it, there was a great community spirit amongst the law-abiding residents, which I had to admire ...

Now at a loss as to what to do, musically, with Andy in The Smiths, Ian and John asked me back to play drums at Andy Couzens' place in Poynton. By this time, perhaps taking Geno to be some wandering prophet, Ian had decided that from now on he was going to be front man and singer in the resurrected Patrol with Andy Couzens playing rhythm guitar, John on lead guitar, and Pete Garner on bass, only under a new name which had yet to be decided upon.

These writing/rehearsal sessions took place during July 1983 when The Smiths were attempting to record their first album with producer Troy Tate. It was decided those recordings weren't fit to release and another attempt was made in October to record the album, sometimes at Pluto Studios with John Porter, the Roxy Music bass player.

I was welcome around The Smiths, I was good mates with Andy after all, and went down to the studio on Granby Row a few times to hang out with the lads, driving Andy back home after midnight, once the day's work had been done.

This time the band had got it right and their rise to the top was assured.

I started following The Smiths during their first small tour of Britain including a miners' benefit gig in the Staffordshire town of Cannock where, after the gig in a marquee on the green, we all had to get away quick after a mean looking bunch of skinheads with National Front tattoos looked like they were about to lynch Morrissey and stick his bunches of gladioli where the sun don't shine.

Later that year I drove Andy Rourke down to London to a gig at the Brixton Ace. Seymour Stein, boss of Sire Records in America, was in attendance after jetting in on Concorde to watch his new signing, The Smiths. He had big plans for the band in the States and he liked what he saw. In the dressing room after the gig whilst quaffing champagne, he got me confused with either Andy or Mike and congratulated me.

'Great gig guy,' he said.

My only thought was *if only!* but it was too late now, I had made my bed and now I was going to have to lie in it.

8

How Not to be in Iconic Manchester Band, Part 2

At the end of the year Terry Hall went for a haircut at Vidal Sassoon's in Manchester, where Johnny Marr's girlfriend Angie Brown was working as a receptionist. They got chatting and Terry mentioned he was looking for a drummer for his new band called The Colourfield, now that Fun Boy Three had disbanded. Angie mentioned my name and an audition was arranged for me around December time at a studio in Leamington Spa, near Terry's Coventry home.

This is what you do if you don't want to be in (another) one of Manchester's most iconic bands: you leave your mates' band (again) for a shot at redemption. Although this wouldn't work out, I still feel I made the right decision here. The Roses weren't really formed or serious at this point, whereas all I wanted to do was drum for a living. This was a lifeline.

Terry Hall was an icon. I was a massive fan of the The Specials and of Fun Boy Three and this, I thought, was the opportunity I'd been hoping to get again after missing The Smiths' parade.

So, after explaining the situation to Ian, John, Andy and Pete and getting their blessing, I moved my drum kit away from Starkey House again where the embryonic Stone Roses were being formed. I got a bit of space in The Smiths latest rehearsal room above a shop on Portland Street in Manchester, called Crazy Face and began to practise for the audition.

The shop was owned by Joe Moss who would become Johnny Marr's mentor and The Smiths' first manager. He owned a property in Marple Bridge, a picturesque village just outside Stockport. Johnny Marr stayed there a while after moving from his lodgings in Bowdon and I would drive out there and hang out with him occasionally.

On one visit, a hairdresser called Andrew Berry was there to cut Johnny's flat-top into shape and offered to cut my hair as well. I liked Andrew straight away and he did a great job on my hair, which was also a flat-top style. He was going out with Tracey Donnelly who worked in the office of Factory Records on Palatine Road in leafy Didsbury and he was a DJ at the Haçienda on Friday nights. He had also set up a hairdressing salon called Swing in the dressing rooms of the Hacienda, directly under the stage. Andrew worked with another hairdresser, Neil Drinkwater, and a dreadlocked colourist called Mike 'Rocco' Arrojo. Andrew was talking about starting a band. It was in Swing that I met my first wife Mandy, a year or so later, after calling in for a chat with Andrew. Mandy was washing someone's hair in one of the sinks before Andrew got to work his magic with his scissors. Tracey also came in to man the phones and I think Mandy was an acquaintance of hers.

Meanwhile, until Alan 'Reni' Wren answered a 'Drummer wanted' advert placed in the A1 music shop in Manchester and joined the Roses the following year, 1984, that legend was on hold.

Ian hitchhiked around Europe and John started a separate band called The Waterfront which included Gary 'Mani' Mounfield on bass. He became mates with Ian and John through his mutual appreciation of all things scooter, before joining the band.

Though I've read reports to the contrary, as far as I remember, the band I was in was never called The Stone Roses so I didn't exactly just miss that in the same way as with The Smiths. I think I played a couple more times with them after The Colourfield but this marked the end of any permanence on my part. When they re-dedicated themselves and became The Stone Roses, I was in The Weeds. Like I say, I think I did the odd thing with them but they understandably ended up seeking someone more reliable. I don't deny that it would have been great to have been in a successful band with my schoolmates, but I was not at all unhappy when they began their ascent as I was, by that time, in The Fall. The lad they got in wasn't too bad either, to be fair. Reni is in a different league to me. One of the finest I've seen.

Back to the story.

Back in Leamington Spa, I passed the audition with Terry Hall's The Colourfield and was offered the gig on the spot. They were to release their first single, simply called 'The Colourfield' at the start of 1984. I met them a week later at Wessex Studios, down south, where I was introduced to engineer, Jeremy Green, who had worked on a lot of The Clash's records in the past.

Come January '84, Terry had set up three weeks of rehearsals in preparation for an appearance on *The Tube*, a live TV show filmed up in Newcastle and presented at first by Jools Holland, but when we were on, by Muriel Gray. I jacked in my job at the fishmonger and threw my lot in with the band.

I set off in my white Dolomite for the first day of rehearsals, above a pub, just outside Coventry called The General Wolfe. The Colourfield were due to perform their debut single, the b-side 'Sorry', and Kim Fowley's 'The Trip' live on the show at the beginning of February. So for the next three weeks I would be staying in a Coventry hotel from Monday to Friday, returning home at the weekends and driving back down the M6 again on the Monday mornings.

After starting work at 11 a.m. every day, we would go through the three songs time and time again whilst Terry got to grips with the emulator computer that was used to record the single. At night we would go into the centre of Coventry calling in at a couple of pubs or the bar of the Trusthouse Forte Hotel for a banana daiquiri.

It wasn't quite working.

Terry never opened up to me once in the three weeks and the other two in the band just seemed to kiss Terry's arse all the time. There were a lot of in-jokes which I didn't seem to be privy to. I found the whole rehearsal experience with them quite draining, and couldn't wait to get back up the M6 on a Friday night.

During the second week, as I was approaching the Coventry exit on the M6, the engine on the Dolomite blew a head gasket, which pissed me off no end. I stuck the car in a garage near the General Wolfe and a quote came back for £500. I didn't have much choice but to fix it. Just great, there went a third of my Colourfield wages straight away. I spent some money running those bangers …

For the third and final week, a young guitarist from Salford joined us for rehearsals. His name was Craig Gannon and he had just come off a gig with The Bluebells, best known for the song 'Young at Heart'. Aged only 17 he could already play his semi-acoustic Gretsch better than most people twice his age. He had an engaging smile which lit up the room and put me at ease for the first time on the gig, not just because we were roughly from the same part of the world. I liked Craig as a person, he was very friendly, and I finally had someone to talk to, as I wasn't getting on with Terry's sycophants. I'm not keen on people who laugh at the boss's private jokes, then ignore you until he cracks another one. Terry was okay but as I said before he was very quiet, withdrawn and never really tried to engage me in conversation. About the most I got out of him was one evening when we all went up to the Haçienda and he spent the night eyeing-up Gina.

She was a bit of a head-turner, to be fair, Gina. The week before I started going out with her, back in 1981, Dave Columb, who was under the impression that he was going out with her - maybe they'd copped off or something - ended up breaking John Squire's nose in some sort of tug of war over her.

So perhaps he wasn't alone in that regard, Terry. Terry Hall is still one of my favourite lyricists from my generation though and I like his sardonic delivery.

Finally we set off one Thursday on the train to Newcastle to do the The Tube, which went out live on the Friday night. It was the first time I had experienced first-class travel. After doing a run through at the Tyne Tees studio in the city, we checked in to the Gosforth Park Hotel. After dumping my bag in my room, I went down to the hotel bar with Craig and got chatting to the singer Sade, who was a real sweetheart. She was performing 'Your Love is King' just prior to The Colourfield's closing spot and made me feel at ease after telling her it was my first time on TV and that I felt a little nervous.

As it happened, I wasn't that nervous at all when Muriel Gray introduced Terry's new project to the nation's front rooms. The songs went well and I was happy with my performance. Back in my hotel room, I wrote the band's manager Pete, who I considered a snake from the moment I met him, a bill for my services then went to party with Sade back downstairs in the bar until the early hours. Before going to bed I pulled Craig off the window ledge as he had had a few by now and I worried he could easily have fallen to his death.

In the morning, Craig and I travelled back to Manchester together after saying our goodbyes to the others. I already knew deep down they wouldn't be asking me to stay on after asking the evasive Pete, what was coming up next.

Despite my bad feeling, a couple of days later I phoned Terry Hall's manager to see if there was any more work with The Colourfield, but he fobbed me off straight away, saying, 'Essentially, Terry's down in Coventry and you live up north. So, no, there is nothing else for you at this stage.'

I came away from the experience with a bitter taste in my mouth. The only positive I got from my time in the band was when I passed Craig's phone number on to Johnny Marr the following year. Johnny ended up appointing Craig as a second guitarist in The Smiths to beef up their sound for a tour in the US.

So that was that. Another opportunity gone. Was it something I'd done - an inability to get along with those three? Maybe I was withdrawn because I was missing the drugs. I don't know really. I felt I'd performed well, though.

It reminded me of the brief period at the start of the decade when I had worked for six months, for a paltry £23.50 a week, on a government sponsored training scheme, for a wedding photographer in Altrincham. It was common practice for employers to take on new staff, paid for by the government, and then discard them like litter before signing up another hopeful, even though the first guy had done a good job, as I had done.

'It seems in this pop game, one minute you're living like a king and the next minute you're down and out, Simon,' my dad said.

You won't be told, I thought.

9

Heaven Knows I'm Miserable Now

With the rejection from The Colourfield, who carried on for a while longer without me, I was, for the first time in my life, miserable. Though I was obviously gutted at missing the rise of The Smiths, I had spent much of that time clouded in a haze of hashish and heroin smoke. Mixed with the joy of seeing my mates doing well and flitting about from one party to the next, I wasn't entirely deflated. But now I didn't even have a job so I couldn't go out or score the odd high.

I signed on for the first and only time.

Johnny and Angie were still looking out for me and set me up with auditions whenever they heard of anything.

I went for an audition with Sheffield pop sensations, ABC, after drummer Dave Palmer had quit the band. I drove over to the YMCA in Sheffield, to be met by a very personable Martin Fry and a miserable bass player who I took an instant dislike to. They gave me thirty minutes but I didn't make the cut.

I got another thirty minutes with the band Prefab Sprout, down at Nomis Studios in London. I thought they were great and the singer Paddy McAloon was very genial, though he did say they'd just auditioned Neil Conti who they were thinking of taking on. So I didn't get that gig. Unfortunately, I just didn't have the experience against the likes of Conti who went on to work with David Bowie.

Still, that was no consolation to me and these rejections didn't do much for my confidence.

I still followed The Smiths, which was good, but yet again that was a reminder of what might have been.

I have one good memory, in March of that year, 1984. I was picking up Morrissey and Eurovision Song Contest winner, Sandie Shaw, from Piccadilly train station in the repaired Dolomite and giving them a lift to The Smiths gig at The Free Trade Hall just down the road.

'What a lovely car, Simon,' Morrissey said, caressing the woodwork.

After the gig, I took my mum and Aunty Catherine backstage for their first time. My mum was a little bit giddy that Sandie Shaw was there as she had bought her hit record 'Puppet on a String' in the sixties. I'd never seen her like that before so I introduced her to Sandie.

'I used to be a fan of yours,' my mum said, a little star struck.

'What happened then?' Sandie shot back, impassively.

I thought this was quite funny but an awkward silence ensued. My mum seemed a bit taken aback as if she'd fluffed her lines but we all carried on and had a good night. I was chuffed she was there and got to meet Sandie, and I also introduced her to Johnny and Andy's mums.

Not long after that, I started hanging about with an acquaintance of Johnny and Andy called Joe. At that time, Joe was a shoplifter by trade. He asked me if I wanted to earn a bit of money driving him around various bookshops offloading stolen books. I agreed and we did this for several weeks until one day we stopped outside a shop in Didsbury and he asked driver to turn fencer. He gave me some story that he couldn't go in there because the guy would recognise him. I was very gullible back then, particularly compared with some of the rogues I used to knock about with. Stupidly, I took these books in and asked the guy did he want to buy them. The shopkeeper kept me waiting a couple of minutes, making an excuse that he just had to attend to something, while he went in the back, and the next thing you know a copper walks in and nicks me. I got arrested for handling stolen goods and was taken to the police station on Brownley Road in Wythenshawe before being moved to a station in Wilmslow.

My parents came to see me later that evening with carrier bags full of food, books and magazines that suggested I'd been sentenced to six months. My dad looked like he'd aged ten years on that very night. I confessed to possession of stolen goods and had to pay a hefty fine over several monthly instalments.

That marked the end of my career as a petty thief.

My parents, perhaps seeing that crime wasn't my calling, started to hassle me about getting a proper job. So, I did a few jobs. I worked part-time at the Wellgreen Beefeater restaurant, pouring out glasses of wine from the dispensary bar for a couple of months. I worked at the Alpine Hotel in Bowdon briefly too but ended up jacking that as well.

I decided to go back to college and so I went to Salford Tech that September to get my City and Guilds in catering. I don't really know why, probably because of my experience in the fishmonger in Wilmslow and the lack of fuel money and funds generally, even though I was still living at home. It seemed as good an idea as any and people always have to eat. I thought I'd give it a try.

I was on day release at County Hall in Piccadilly Gardens, the large council canteen that provided for staff at the Greater Manchester Council, whilst learning how to make béchamel sauce and how to mirepoix vegetables correctly with my new set of kitchen knives and chefs' whites. After two months of attending Salford Tech, the catering manager at County Hall asked me if I wanted a full-time position in the kitchens there. It wasn't exactly the gig I was looking for, but as I'd blown it with The Smiths and Terry Hall, this was what I was going to have to do for the time being, just to have my own independence and freedom to get back into the music scene.

I had to get the train past Morrissey's mum's house on Kings Road every morning and night. On more than one occasion, the lyric to 'Nowhere Fast' would float through my head as I went past, feeling sorry for myself. *'And when a train goes by, it's such a sad sound.'*

I became friendly with the pastry chef at County Hall, a guy called Pat who looked out for me and kept the alcoholic head chef Neil off my back. Neil used to get on my case about being a posh kid from Hale Barns. I never considered myself posh, though I don't deny I did have advantages. Advantages I didn't make the best use of. Anyway, Neil saw himself as some kind of working-class hero for scorning my roots.

Off he'd toddle into the walk-in fridge, sneak a great slug of brandy and come back as if nobody knew, reeking like he was about to be flambéed.

'Put them chips on posh boy, what? Is your dad going to come and do it for you?'

'Fuck off dickhead.'

Pat was good to me though and had his own dislike for Neil, like most of the staff. Pat lived in Prestwich and had a mate who knew Ian Nance, the guitarist in punk hopefuls V2 who had scored a hit in the punk charts of the late seventies with the single, 'Man In The Box.' I had gone to see V2 at the Bowdon Vale Club whilst still at school. After this initial success, the group imploded amongst the usual volatile mixture of sex, drugs, and rock 'n' roll and now Nance was hoping to resurrect the band with himself on lead vocals and guitar. He let it be known that a drummer was required in the new line-up of V2 mark II, so a freezing lock up in Salford was my next port of call.

Nance and the bass player, whose name I can't recall, were keen to have me in, but again, my heart just wasn't in it. Music is a very subjective thing, and I felt, unless I was getting paid, I'd rather take my chances with something I was into. There seems to be a recurring theme here don't you think?

Sometimes during the working day, Ian Brown, who was back from hitchhiking around Europe, used to appear at lunchtime on the pavement outside County Hall. I would peer down from the kitchens every day at one o'clock, just to check if he was there, and if so, we would go to the Piccadilly Cafe over in the bus station for a brew and a bag of chips on my dinner time. This cheered me up no end.

10

The Weeds

I wasn't a total recluse. I'd begun hanging around regularly at Andrew Berry's Swing hairdressing salon, where I would sometimes find him coiffing Morrissey's quiff or shooting the breeze with other clients like Bernard Sumner or Gary 'The Chef.' He was a great raconteur, Andrew.

I began driving to work and parking the Dolomite near the Haçienda, so at 4 p.m. when work was done, I would call in for a bit. I sometimes gave Andrew's girlfriend Tracey Donnelly, who was working in the salon or in the new Factory Records office, above the Haçienda, a lift home as she lived near my mum's. She used to give me two quid a time, thus sharing the cost of the fuel. Pound coins had not long been out.

'I'll cross your palm with gold, Si' she'd say, so I gave her a lift.

Plus I fancied Tracey, if I'm honest. Tracey had two brothers, Anthony and Chris, who went on to establish the Gio Goi casual clothing company, which was everywhere in the Madchester years.

I knew Andrew wanted to start a little group and on one of these journeys with Tracey, we arranged to all go round to Rocco's flat in Hulme to discuss the new band.

'Alright Rocco.'

'Alright. Fancy a toke on this baton?'

Andrew asked me to be part of a trio called The Weeds, inspired by a little hobby one or two of us got up to.

The first place The Weeds got together was in a two-bed flat on Epping Walk in Hulme that belonged to bass player Rocco's girlfriend Kaz. It wasn't one of the notorious crescents, but it too was infested with cockroaches.

The interior walls were cheerfully painted black and you could look out over Princess Parkway, which wasn't the most scenic. It was near where the iconic picture of the band Joy Division, standing in the snow on the footbridge from Epping Walk over Princess Parkway connecting the two sides of Hulme, was shot by Kevin Cummins, the rock photographer.

Slowly, we began to pick up the instruments again. I brought the Tama drum kit round and the band began to settle into a blues-rock sound.

It was only a ten-minute walk from County Hall, so I would park outside the flat early in the morning and walk into town, then after work call in at the flat for a smoke before heading home.

In part due to the noise and in part because we needed a better space anyway, The Weeds started rehearsing at The Boardwalk, a dingy nightclub and concert venue in an ex-Victorian church school on Little Peter Street. I started to sleep at the flat more often, although my car got broken into a couple of times - a new sheepskin coat got nicked once.

It was in Hulme that I was first introduced to speed. It was plentiful and cheap and helped fuel our hectic lifestyles with work and the music and going out. You could score any drug you wanted within a half-mile radius of The Eagle pub, on a communal green in the middle of one the crescents.

I remember one day in the summer of 1985, our musical trio were watching *Live Aid* on TV at our mate Andy Cadman's flat on Bonsall Street during the scorching hot day, with the front door wide open to ventilate the place. Somebody managed to sneak in and run off with a guitar that was left in the hallway without any of us noticing a thing. This sort of thing happened a lot in Hulme as there were so many addicts on the look out for money for their next fix. Thankfully, I never got that desperate for a hit.

The council were giving away keys for flats to practically anyone who wanted one for a minimal rent. If you didn't want to pay rent, people just broke into an empty one and started squatting there anyway and the authorities turned a blind eye. Very rarely did you see any police about. They seemed to be happy that all the drug trafficking was contained in the concrete monstrosity. Only when someone was attacked or as happened on rare occasion, murdered, did you see the police intervene. Soon, younger kids on mountain bikes could be seen openly selling drugs to the tenants and to strangers travelling in from other areas - as far afield as Leeds, Liverpool and Birmingham - just to score.

I got into a bit of trouble at work, during the trial of Dr Máire O'Shea, who was charged under the Prevention of Terrorism Act and appeared at the Crown Court on Aytoun Street in Manchester, just at the rear of County Hall. For a week or so in the morning, after arriving at work at about 7.30 a.m., a huge convoy of armed police vehicles and motorcycle outriders could be heard escorting the prison van that contained the accused around the back of the Greater Manchester Council headquarters to the Crown Court.

One day I decided to come in early and have a nosey at the prisoners' cavalcade. I made my way to the roof of County Hall which was out of bounds to a trainee chef like me and watched the arrival of the convoy. I noticed a police sharpshooter positioned in the clock tower of the courts opposite, with his high-powered rifle easily visible, staring at me for ages, through a huge pair of binoculars, as the multiple sirens heralded the convoy's arrival.

About two minutes later the catering manager and an unidentified man in a dark suit came bounding out on to the roof and shouted at me, 'Come back inside. Off the roof! Now!'

For my sins, hardly the crime of the century, I was sent out into exile to run a small canteen, full of bin wagon mechanics in Farnworth near Bolton. I enjoyed my time there. I worked with two local girls, who did all the washing up for me - heroines both. It was all egg and chips mostly, and the rest of the time feet up in the office, reading the papers, so I had an easy life and made a bit of money on the fuel expenses incurred from driving to work every day.

One of my favourite clubs at the time was The International 1, on Anson Road, just outside the city centre. The same management team also had the International 2, which was bigger, more decrepit and was rough to be honest. The manager of The International 1 was Gareth Evans, who would go on to be the manager of The Stone Roses, replacing Howard Jones. I saw quite a few bands there. I went to see Simply Red just before they went massive, as well as the Go-Betweens, Husker Du and at Christmas, The Damned. Along with the Haçienda it was a good place to go and watch any interesting bands coming through.

It was about this time that someone introduced me to the album *This Nation's Saving Grace* by The Fall. I wasn't a fan of the band back at Altrincham Grammar School, like Andy Wake was, but I really liked this record a lot. It seemed a lot easier on the ear than the earlier stuff. Via

The International, I was introduced to Karl Burns, The Fall's drummer. He lived in Hulme with his girlfriend, Sue Dean, who was photographing a lot of the upcoming bands at Gareth's club, where The Weeds would play one of their first gigs at the start of 1986.

Marc Riley, who happened to be an ex-patient of my dad's, and who had left The Fall after a punch up with Mark E Smith whilst on tour in Australia, lived in the same block of flats as Craig Scanlon, the guitarist in the current Fall line-up. He had started up a record label, called In Tape Records, and ran the label with his partner Jim from the large flat in Sale, just down the road from the Rourke household, where he kept a huge python in a glass tank.

Andrew Berry knew Marc Riley well - they both grew up in Wythenshawe - and when the In Tape boss heard a live recording from the International gig, a recording session was set up at Suite 16 Studios in Rochdale, with a view to recording 'China Doll' as a one-off single. It was a good first effort that sounded like a cross between The Stooges and The Rolling Stones, but didn't set the world on fire. Ian Tilton, the rock photographer, did a photo session with us for the cover of the single in a weed-strewn meadow by the side of the M60, near Sale Water Park.

The band had already played support to Psychic TV and Strawberry Switchblade at the Hammersmith Palais and opened for Felt at the Clarendon Ballroom, in London, and we were keen to do as many gigs as possible. Neil Drinkwater would make all the phone calls and do all the fixing that needs to be done when a band puts on its own gigs.

A gig was booked to play support to a band called The Bodines at The Boardwalk. We knew the place and its owner, Colin Sinclair, from rehearsing in one of the rooms in the basement. A lot of Manchester bands honed their sound there, the Mondays, The Charlatans, Oasis. We would often play pool with other bands such as Inca Babies, or hairdressers' favourite Swing Out Sister, before going for a night out at the Haçienda.

On the night of the gig, I went to pick up Andrew at tea time from his mum's place in Wythenshawe, before making our way in the Triumph Dolomite, which Neil had nicknamed The White Chariot, to pick up Rocco and his bass guitar from a residential address in West Didsbury where his mate lived. After that we were to carry on in to Manchester to meet Carrie Lawson, the new guitarist, at the soundcheck.

Carrie, Karl Burns' new girlfriend, had moved up to Manchester from Derby where she had been working at the local BBC radio station, interviewing bands on the weekly 'Indie' show. If there was ever a template for a 'Rock Chick', she was probably it, with her Barbie doll looks, big blonde hair, and leather kecks which she always wore. I guess it was something to do with adding a bit of glamour to the band. She added some nice guitar licks too though, so it wasn't a token gesture.

I pulled the car up near the terraced house in West Didsbury and Andrew went to go and get Rocco whilst I waited outside. After waiting for twenty minutes I started to get a bit concerned about making our soundcheck in time and I went to find out what the delay was. I pressed the doorbell and a balding middle-aged bloke opened the door. Before I had time to think, the drug squad officer gripped both of my wrists and dragged me into the rear room of the house, past the front room where Andrew was already being searched and questioned. After protesting my innocence, the drug squad officer said they had a warrant to search the premises for illegal drugs, which they showed me. They were now going to strip search me right there in the back room of someone's house, who I didn't even know.

'Have you got any drugs on you Simon?' he asked.

I knew the answer to this one: 'No.'

Unconvinced, the intimate search began, finishing up with me being bent over naked with a hairy-arsed copper shining a Maglite up my nether regions.

Nothing.

It was only when he took a closer look at my socks that were discarded on the floor that out popped a tenner's worth of Afghani Black.

Shit. Busted.

In the room next door the same thing was happening to Andrew. We were both read our rights and carted off in two cars to Platt Lane cop shop, where we were charged with possession of a Class C controlled drug with a court appearance in a couple of days' time.

The annoying thing was, Rocco wasn't even at his mate's house that had been under police surveillance for weeks. The cops believed there to be a speed laboratory operating inside. They were wrong and snagged the wrong people, but they did release me and Andrew later that night and we belatedly got to the gig, and played better than we ever had. Rock and roll, eh?

At our court appearance, where the pair of us both received a £50 fine, the elderly judge stated that when he was younger he too had been into jazz music, almost apologising for imposing the fine on us.

This would not mark the end of my drug use, nor my last bust.

A couple of years later I got caught with a lump of resin I bought in The Spinners pub in Hulme and loaded into a riot van. I swallowed the resin, about fifteen quids' worth, and was clocked doing it.

'Open his mouth, open his mouth!' the officers were shouting, 'he's trying to swallow it.'

I did manage to swallow it but it was so dry.

The coppers held me down trying to get it out, forced my jaws open saying it was on my tongue. My tongue was stained with the thick resin.

I got off on a technicality because there was no doctor present.

Another time, I was held up outside The Spinners, before all the crescents there got demolished. I was sat in my car, putting my seatbelt on, when a young lad on a mountain bike pulled up alongside, opened the door, sat in the passenger seat and pulled a gun on me.

'Give us your money.'

'I haven't got any. I've just spent it on a draw.'

'Hand it over.'

I didn't stop to see if the gun was real or not, just passed him the draw.

'My name's Turbo,' he said, boastfully, riding off into the crescents in broad daylight.

Some years later, I heard on the radio that a dealer with the street name Turbo had been shot dead in Moss Side. I'll never know if it was the same guy. Things got out of hand in Manchester in the late eighties and early nineties.

In February 1986, The Weeds were offered the first of several support slots with The Fall in Bristol, London and Lancaster, probably due to the fact that Andrew was now also cutting Fall singer Mark E Smith and his new wife Brix's hair on a regular basis.

Watching The Fall on stage was a real eye-opener. There was a massive slanging match going on at the Harlesden Mean Fiddler gig in London, between Mark and the drummer Karl Burns, about who knows what and I would soon find out that manic interband arguments were a regular occurrence in the wonderful and frightening world of The Fall.

After the gig was over and we were packing our equipment away in the Salford Van Hire Transit we'd hired for a couple of days, I noticed Mark walking over in my direction as if to ask me something. I had never spoken to him before, so was wondering what it was he wanted.

'Excuse me cock. Can I have a quick word with you?'

'Yeah sure,' I replied. 'Shall we sit in the van?'

After we climbed in the front of the Transit, Mark offered me an Embassy filter from a dog-eared packet, pulled out of his expensive black Armani jacket.

'How do you feel about joining The Fall?'

'What, now?'

'Keep it to yourself, cock,' he said, 'Come round to my house for a chat on Monday afternoon.'

It wasn't explicitly stated that Karl was going to be sacked but it was obvious to everyone that there was trouble between the two of them.

He wrote down his telephone number for me on the remnants of the Embassy packet. Twenty minutes later I was driving the van back up the M1 towards Manchester thinking of nothing but the brief conversation with Mark. I thought it best not to say anything to my bandmates until I had met with Mark and heard what he was offering. I was also aware of the fact that The Fall was booked to do a tour of the US that would take up most of the next month and that the Weeds had also been asked to support The Fall again on a tour of Scotland in April on their return from America.

So on the Monday at the agreed time of 1.30 p.m. I went to Mark's house in Sedgley Park, near Prestwich village. I rapped on the door of the semi-detached on the small suburban street and saw the venetian blinds twitching. After what seemed like an eternity the door was finally opened and there stood a smiling Mark, who welcomed me into his world.

'Hello cock.'

We went into his dining room/office overlooking the small garden at the back. He made me a cup of tea in a huge cup and saucer in his state-of-the-art kitchen and we sat down at the black dining room table that I instantly recognised from the cover of a recent Fall single 'Couldn't Get Ahead'. The table was strewn with handwritten lyrics, a typewriter, and half a bottle of Bell's Whisky from which he offered me a glass. A relaxing bubbling noise emanated from the filter of a large fish tank filled with tiny silver fish that darted in and out of a partly-sunken galleon.

Mark told me he wanted Karl out of the group on completion of The Fall's latest jaunt in the US, which would be in a month's time. Did I want the gig bearing in mind I had The Weeds going and was holding down a full-time job at the canteen in Farnworth?

It didn't take me too long to come to a decision. I wasn't going to miss this opportunity, though I felt a bit guilty about Karl, who I considered a mate although I had only met him a few times at this point.

Andrew had turned down the offer of a recording deal with Factory Records after Tony Wilson saw The Weeds supporting The Happy Mondays. It was at Corbieres, a tiny subterranean venue that looks like a whitewashed wine cellar, that was (and still is) renowned as having the best jukebox in town. Wilson wanted to sign us - he signed The Mondays, the same night - but Andrew had it in his head that he wanted to be on EMI or one of the other majors. It seemed stupid to me not to sign for Factory - The Weeds didn't exactly have loads of label interest.

The Fall, on the other hand, were signed to Beggars Banquet, had gigs lined up, a new LP which I liked, and a large cult following.

So for me, as long as I was offered something like the wages I was on with the council, it wasn't a hard decision to make. Mark offered a three-month trial period at £100 a week - £50 less than I earned in Farnworth. I was happy with his terms and said I'd do it there and then if he'd put it in writing. He scribbled the terms down on a scrap of paper off the desk and handed it to me.

Of course all this was subject to me passing an audition, which I knew I could breeze through easily as I now knew all the songs off *This Nation's Saving Grace* and a lot of the band's single releases. Mark seemed to already have made his mind up about me joining his band after watching me warm up with The Weeds, but said he would get bass player Steve Hanley to set up the audition at The Boardwalk after their return from the US.

With that, the business was concluded and he offered me another whisky, which I accepted though I couldn't stand the stuff, and chopped out a large line of speed for me. He put a Link Wray album on his turntable, which I really enjoyed listening to for an hour.

We chatted for quite a while about all sorts of things before Brix, Mark's wife and bandmate, returned from a shopping trip to Kendals in Manchester, laden with carrier bags.

She seemed excited that I was replacing Karl and joining the group and asked if I would stay for dinner. As I had just tanned a large line, I made my excuses and left after an enjoyable afternoon getting to know Mark. My thought as I drove home was: when shall I hand in my notice?

I waited another month while The Fall were away, then found out Karl hadn't been sacked yet after their return from the States. They still had three dates in Scotland: Glasgow, Edinburgh, and Aberdeen to play, before I eventually got the green light. Knowing that The Weeds were the support in Scotland and so I'd have either one or the other gig, I decided to jettison my catering career and handed in my notice at work. They were very supportive towards me and the two girls organised a whip round to get me a card and a nice new stick bag as a leaving present which was very touching I must say.

ACT II

11

The Wonderful World of The Fall

Off we went in my Triumph, up the M6 and over the border into Scotland, to begin The Weeds last tour, Neil skinning up all the way in the back.

We stopped at the services and as we got out for a piss, a cloud of marijuana smoke billowed out of The White Chariot.

The Fall pulled up behind us as we spilled out of the Dolomite.

Mark thought this was hilarious.

'Look at 'em, they look like the Furry Freak Brothers,' he cackled.

The Weeds sets seemed to go down well enough, though most people stood at the bar waiting for The Fall to come on. I watched their set as well, but with vested interest. All the while I was keeping my hastily drawn contract with Mark quiet and learning the drum parts that I would soon be playing at the 'audition', on the small stage at The Boardwalk, upon our return to Manchester.

The day arrived and went without a hitch. It was just a formality really and after an hour's run through The Fall's set list, Mark said, 'OK cock, you've got the job, do you fancy a pint?'

I can't remember what I said or did. Probably just said thanks and smiled as I had been around the band a bit by now and I felt I had the gig in the bag. I was pleased though, because I was getting roughly the same sort of wage as the canteen work and it was doing the one job I really wanted to do.

So. I was going to play with the Smiths after all.

I let The Weeds know first and they gave me their blessings. I obviously owed The Weeds, because if it hadn't have been for them, I'd never have got The Fall gig. Who knows, I might have drifted out of music altogether.

The only person who seemed a bit put out was Carrie.

'It won't change your life, you know,' she said, tartly.

It was an angry reaction, but then, I had just more or less disbanded The Weeds and taken her boyfriend's job. Deep down I knew joining The Fall wouldn't change my life, but I didn't think it needed pointing out! Despite this, I was genuinely excited about where this new opportunity might take me

Next, I told my parents who had different opinions regarding my decision to join. My dad didn't like the idea at all after my experience with Terry Hall and The Colourfield, watching me throw in the towel at the job for life in the council kitchens. My mum on the other hand was really pleased for me and said, 'Simon, just do whatever makes you happy and your father and I will support you.' My mum dropped me off at Mark's one day when my car was off the road and wanted to meet Mark. It was a bit awkward, my mum wanting to meet him, but he was all charm and good manners and my mum liked him.

I would have joined the band regardless of any endorsement - I couldn't refuse - but it felt good to hear after the ups and downs of the last four years.

I told a few mates but before I knew it, most people I knew in the Manchester indie music scene seemed to know and congratulate me on the news.

Johnny Marr was made up for me and gave me some advice.

'Don't mix your drugs and eat plenty every day.'

I was eating fine - I had worked at a canteen - but I was mixing the drugs, still scoring the odd fiver-bag of heroin.

The Smiths were having their own drug issues. Andy Rourke was temporarily kicked out of the band after his heroin use went public. I saw him at Johnny Marr's house just after he'd been given the news. He was white as a sheet, cradling his head in hands. I really felt for him. I knew that he was coming down and it must have felt like his world was imploding.

I don't really know why Mark took me on. I knew things were bad with him and Karl. I can only surmise that he wanted a bit of harmony in the band. Mark took me for a drink and told me that he'd been asking around about me.

'Not a bad word has come back about you, Simon,' he said, handing me a pint. I was gratified, but I didn't think much of his network of informers. Least he didn't know about the gear.

Anyway, Brix and Mark both made me feel welcome. I hit it off with Brix straight away. I fitted Mark's criteria at the time (it was never consistent over the years) in that I wasn't really a Fall fan and kept the drumming simple. Beyond that, it was maybe just a case of being in the right place at the right time.

I wasn't really concerned with why - I was getting paid for doing something I loved.

Within a week, Mark and I drove over to Amazon Recording Studios just outside Liverpool to work on the song 'Hey! Luciani' with producer Ian Broudie. It was Mark's intention to use the song as the title track in an upcoming play he was writing about the allegedly suspicious death of Pope John Paul I, several years earlier.

Mark had read a bestseller by David Yallop called *In God's Name* the previous year and found the subject matter very interesting indeed. His intention was to put on his own slant on the late Pope's death, performing a play in London later in the year.

Much of the song had already been completed in a previous recording session the band had done. Producer Ian Broudie, who went on to form The Lightning Seeds, recorded me playing a floor tom over the middle eight. Mark wanted quite a primitive driving sound.

'Play it like this, cock,' he's going, hammering an out-of-time beat on the studio desk.

This was the first thing I recorded for The Fall. Not much really, but at least it was a start. I think Mark just wanted to get me on the record and get me involved because all I did was hit this floor tom for eight bars. But it was a gesture I appreciated. I felt I was part of the band now.

My first gig was at Folkestone's Leas Cliff Hall in June of 1986, followed by a series of shows in England and a number of European festival dates. We had a Scouse driver/roadie called Colin, who had worked with The Kinks and took us everywhere in a black customised Dodge van with a shagpile carpet-covered interior. It was like getting in the Scooby Doo Mystery Machine, except Shaggy had to share his stash. He looked like Guns N' Roses' guitarist Slash, from a distance. He had black leathers and corkscrew perm. He sounded like a tambourine with all his bracelets and skull-adorned bling. He liked to inhale (via the nose) something he called 'Bolivian marching powder'. He was very generous with it, as well, and after breakfast in whatever hotel we were staying in, he would always invite me to his room for a livener before we set off on the road again. He made me laugh did Colin with his larking about and his general Scouse cheeky-chappy banter. I could tell he'd been doing this sort of thing a long time.

One day he reversed the Dodge van at high speed into the side of a new Mercedes, parked at Watford Gap Services, before driving off quickly with all the band inside. He must have thought that none of us had noticed which, of course, we all had. He was with us for another year or so. He went on to be Ray Davies's guitar tech before returning in the early nineties for a while. He was the fastest stringer of a guitar I ever saw. I sometimes wonder where he is now.

I'd landed on my feet. While I thought The Fall were a league below the likes of The Smiths, any regrets about not playing with them soon vanished.

We did a gig supporting Talk Talk, who really struck a chord with me, inside an aircraft hangar at Duxford Airfield in Cambridgeshire, amongst some classic British aircraft from World War II including a de Havilland Mosquito fighter. I'm a bit of geek about aeroplanes too, so this was brilliant.

We played in London where we had a similar sort of audience to anywhere else but it felt different in the capital. You'd have all kinds of journalists and photographers showing up, who never seemed to bother us when we played in the provinces. The music journos would hover backstage for an interview and ask Mark or Brix a few questions. Mark was also good in granting interviews to young trainee journalists if he thought they were going to ask intelligent questions. They never really asked me anything, it was the Mark E Smith show after all. It was only when Mark couldn't be arsed that he'd thrust me forward - if there was nobody else!

I knew what some of the songs were about as there were obvious references to people or places we knew or experiences we'd had. But honestly, half the time I didn't know what he was singing at all. I didn't mind as long as the fans were engrossed, which they were. Mark never printed the lyrics to the songs which I think was half of the mystique. People could make of them what they would. A lot of intellectual types would be poring over the words and discussing the wider meaning. Mark loved this kind of thing. He was always a bookworm and wanted people to work out the songs themselves. That said, he did let his mate 'Big' Dave Lough travel with us, flogging *The Fall Lyrics Book* from a suitcase at the back of the venue. Dave had transcribed the lyrics himself from the band's earlier material.

When I couldn't hear or decipher the words, I never really contemplated their meaning. Plus, I suppose, I'm like a lot of drummers, I'm more interested in the music and the tone of the singer rather than the actual lyrical content, as long as it isn't offensive. So call me a heathen, but that's how I feel about it.

Back then, I was far more interested in girls and drugs.

While we were in London, the band had a resident speed dealer at a flat in a tenement block opposite King's Cross station. I was a speed freeloader at first, never bought it. I stuck to weed and beer on the road. I suppose I just got into doing speed because it seemed everyone was doing it, like going for a pint with your mates.

'Fancy a line, Si?'

'Yeah alright then - just to be sociable …'

It was a bit of a bonding ritual. Have a line then get on the vodka and orange if we didn't have a gig. I personally couldn't have a proper drink if we had a gig or recording session, but taking speed was totally normal in those days. It smelt like cat piss, burned the inside of your nose, and kept you up for two days.

The highlight of the summer was a gig at G-Mex in Manchester, for The Festival of the Tenth Summer, a celebration of the ten years since the explosion of punk rock. It was the first gig in the new exhibition centre which had been Central Station. It was the biggest gig I'd played, about five thousand people. We played support to The Smiths and New Order, who were headlining, but it was busy even when we went on at tea time. I went to watch my mates from The Smiths, who seemed at the top of their game. Morrissey was gyrating and waving a sign in the air that read 'The Queen is Dead'. I don't think they did 'Suffer Little Children'. Morrissey would no doubt have known that the site we were playing was where Moors murderer Ian Brady had kept tapes of his and Myra's victims' screams in a coin-operated locker on one of the platforms. Anyway, sorry, what a horrible little fact that is.

There was a great atmosphere backstage as there weren't enough dressing rooms for everyone so we were mostly together in one open plan area, with the late Tony Wilson from Factory Records doing the rounds.

He was a mate of Mark's.

The gigs were great fun and I learnt a lot from Mark. Brix spent most of the time hanging out with us. She'd certainly made The Fall's sound a lot sweeter than the sound I remembered from school and she looked good too, with a pink Paisley Telecaster - it looked like something Prince might play.

Soon after, less than six months since egg and chips in Farnworth, I was in Abbey Road Studios for the first time, recording tracks, including 'Mr. Pharmacist' with John Leckie, known for his work with heavyweights like Pink Floyd and John Lennon. He made things easy for me in the famous St John's Wood Studio Two, which The Beatles had used. I was aware of the history of the place. It's probably cliché to say but I really did feel a special 'vibe' when recording there. It was a hive of activity. Everyone seemed to have a real sense of purpose about their art and the acoustics are superb.

Leckie wore something purple coloured every day and had an inner peace about him, and this wound up an alcohol and speed-fuelled Mark E Smith no end. Mark hated anything vaguely hippyish. At one point in the sessions, Mark spat at John, shouting 'Get some work done cunt', which made me feel very uncomfortable. John was a really nice guy and didn't deserve it. I must admit, I didn't mind if it was someone who needed cutting down, but this wasn't one of those cases. Still, it wasn't long before I got used to this kind of thing and it'd be in one ear and out the other. As long as he wasn't shouting at me.

Beggars Banquet, The Fall's record label at the time was footing the bill for the recordings and the hotels in London. Mark seemed to like Beggars as they gave him freedom to record what he wanted. We had a new manager, John Lennard, who promoted lots of other artistes at the time, under the name JLP Presents. He was a real life playboy - tanned, long flowing black hair, Porsche, massive mobile phone. I liked him though. He had an office in Gospel Oak and took a shine to Brix and Marcia Schofield, the band's new keyboard player. Marcia was from Brooklyn, New York, and joined The Fall not long after I had done so, at the end of the *Bend Sinister* sessions. She had a bit of attitude she did. In a good way though - like Brix.

One afternoon as we were grafting in the huge studio, I gazed up at the control room at the top of a steep staircase. Through the thick glass window, I spotted Simon Le Bon, singer with Duran Duran, accompanied by one of the Taylors, staring back down at us in their fedoras and pastel-coloured clothes, jacket sleeves rolled up à la *Miami Vice*. He was chatting to Leckie who was sat at the mixing desk - on The Fall's time. I think Leckie invited Le Bon in while Mark was in the pub, in case it kicked off, but actually, I think Mark would have really liked that. Not that he's a name-dropper or that he particularly liked the band but I'm sure he would have liked the kudos. Mark wasn't above hobnobbing with the stars, showing he belonged in the same world.

There were two sides to Mark, one being his caring, sharing, dare I say it, paternal side, which was a lot more evident at the beginning of my eleven years in the band.

The other side of Mark is his well-documented dictatorial streak. He could treat people like shit. Nasty, unnecessary stuff. Try to find people's soft spots and needle them. I do have to say though, that while there were unmistakable flashes of that kind of thing from the off, he was, actually, mainly, great fun to be around and genuinely wanted to look after his band. You can't last as long as he has simply by being an arsehole.

I've heard Mark likened to the late football manager Brian Clough and I discovered that Mark was an admirer and could see similarities in their man management style. They both liked to be very hands-on with their players and didn't suffer fools gladly. If Mark saw potential in a 'new signing' and actually liked you, he would encourage you to develop your style. In my case he kept telling me to keep the beat simple and to keep drum rolls to a bare minimum. He told me on more than one occasion how James Brown would fine his drummers $5 (or $1 - it changed all the time) when they threw an unnecessary drum roll into the mix. He tended to leave bass player Steve Hanley well alone most of the time, but often shouted at guitarist Craig Scanlon to, 'Wake up and play it with feeling will you', then making him do several passes of the same riff, while he went to the pub for an hour or so.

Upon his return, Mark would storm back into the studio, with renewed vigour and start shouting and bawling at whoever was in the firing line or whoever was pissing him off the most that day.

Also in the band's line-up when I joined was another Simon, Simon Rogers. A very talented musician, he had been writing and producing for The Fall as well as playing guitar and keyboards in the live set-up, for a couple of years already. Mark really respected Rogers. When 'Mr. Pharmacist' was released as a single later in the summer, Mark introduced me as 'John S. Woolstencroft' on the back of the record sleeve, perhaps because he thought it too poncey to have two Simons in the band, I don't really know for sure.

Relocating to Stockport in Yellow Two Studios, we carried on recording the album at an astonishing rate. Mark loved recording there because it was next door to The Black Lion, which served Boddingtons Bitter. I thought it tasted like dishwater.

The album was engineered by Chris Nagle, married for a time to Julia, who would eventually join the band in the mid-nineties.

I am proud of some of the tracks we did there, including 'Terry Waite Sez', 'Realm of Dusk', and 'U.S. 80's - 90's', but in the main it was recorded at a frenetic pace with Mark barking out orders to play it faster, usually depending on how much whizz or booze had been taken earlier in the day. Brix kept her husband in check, some of the time at least, and kept the quality control higher than it might otherwise have been.

When 'Mr. Pharmacist' was released as a single, it got quite a lot of airplay, especially on John Peel's night-time radio show, swelling the number of punters who came to see us play. I made the first of nine visits with the band to the BBC Maida Vale recording studios to record a live session for the Peel show. The sessions were great fun at first, but then the novelty sort of wore off over the years and the reality of the gruelling long days, requiring travelling from Manchester and back, kicked in.

Whilst the band were playing up in Glasgow in September, Mark announced that our wages were about to be increased overnight to £300 per week after an upturn in The Fall's popularity. This was brilliant. In 1986 that was a lot of money; worth more than double that today.

This was in the lobby of the Holiday Inn just by the train station, so while we waited for Brix to join us, I bought a round of Bloody Marys at the bar for Steve, Craig and myself to celebrate the good news: a toast to 'the engine room' of the band.

After a quick visit home we flew off to Austria for dates in Graz, Dornbirn, Linz and Vienna. Linz, in particular, I thought was beautiful - the Danube, a sliver of mercury, snaking through the fairytale castles and medieval halls.

We had to drive for hours and hours over the Alps to get to Dornbirn, nearly falling over the edge of a single-track road when Mark and Brix started having a violent row about something or other. Perhaps it was the prototype bright orange MDMA crystals that Mark had been given in

Linz by a couple of his mates, who worked for one of the big drug companies there and always brought along goodies when we were in town. It must have been strong because at one point Mark was curled up on the minibus floor, shouting 'I'm a snail, I'm a snail.' Either that or he was just winding Brix up for a laugh.

I took some of this gear and my recollection is a bit hazy after that. Years later, Craig told me that in the morning, whilst boarding the bus, I looked like I'd seen a ghost and had told him that me and Mark had got wrecked and woken up that morning both bollock-naked in the hotel room. I've either forgotten that one or blocked it out …

When I first joined, Steve and Craig were both very welcoming towards me, as everyone was. Steve was punchy and solid on the bass, disciplined and driving. Craig would urgently stab out his chords and riffs.

I started sharing a room with Craig at first and, later, Steve. We would spend a lot of time together on the road. I didn't really drink with them too much when we were back in Manchester. Steve was married and Craig had a long-term girlfriend in my early days and I'd go out with Mark and Brix more. We never socialised as a whole band.

Craig called me 'Oracle' because unless he knew somewhere, he left the choice of bars or whatever up to me.

'Where we going tonight Oracle?'

I thought we could go wherever we wanted.

12

Up and Away

And off we went over the ocean.

In September 1986, I flew out for my first tour of North America with the band, arriving in a sweltering Atlanta. Like most of the tours I did in America with The Fall, it lasted for just under a month. It always felt like I was on holiday when we went.

On this first tour, we had the budget to fly everywhere, which suited me - I love flying. Plus it was dead easy to take a nugget of hash with you in those days. Just put it in your pocket and smile.

The dry heat hit me as I walked down the steps of the jet at LAX for the first time and I couldn't stop thinking: I've fallen on my feet here. The whole yuppie thing of the States and London in the mid-eighties hadn't spread to Manchester. Manchester was grey, dour, damp, still characterised by industrial decline and the sounds of Joy Division and The Smiths. LA was all palm trees, convertibles, Hollywood smiles, boob jobs - and year round sunshine. Until I grew to appreciate New York, California was my favourite. I'm a bit of a sun worshipper.

My only regret at this point was that I missed my sister Jane's wedding. I had sent a telegram to the Mere Country Club, where Jane held the reception, but it didn't arrive my sister said later. I paid $50 for the privilege, so I was none too pleased. I think she believed me.

While we waited for our bags, chatting to Bad Seeds guitarist Kid Congo, who had been sitting next to me on the plane, I spotted the little guy who played Tattoo from TV series *Fantasy Island*, walking by in his trademark white suit. I'm not very good at star spotting generally. It was Steve who would usually spot so and so, from such and such.

Steve, Craig, and I, went for a couple of pitchers of beer and a game of pool at Barneys Beanery, where singer Janice Joplin once used to hang out. Steve and Craig told me they always went to Barneys when in LA, and thus we began our tradition of Steve winning the pool and the two of them drinking me under the table. Those lads could drink more before a gig than I could in an entire night. I was plastered after four or five pints, less than that these days. It wasn't unheard of for them to get through four or five times that amount.

We drove to a Denny's restaurant on Sunset Strip that September - it was my first experience of the American diner culture, which I loved instantly. I made a point of visiting as many as I could in the States. A few efforts have been made to open diner-type restaurants in the UK but they're never as good: the food, the coffee, the service, the value for money - they don't even open all night.

The following night's gig went well, especially performing 'LA', a firm favourite of mine off the album *This Nation's Saving Grace* that Brix, who had lived in LA for many years, made her own.

The Roxy was only a tiny club, crammed full of excited fans, many of them ex-pats, including my childhood next-door neighbour, Keith Murray, who now had a successful career in accountancy, like his dad, David.

We didn't know who to score speed off in LA, so we bought a couple of grams of bugle off someone who worked at the club. It was as normal as buying a beer. The rider was ice troughs full of Corona with slices of lime, which was the first time I'd come across the now ubiquitous combination. Always Corona though. The locals reckoned that the Mexican brewery workers pissed in Sol.

Back at the hotel, we partied by the rooftop swimming pool until the dawn chorus. It was the same swimming pool featured in the *This is Spinal Tap* film/rockumentary/piss-take, which after its release in 1984 could be found in the video collection of pretty much every tourbus driver from then on. *Fawlty Towers*, *Only Fools and Horses*, and *Blackadder* videos, were also staples, even on American buses, back in the mid-eighties.

We went up to San Francisco for a couple of dates at The I-Beam club with Nick Cave and the Bad Seeds, who we kept bumping into everywhere we went. I loved San Francisco. I think I loved it before I even went there. It felt like I was on a film set or a show like *Starsky and Hutch*. I rode the trolley buses up and down the steep hills, and then I took a ferry that sailed under the Golden Gate Bridge and went to see Alcatraz

Island. Powerful currents met and swirled in the Bay.

I visited the famous fish market at Fisherman's Wharf, thinking old Si from Pimlotts might be able to show them a thing or two, but this was something else. The fish and the crabs were from another world. Enormous spider crabs, shrimp as big as your hand. I'd never seen such variety before.

We stayed in Japantown at the Miyako Hotel and partied late into the night with Nick and his band in the room next door.

I went next door for a drink with the Bad Seeds and met a local girl, which is fine, except I had been seeing someone else back home.

In the morning, she couldn't get out of the hotel fast enough.

'Something really bad's happened in this room,' she said.

I wasn't sure if she was going on about getting bad vibes or our own illicit liaison. I was still half-cut and didn't care either way.

Admittedly, this wouldn't be the last time I played away.

I don't really know what to say about all that without sounding awful. But I can't honestly say I felt guilty, as selfish as that sounds. I have to confess to that: I can be a bit selfish. It's probably really sexist to say this but it just seemed like a bit of a perk of the job. There were no mobiles and internet so you were never going to get caught, unless this girl turned up on your doorstep, as happened to Mark a couple of times. For me, it was either sit hunched over another pitcher of beer talking bollocks or chat up a pretty girl. Especially appealing if we'd just played to an audience that was mostly blokes which was usually the case.

Obviously wracked with guilt, I struck up a friendship with a Mormon TWA flight attendant called Kerry, on our next flight, where she taught me some card tricks and some sign language, as the cabin was empty.

'Keep this,' she said, and dealt me the Queen of Hearts with her phone number written on it.

She put me up in her apartment for the night - she's the only person I've ever known who had a water-bed. Transparent it was. I had a go on it. Don't know what all the fuss was about to be honest.

Such is the terrible grind of touring in a band.

I loved the hotels we were staying at in the States. Even the cheap ones had 24-hour room service and cable TV. Still, I tried not to spend too much time in them, and to explore each city we landed in.

In New York City, we stayed right by Times Square, in the Omni International, where I had my own suite, for the first time. This excused me from listening to Craig grind his teeth while he slept, eyes wide open, pupils in the back of his sockets. He was probably pleased to be away from my 747-style snoring to be fair.

Whilst checking in, I got talking to Janet Jackson's drummer. We briefly talked snare drums. I don't think I told him you could make your own with a Quality Street tin and a bit of grit.

Played it cool, you know.

I dumped my bags and went for a look around.

Times Square has so much energy. I only knew it from seventies detective shows so again it felt like I was on a film set.

The locals struggled to understand my accent, however, and kept quizzing me about where I was from.

'Are you from *Australia*?'

'No. England.'

'*London*?'

And on and on. I found myself slipping into an American accent to save the bother.

On our night off, I wandered over to Steve's suite and did the special knock - the intro beat to 'Lucifer Over Lancashire' - so that he knew it wasn't Mark coming in to spoil our party. I didn't know why we had to avoid Mark - I liked his company, he could be dead funny and I've never been one for cliques, but I went along with it. Steve let me in. As usual, he had the ironing board out, pressing his stage attire, so I helped Craig carefully re-fill the minibar vodka bottles with water. Inevitably we made for the nearest Irish Bar. Colin, who had been a roadie for years, had all the contacts and sourced us pharmaceuticals. The coke was not only a lot purer than the stuff we were used to back home, but half the price as well. We headed down the street to the Limelight club to check out the sights and sounds, my face contorting independent of my brain. Again, it was at another level to anything in Manchester.

The gig at the New York Ritz was sold out, with a crowd of about 3,000, which blew my mind. New Yorkers are one of the hardest crowds in the world to please, if they think you're shit, they'll let you know. They loved our show though and that first gig in the Big Apple, stands out as one my favourites of my time in The Fall. The crowd in New York was much more vocal than anything I'd experienced in the UK where people would stand around trying to look cool.

'Hey!' shouted one of the punters, 'where the fuck's Karl Burns at?'

I guess it was a question many Fall fans wanted to ask but didn't voice. At least not to my face. It caught me off guard and I wondered if I'd ever be accepted by the fans.

We re-crossed the continent.

As well as our own gigs, New Order had given us support slots on two shows at an arena in San Diego and a stadium at Irvine Meadows, Orange County.

I went with John Lennard and Brix to SeaWorld for the afternoon, to check out the dolphins and killer whales. Brix was pumping me for information about Kerry. What was I going to do? Did I love her? Would I move to America? Brix seemed a bit wary of her.

Kerry came down to visit for the San Diego show and I had a walk around the old Navy docks, which were vast, while jet fighters screamed overhead en route to base. As she could fly for free, Kerry made her way over the Atlantic several times to visit me, but it fizzled out after a few months.

Whilst we were over in California, we were looked after by a tour manager called Greg, who Brix and Marcia christened 'Greg Smeg' because they thought he was pure sleaze. He looked like TV detective *Magnum PI* with his mullet and trimmed moustache and travelled separately from us in his Trans Am with a young girl who looked like a gangster's moll. She was young enough to be his daughter and was off her face all the time I saw her. One morning, I went to knock on his door to ask about a flight, nicking the bread rolls off the room service trays outside the hotel room doors along the way - our per diems tended to go on drugs so feeding yourself was either off the rider or beg, steal, borrow. After opening the door wearing just a white towel, he invited me in the room.

'What's up Simon?'

Embarrassingly, I hadn't cottoned on yet that 'what's up' was just the local lingo for 'how are you?'

'What do you mean what's up?' I blurted out, mouth full of bread roll. '*Nothing*. Everything's *fine*. Why?'

He looked at me curiously.

'You look kinda worn out Simon. Would you like a little kick start?'

He led me over to a bedside cabinet next to where his naked girlfriend was asleep. He opened the draw and I saw a Smith & Wesson .38, lying next to a huge bag of cocaine which he took out and then proceeded to chop out two of the biggest lines I had ever seen. It turned out he was selling the coke to everyone backstage at the New Order gigs. He invited me to travel on the cramped rear seat of his Trans Am, for the two-hour drive to Irvine Meadows with the moll in the front leaning back over every ten minutes and shoving a full coke spoon under my nose.

I was a bit concerned about being ostracised for this and I got back on the tourbus to the usual groaning, eye-rolling and piss-taking from Steve and Craig about never leaving the bus. Marcia and Brix wanted to know all the gossip and gave me a bit of good-natured banter about hanging around with Greg.

At the arena shows, the huge crowd seemed to appreciate us. It was amazing to see how big New Order had become over there in a short period of time. People loved them, me included. But more than that, it was great to see so many familiar faces from back home in Manchester, especially Ed and Di, our sound engineers, who for the moment were on New Order's payroll.

After the second gig was done and dusted, we all got taken out by the promoters for a Chinese meal at a nearby restaurant where I ordered a whole crab that was as big as a toilet seat.

13

Frenz

Two days later I was back in Manchester, sat with Mark in The Wood-thorpe pub opposite Heaton Park, freezing, listening to Fred the landlord slag all his customers off.

Home sweet home.

Before long I found myself sat in pubs with Mark on a regular basis: The George, The Ostrich, The Forresters. He'd ring up at lunchtime.

'Fancy a pint Simon?'

Brix was away a lot working with her band Adult Net and I think he liked the idea of having a driver as well as a mate.

'Yeah, I'll be round in an hour.'

I didn't have anything else to do anyway. I'd go to his house, have a line, and chat about this or that. We had a bit of a running joke about a song he'd written called 'Chi Chi Chi' which he wanted to submit to the Eurovision song contest. I'd be going, yeah, it's good that, it could work in any language. Mark would bring it up every now and then, usually when we were on the continent.

'We need to get the music done for this "Chi Chi Chi".'

As daft as it sounds, I think it would have stood as good a chance as any of the piss-poor entries we normally put forward.

My new home was on Slade Lane in Levenshulme. Before the American tour, I'd finally moved out of my parents' house but I hadn't spent much time at the place. It was a tiny studio flat full of damp, but at least it was mine.

Andrew Berry, now noted as a bit of a celebrity hairdresser, had moved from his salon in the Haçienda to a new address on Tib Street in what is now called the Northern Quarter. The street was a real dump back then. An underworld figure from Oldham had put up the money to start up the business which was to be called 'Vanilla Fudge' and located up some steep stairs above an electrical shop. It was all kitted out. New fixtures and furniture, a sofa in the reception area and a custom made stained glass window with the name Vanilla Fudge fashioned into it.

On opening day, I had a couple of hours spare so went to visit Andrew and Neil for a chat and promptly burned a hole the size of a fist in his brand new settee.

I was smoking a joint and, as sometimes happens, I was a bit absent minded about the spliff and having a laugh so didn't notice a burning ember had fallen off as I sat on the new sofa.

'Can anybody smell burning?' Andrew asked, concerned.

I looked around the room half-heartedly and then looked down to see a smouldering ember boring into the foam, emitting a noxious toxic smell. I jumped up.

'Oh Shit! Sorry mate,' I laughed, stoned, slapping at my jeans in case they were on fire. Andrew looked a bit pissed off.

Being a good mate he laughed it off. He was just happy for me now I was a member of The Fall. Unfortunately for Andrew, his investor was banged up a few months after.

All the Fall gigs were packed. We were on a roll.

However, for the wrong reasons, one gig stands out more than any of the others: Sheffield Polytechnic. Towards the end of the set, Mark got up on my drum riser and started to pour a bottle of water over my head while I was playing. Only for a second or so, but I could hear a load of the fans cheering. I didn't consider this to be part of the show, but even in these early days the punters and Mark did.

What was Mark going to do next?

I think Mark was seeing how far he could push me. I carried on playing and finished the gig but I was fuming.

After the gig had finished I sat on the tourbus on my own seething, contemplating my next move. Steve and Craig came to find me. They were concerned that I was going to quit there and then and boarded the bus with a bottle of Moët, and sat down at the table with me. The champagne seemed to have a remarkable effect because by the time we had polished it off, I told them both I was going to stay. I did love being in the band and told them so. They were relieved and I appreciated their concern. I considered them more than just bandmates after this gesture.

I think it was Mark's way of testing me but I made a pact with myself that night that if anything like that was to happen again, I would quit. You might say it was just part of the act but I wasn't going to be anybody's whipping boy, not for £300 per week, anyway.

Despite that incident, I really enjoyed my first British tour with the band and loved living out of a suitcase, something I still like doing today.

The gigs were full the next year as well.

In my early years in the band we spent more time in Germany than anywhere else. I always enjoyed touring Germany as the crowds were bigger, the wheat beer was great and they had some good techno clubs, particularly in Munich. Munich was a lot bigger for techno in those days, much more so than the current hotbed in Berlin. For some reason, when we were in Germany, the hired PA was shipped around in a van advertising flowers.

Speaking of big crowds, in the summer, The Fall was asked to support U2 on their 'Joshua Tree' world tour date at the home of Leeds United, Elland Road football stadium. The original support band World Party had pulled out at the last minute and we stepped in. It was a beautiful sunny day in Leeds and I was excited at the prospect of playing my first stadium gig, even though I wasn't a fan of U2 whatsoever.

The thirty-minute set went well overall with a smattering of applause coming from pockets of the huge crowd. The fact no one had thrown any rotten fruit at us or booed us off, I considered a success. We all went to our dressing room up inside the stand behind the stage and got stuck into the hospitality there to celebrate. We started glugging down red wine and went to have a look at U2 who were just about to go on. As we were walking down the terracing in the backstage area, I glanced round behind me and saw Craig being physically thrown down the steps of the aisle, still clutching a bottle of wine in his hands, by U2's security detail, who were clearing a path for the band. Craig shouted 'I pay your wages, you know!' to one of them, but it seemed a bit of a futile gesture as the entourage walked over him, oblivious, while he lay prostrate on a concrete step.

Before long we were back in Germany at the Knopfs Music Hall in Hamburg, playing alongside Nick Cave and the Bad Seeds again, as well as the Butthole Surfers.

Too many tickets had been sold and an actual riot ensued outside the gig next to a petrol station. Some of the punters weren't allowed in as the gig was already bursting at the seams. Making our way to the gig on foot, we saw someone set fire to a pile of car tyres and start rolling them across the garage forecourt towards the petrol pumps. I started walking down the street away from the danger with Brix and Marcia and watched as the fire brigade and riot police brought the situation under control as the sun went down.

The gig was obviously packed and went down well but there were a lot of understandably unhappy people about.

I liked Hamburg: a beautiful city, tall striking blonde women. It crossed my mind what it must have been like for The Beatles to have washed up here all those years before. It reminded me of Liverpool actually, probably with them both being ports.

We stayed in a skyscraper of a hotel where someone threw a duvet out of the window that floated and flapped to the ground twenty-three floors below in an amateurish rock and roll gesture. Why a quilt (or anything really) I don't know. Brix and Marcia sheepishly went to retrieve it.

Shortly after, we flew back to London for our first appearance at the Reading Festival, which on the night we played was headlined by goth rockers, The Mission. The crowd fucking hated us. During our spot, several plastic bottles of Ruddles Bitter filled with piss, were thrown at Mark, who after reading the Ruddles label, shot back at them, 'No wonder you're throwing that shit away', unaware it was piss.

Good job they weren't throwing Boddies because he might have taken a mouthful.

THE GROWING STONE

Ian used to come to visit me a fair bit in those days as the Roses were rehearsing at International 1 nearby. They'd played a gig there and had done a couple of successful word-of-mouth gigs, set up by Steve Adge, in one of the railway arches under Piccadilly Station. Because I was mates with the band and in The Fall, new manager Gareth would welcome me whenever I turned up to see a gig there and told his bar staff to give me free drinks all night. There may be no such thing as a free lunch, but if you're lucky you can have a free drink every now and then. And who am I to turn it down?

Ian was interested in what Mark was like since he knew of The Fall and listened to all my stories of life on tour over cup after cup of tea. He also had a particular interest in the logistics of putting a tour together. How many roadies did we have? How does the equipment get shipped? Who gets paid what? Seemed like he was preparing for the possibility of his own tours. The Roses now had a bit of a following and were working on songs all the time. I must admit 'So Young' passed me by a bit. Didn't think much of it. 'Elephant Stone' was when I started taking notice.

Ian was made up for me, though.

I remember him saying once to Gina, 'I always knew Si would get the furthest.'

With hindsight, I beg to differ …

I first met Reni in a rehearsal room in Chorlton before they moved to the International. I was impressed. I ended up selling him the blue Beverley kit that my mum bought.

While I was there, I ran into Docker who happened to be working at a burger factory next door with our mate Nick or 'Two Pound' as we called him. Whenever you were buying a bag of gear he'd go, 'I've only got two pound', in his deadpan Manc drawl.

He *always* said it. There was never a time he'd just throw in a fiver or whatever.

'I've only got two pound.'

Alright then Two Pound.

Docker had been in and out of the nick in the years since I'd seen him. The last I really saw a lot of him was our shambolic holiday together in Ibiza back in 1983. Docker was still shifty. He tried to sell me a box of minced beef outside the rehearsal rooms. I was doing alright in the The Fall but I didn't have much room in my tiny flat and my only cooker was a portable two-ring Baby Belling so I declined the offer. What the hell was I going to do with a massive box of mince meat?

HEY! LUCIANI

After recording *Bend Sinister* and touring for nearly six months, we turned sharply, as is Mark's artistic wont, and returned to the music I had first briefly recorded.

It was December, and we came straight off the tour and decamped to London to perform the play *Hey! Luciani* about the life and death of Pope John Paul I. John Paul I had only held the big gig for a few weeks before white smoke could be seen billowing from a chimney on the Vatican roof and Mark, who described his own work as 'a cross between Shakespeare and *The Prisoner*' (also favourite viewing on the tourbus), interspersed the story with conspiracy theories involving the Mafia and Nazi war criminal Martin Bormann, who he had hiding out in the Brazilian jungle.

The band was to perform the music in the show as well as a bit of acting. Steve looked just like a pope in his white robes, mitre and staff. He seemed as nervous as I was, in my role as a bent cardinal, though Australian performance artiste Leigh Bowery, who was central to the performance, reminded me of my lines when I forgot. I stuttered a few times and he'd come over and whisper behind his hand to nudge my memory. Because Leigh was quite outrageous and comical when he did this, people thought it was funny and I got away with it, like kids at a school nativity. I was happy when the show moved into musical mode and I could get back behind the kit.

On the press night, Mark could be seen menacingly prowling around the aisles amongst the seated gentlemen of the press, in shiny black riding boots, holding a leather crop in the style of Bormann himself. A number of heavyweight newspapers were there, but like me, they couldn't fathom out what the hell was going on either. It got slated in the *The Times*.

Still, we had a great time doing it for the two-week run. I remember the Happy Mondays came down one night to watch us, god knows what they made of it!

At the end of the show we'd sit out front in the theatre stalls and have a few drinks, listening to music through the PA and chatting to various actors and extras, then nipping off to the dressing room for a quick line.

Leigh was a mate of Boy George and he used to go clubbing every night after the performance in his various costumes, one of which included a motorcycle helmet with foot long spikes sticking out of it and wearing tights. You should have seen the look on people's faces on the tube as we headed towards Soho. Priceless. Sadly, Leigh died of AIDS several years later.

On New Year's Eve, I went out with Mark and Brix to the Haçienda, partying the night away to the likes of 'Word Up' by Cameo, wondering where this strange adventure would take me next. The Haçienda was by now a hot ticket and huge queues of excited music lovers snaked their way around the corner of Whitworth Street West. Ecstasy had arrived on the scene, introduced, so the legend goes, by the Mondays themselves.

Dave Haslam was packing them in to the Haçienda for his midweek

'Temperance' nights where the likes of 'Mr. Pharmacist' would regularly be played. It sounded amazing and it felt great to be part of the band. The 'Nude' nights run by Mike Pickering at the weekends were doing even better. I had first met Pickering, who went on to form the pop band M people, after auditioning for his band Quando Quango in 1982. I spent many happy hours in the little wooden DJ cabin on the balcony overlooking the dance floor, making a lot of new friends and, as always, getting into a lot of new music.

It was a great end to a great year.

NOEL'S CHEMICAL EFFLUENCE

I had been in The Fall for less than a year. It was a virtually non-stop schedule of touring and recording. Like any job, there is that double-edged sword where you'd rather be busy than not, because if you're sitting around doing nothing for weeks, well then, the writing could be on the wall. Still, it was a hectic first year. The next few years would be no different.

The Fall had just begun hiring proper rock and roll tourbuses with the bunk beds, a lounge, tinted windows, glittery signage and all that. They'd always had Salford Van Hire minibuses up until then.

Noel from Darwen was our first regular driver. Small, fat and bald, he was an ex-Navy 'stoker' that had worked on the HMS Ark Royal for many years before running an ice cream van in deepest Lancashire. Like most drivers he loved his Chris Rea and Dire Straits CDs and liked to keep a tight ship.

Usually when we met outside Mark's house, we would end up waiting for an hour for Mark and Brix to appear, so we'd watch a video. Once, we were watching *The Yob* starring Keith Allen, which we thought was really funny, until Mark eventually boarded the bus. He climbed on with his plastic bag full of scrawled lyrics, cassettes and a deafeningly loud gold-coloured loudhailer that he set off to the tune of 'Yankee Doodle' to announce his arrival. It used to wind everyone up, which Mark got a kick out of.

He could see we were enjoying the film - we were halfway through it - but he walked up to the VHS player and began stabbing frantically at the machine trying to find the eject button.

'We're not watching this shit.'

We sniggered like school kids watching some out-of-touch teacher fumbling with this newfangled technology.

Finally, he got Noel to get the tape out and put *Zulu* in and cranked up the volume to the maximum. This special showing of *Zulu* would happen at regular intervals over the next few years. He just kept putting the fucking thing on.

Years later, I met Keith Allen and told him how Mark had turned off *The Yob* and put *Zulu* on because it was his favourite film.

'Facking hell, that's my favourite film as well,' Keith chortled.

We rarely listened to our own CDs on the bus. If Mark was travelling with us, we always had to listen to what he wanted. This could go one of two ways. I liked krautrock band Can and some of his Northern Soul stuff. He'd regale us with tales of his pill-popping dancing days. 'Purple hearts' and 'blueys' and flairs at Wigan Casino.

On the other hand, things like Captain Beefheart I couldn't stand.

He who pays the piper calls the tune.

I would go and lie down on my bunk, as far away as possible from the TV lounge and the pissy smelling chemical toilet. Even if everyone on the bus adhered to the strict 'no taking a crap' rule, those toilets always reeked once the bus was a few years old.

Or, I would go and sit with the driver and keep him alert if we were travelling in the dead of night. We used to do a lot of overnight runs, especially when we were crossing the huge distances over mainland Europe or the US.

Failing that, I would drink huge shots of vodka with Craig, have a couple of spliffs then feel my way to my bunk, fully dressed, shut the curtains and fall asleep listening to the sound of the whirring prop shaft beneath us, as the miles flew by.

I can imagine travelling this way is sometimes similar to being a submariner. Stuck in the close atmosphere until we reached our destination or the driver ran out of time on his tachograph. Sometimes though, in those days, there were inexplicable instances of tachographs unaccountably flying out of windows and drivers somehow two hundred quid richer for the error. The show must go on.

After two or three days, you can get sick of certain people you are travelling with. Not that you dislike them, it's just what too much proximity can do. Part of the sitting at the front making brews and reading maps was keeping my own sanity. Noel, in return, would lend me cash until the next payday or stash any cannabis in the wheel hub of the bus when crossing any borders - he reckoned the brake fluid covered the scent from any sniffer dogs. He'd get me up before last orders in the dining room at breakfast.

'Alarm call, Si?'

THE ARTIST AT WORK

As we pulled into each new town, Mark would often go off on his own to do an interview in a pub round the corner with some journalist or other.

Brix and Marcia often had their own dressing room and would spend a fair amount of time trying on different outfits and applying makeup and so on, with Brix asking your opinion as you walked past the open door.

'Simon! This dress or that?' I'd pick one.

''kay, sweetie.'

The engine room would go for a couple of drinks in a different pub to Mark and sometimes fans would come up and buy us drinks. I'd accept the odd one. I was happy just having a smoke.

Though Mark didn't bother me about smoking, his general view was that it was for hippies, although he had the odd toke with me, late at night, only us two still up.

Mark's grouchy stage persona, it took me a couple of months to realise, was pretty much part of the show. Eventually, it seemed to be expected by the punters who lapped it up. Even before the show he'd make a song and dance about the stage, insisting that somebody swept it before he went on and made sure there were no old bits of gaffer tape left from previous shows.

Once we were on, he would stalk the stage, scowling at the monitor man or anyone catching his eye. He'd wander off and sit in the dressing room for a bit while we played on and on. If he wasn't happy with the sound he'd frantically try to move a 10-foot stack of speakers to no avail. Like a toddler trying to move a fridge.

Hardly ever talked between songs.

'Good evening-ah. We are The Fall-uh ...'

He had good microphone technique, so he told me, like the greats from yesteryear - Elvis, Sinatra - he was up there.

He'd play snippets of undecipherable ramblings from his Dictaphone. He'd stop songs all the time, say, 'this is shit, start again, get your fuckin' act together' - even if the song was going fine. Then he'd start messing about with our equipment, looking to knock us down a peg or two.

Marcia just laughed it off when he would come over and budge her out of the way of the keyboard and play something ridiculous and off-key, hammering at the instrument with his fists in the style of 'Great Balls of Fire'. She'd just pick up a tambourine and play right along, shaking her long black hair.

In those days, Brix would come over and play next to Mark, smiling: the happy couple. Mark would smile on the odd occasion but didn't really look comfortable and would wander off, only to return, messing around with her amplifier. In later years, he backed off a bit with Brix because she went absolutely mad, shouting aggressively and standing her ground.

Steve would stand guard over his amp like the Colossus of Rhodes wielding a Rickenbacker bass, and so kept Mark at bay.

Probably the most consistent victim was Craig. Most gigs, at some point, Mark would go over to Craig's amplifier and fuck about with the knobs. There didn't seem to be any rhyme or reason to what he was doing, just going over and twiddling pot luck. Sometimes it worked, sometimes it sounded shit, sometimes it fed back excruciatingly. What appeared to be the main purpose was to wind up Craig to make him play more aggressively.

To an extent this did sometimes work as it would piss off Craig, but I think he got more wound up when Mark would go over and physically try to improve his posture as he stood, playing away. Mark hated it if you slouched about and would say to me 'stand up straighter Simon, you look like an old man', which I thought was rich coming from him.

Another favourite tactic in America was to pull the plug on the massive cooling fans that were generally provided on the sweltering stages, so we would all sweat our tits off.

I wasn't immune to the interference. Mark used to move the microphones off my kit because he thought the best live bands were from the sixties when there wasn't anything more than one microphone hanging above the kit. I got round it by having Colin clamp a mic inside the bass drum and rigging up a dummy mic in front of the drum. Colin also miked up the snare drum from underneath so Mark couldn't see it. That way I had the two most used drums going through the PA at least.

Seeing the dummy mic sat temptingly in front of the kit, Mark would take the bait and move it away from the kit. Colin dutifully came on stage and went through the charade of re-miking the bass drum, laughing. Mark got wise to this eventually as the sound never changed and he did stop doing it, but it took a few years.

It was a spectacle. I'll give him that.

JOHN PEEL

On our return from Europe, we released the next single, 'There's a Ghost in my House', with Grant Showbiz producing (and staying over in my mum and dad's spare room). We shot an accompanying video in woodland next to The Woodthorpe. It was the first time a Fall single had entered the Top 40. I hoped this was a sign of things to come.

We recorded it live as always in a couple of takes. I knew the old Motown classic as my mum used to play it when I was a kid, so I didn't have to learn it.

At the end of the April, The Fall was invited to do another John Peel session at Maida Vale in London. The Peel sessions were good for the band and no doubt turned many people on to us. His radio show was an institution in Britain and for him to constantly cite The Fall was great kudos.

They were long days though. We would normally set off in a minibus at the crack of dawn from Prestwich after picking up the gear from Steve's dad's bakery in Wythenshawe. We'd arrive at the studio around mid-morning and carry the equipment up corridors that seemed to go on for miles. Once we set up the gear, we'd get a decent live sound and run through a couple of practice passes for the studio engineer. We often got Dale Griffin, ex-Mott the Hoople drummer, who got on with Mark.

As we set up, Mark would go to the pub and after a wait of a couple of hours in the BBC canteen, he would return fired up, and start barking orders at Craig to step it up even though he had been playing exactly the same thing earlier. We'd do a few live takes before the engineers went for their tea. More sitting about waiting. When they came back, they'd mix the tracks, usually until about midnight. Then it was break all the equipment down and load it back on the bus and drive back to Manchester, arriving in the early hours of the morning. Knackered. No wonder we took speed.

The Guest

Meanwhile The Smiths were recording their latest album. I was too busy with The Fall now to think about what could have been, though Mark ribbed me about it on a few occasions.

'You're not in The Smiths, you're in The Fall so you'd better get used to it,' he'd say.

Then he'd say, 'You're not like them Simon.'

I've no idea what he meant by that.

I still kept in touch with Johnny and Andy though and drove down to The Wool Hall Recording Studios near Bath where The Smiths were recording *Strangeways Here We Come*, to hang out for a couple of days. Morrissey and Johnny were both tied up in the studio working on the track 'I Started Something I Couldn't Finish', which sounded great. I played a lot of snooker and darts with drummer Mike Joyce in the games room.

I always got on well with Mike, a genuinely funny guy. Though I regretted not taking The Smiths gig, I never begrudged Mike. How could I? I turned it down. It was the same with me and Karl Burns - we were good mates.

When Andy and Mike had finished recording, the three of us went for a drive through the narrow lanes that surrounded the residential studio. We motored past Stonehenge a few times in my Datsun Laurel while blasting out Barry White on the cassette player.

I suppose, in hindsight, Barry White's deep-voiced, unsubtle bedroom innuendo was a bit out of place next to a mysterious site of Druid and pagan ritual.

We ended up calling in for a drink in a tiny little pub with a thatched roof in the middle of nowhere until closing time after which I drove back to the studio for the night, pissed up, high on life. It reminded me of a scene out of *A Clockwork Orange* where the gang tool about in the Durango 95.

The band was noticeably fractured, but little did I know that The Smiths were nearing the end of the line. They would split up before the year was out.

The Renegade

Some time that year, I was with Mark in a club in Manchester called

Precinct 13, when suddenly I saw Ian Brown approaching me to say hello.

Mark knew who Ian was - The Stone Roses were on their way up by now and were appearing in the weekly music press even more than The Fall were - but Mark refused to shake Ian's outstretched hand and turned his back and went to sit down. Ian bought a round and came and sat down anyway while Mark did his best not to talk to Ian. Later, when it was Mark's round, he went to the bar and returned with two drinks: one for me and one for him.

This left me in a bit of an embarrassing position and I was pissed off at Mark for snubbing my friend so blatantly.

Ian was speechless and while he didn't hold it against me, he didn't forgive or forget it with Mark.

He got up to leave and as a parting shot said he'd burnt 'It's The New Thing' over an open fire because it was shit.

FRENZ

By the end of June 1987, work had begun on the next studio album, *The Frenz Experiment*.

Mark had a thing that musicians in his band should be no different from any other workers. Bricklayers, bakers, whoever, you need to turn up on time and get on with the job, no airs, no graces.

I thought it was a good attitude to have as I've never been work shy, but I thought he took it too far. We were a good band and I thought we could have produced better work than we did if we'd have spent more time on it, if we didn't work quite so off the cuff. This wasn't what Mark wanted though; he wanted to relentlessly put out album after album. In those days you couldn't just download one track off the internet, so if you liked one song you had to buy the whole album, which maybe was Mark's theory. I felt it was quantity over quality.

The Fall has some really good tracks but you have to weed them out amongst a lot of filler. On the other hand, a lot of fans like Fall songs that I can't stand. It's all a matter of opinion.

The first *Frenz Experiment* sessions took place at Pete Hook's studio, Suite 16, where the late Rex Sergeant was engineering for us. Later sessions were at Richard Branson's Manor Studios in Oxfordshire.

I remember it had a huge oil canvas in the entrance hallway probably about 20 x 15 feet that had all the Virgin stars like Phil Collins and Boy George painted on it. It made me laugh every time I walked past because it was horrible and the likenesses of the musicians were terrible. Really, you should have seen this thing, it was ridiculous. Tacky as anything. We had an in-house chef though who would get in whatever you wanted so it was pretty cushy. A lot different to Suite 16.

We stayed in the manor for the recording. Like the tourbus, it was first-come first-served with the beds. All the bedrooms had names. I got in early and had a great room with a four-poster bed overlooking the extensive grounds. Craig ended up in a box room called 'The Pit'.

We went in a few pubs round and about and the locals didn't know what to make of us. Here we were in middle England, a load of northern oiks speeding off our tits. Luckily, the more endearing Brix and Marcia managed the charm offensive and reassured the staff that we weren't going to rob the till.

Despite my reservations about the time we spent on it, I felt there was some good work on there.

The album is most notable for its cover of the Kinks song 'Victoria', which was recorded back in Abbey Road Studios and would be released as a single. Another cut off the album that still sounds great is 'Bremen Nacht'. It was always great to play live - you'd see some of the crowd almost going into a trance.

FILM

There was always something going on.

In October, the new single 'Hit the North' which we had been performing live for several months, was released. People really seemed to like the song, no one more so than me.

We later made a video where I can be seen wearing a shiny pink shirt and doing some really dodgy dance moves. I cringe with embarrassment every time someone mentions it to me, which fortunately isn't that often.

It was quite ground breaking musically for The Fall - really different, a lot of programming and sampling going on from Simon Rogers. Mark may have lost a few Welsh fans though, by calling them savages in his lyrics. I even heard the song played on Gary Davies's Radio 1 lunchtime show one day as I was driving up to Mark's house and it was played regularly at the Haçienda, on the Temperance nights.

I think it still sounds good today.

Barely a month after this, Beggars dug a bit deeper into their pockets to finance a video for 'Victoria'.

We all dressed up in Victorian attire and larked about with a large cake that was supposed to be a model of the original Crystal Palace that went up in flames. Brix was shown being stitched into a whalebone corset, by Marcia who was a servant. Mark, in military dress, surveyed a large globe. There were references to the birth of football with Mark and dancer Michael Clark playing soccer at a small football ground, where we were filmed on a magnificent iron spiral staircase that led down into the Rotherhithe tunnel which runs under the Thames. It looked like something you'd find in a Jules Verne novel. I am wearing a black dress suit with large top hat, waving a small Union Jack, inanely. This also makes me cringe.

On the single's release in January, it also managed to dent the Top 40 and was played in the background in the cafe on an episode of TV soap *EastEnders*. I don't think during my time in the band we were ever again as absorbed into the mainstream.

FAMILY

My parents came to see the band for the first time at a one-off gig at Maxwell Hall in Salford. I could see my mum looking very proud up in the balcony as I played, but my dad just sat there hating every second of it. His only comment to me about the gig was the usual, 'The music's much too loud'. It was all I expected from him really.

'I can't hear a word the singer's saying.'

I didn't see what his problem was - neither could I.

14

Kurious

Next.

In Greece, a promoter gave Mark a couple of tabs of acid which he shared with me. It didn't seem to have any effect until later in the night when I felt an excruciating pain in the pit of my stomach which floored me. I was used to having pains in my stomach - I had trouble on and off since I was seventeen with a stomach ulcer - but this was different. I don't really know what started the ulcer off to begin with, but I am a bit of a worrier.

The alcohol and the drugs that I was taking can't have helped much either.

Still, this pain was more severe and it must have stemmed from the acid. Mark speculated there was strychnine in the tab, a red window-pane. I was rolling about on my bed all night in agony and however many Zantac tablets I took or glasses of milk I drank, the pain wouldn't go away.

All the next day I was just thinking … shit, I've got a gig to do, as the pain carried on gnawing at the lining of my stomach. I didn't make the soundcheck, so I just arrived five minutes before the gig started and hoped for the best.

It was horrible.

I left the acid alone after that.

On the day of *The Frenz Experiment*'s release, we performed a selection of new songs off the album, and did a record signing session afterwards at HMV Records on Oxford Street, London. It was a novelty at the time, well, for us anyway, and made the news in the following week's edition of the *NME*, where at that time there was still usually a story about the band every week.

Speaking of the *NME*, we did a cover version of The Beatles 'A Day in the Life' for a charity album which reprised *Sgt Pepper*. I'm not even a massive Beatles fan but it really suited Mark. Our interpretation was pretty true to the original and I think it's the best cover we did while I was on board.

Anyway. It was 1988. Raves. Smiley faces. Acid House. Tabloid panic. The youth of today. S'Express topped the charts. The Fall toured relentlessly.

At the Paradiso gig in Amsterdam, Brix was electrocuted at the sound-check and refused to play the gig because she was so traumatised.

In Frankfurt, I was sitting in the hotel lobby when I saw Bo Diddley in his boating shoes, navy blazer and white captain's cap, struggling with a huge silver platter, groaning under the weight of fried chicken. He shuffled his way at a snail's pace towards one of the lifts, across the marble floor. As he made his way into the empty box car, the doors suddenly started to close on him, sending the silver platter and the mountain of fried chicken and white china plates, crashing all over the marble floor. Poor old Bo froze. I was on my way over to help him when a bellboy rushed to his rescue.

More gigs.

On the flight over to America, I nursed my stomach condition by getting stuck into the Bloody Marys with Steve and Craig, as per ritual. By the time we touched down, I was a mess.

We were met at the airport to be told that Mark, who had arrived a couple of days before on promo duties, had arranged a gig that night. We drove straight to Maxwell's in Hoboken. This was the only time I've been pissed up before a gig and it didn't make me want to do it again. It was another bad (self-inflicted) experience, shortly on the heels of my bad trip in Athens.

Drumming is a very physical thing, particularly with The Fall where the beats were mostly fast and hard hitting. The last thing I needed before this was a load of booze.

We gigged across the continent again.

Immediately after the show in San Francisco, the whole band, including Mark and Brix, who occasionally travelled separately, boarded the silver sleeper for the drive overnight to Los Angeles. Everybody grabbed their bunk and went to sleep except me, Mark and Eddie. We drank neat vodka, sniffed a bit of charlie and Ed and I smoked some skunk, whilst we put the world to rights. I can't remember what specifically we talked about. We were out of our heads.

Talking shit.

The sun was just coming up as we thundered down a stretch of the Pacific Coast Highway, so Mark asked our driver to stop for a while so we could get out and breathe in some of the fresh sea air down on the deserted beach below. It was a glorious morning and it felt good to be alive as the three of us climbed down the steep rocks to the Pacific. Mark and I started to climb back up to the bus after twenty minutes, thinking Eddie would follow us, but instead he started to walk out into the ocean in the white bed sheet he was wearing. When he finally got back on the bus he was dragging handfuls of yellow seaweed in his wake. Me and Mark were doubled over laughing at this vision of Eddie, in his makeshift toga. Mark got down on his knees going, 'Oh Squid Lord, all hail Squid Lord' etc. Hence the song 'Squid Lord'.

It was one of the few times I found out where the inspiration for Mark's songs came from. Like 'Pumpkin Head Xscapes' which started out as a joke about Craig's cat going missing.

We'd get all sorts of weird and wonderful visitors on the tourbus. I remember once in LA a guy who looked like a tramp wandered up to the open door and was after some money for a drink. We invited him on and said we've got loads of drink here, help yourself. He started rummaging around the ice cooler going no I don't like this, don't like that, turning his nose up. Cheeky bastard! Finally, he found something that didn't offend his sensibilities too much and sloped off. What's the saying about beggars can't be choosers?

Fresh from the beaches of Southern California, we got back home and started to record *I am Kurious Oranj* in Rochdale. Mark had been writing and producing a show called 'I Am Curious Orange' loosely themed around the 300th anniversary of William of Orange's accession to the English throne. After being part of the *Hey! Luciani* production, I had no idea what to expect.

I never thought I'd be doing ballets and the like but I admired Mark for trying something different. He was always quite innovative. His output was remarkable - I don't know where he got the time to write so much. At this point, he was never short of ideas or lyrics and sharp, but cynical, observations on a wide array of topics.

The recording sessions were done in fits and starts at Suite 16, which was above a music shop, on a cobbled backstreet in Rochdale town centre. With the studio being so close to Manchester, it was handy.

Mark wrote his songs a lot by singing lyrics and rhythms into his ever-present Dictaphone whenever the inspiration struck him. He would play the tape back to us on the bus or in the pub or wherever. It could be anything. Plastic guitars, traffic, working men's clubs, TVs talking to themselves. There were bits worked up from loudhailer and drum machine pre-sets. Anything was a song.

The next time we were at a soundcheck he'd play the Dictaphone through a microphone and we'd try to come up with something to go along with it. Sometimes it worked instantly but most times it'd collapse and turn into a farce as we were unable to follow all this horrible noise squawking out of the Dictaphone. Such is the creative process.

I am Kurious Oranj was finally released to mostly favourable reviews. Again, I thought there were some good things on this, stronger than Frenz for me. The single 'Big New Prinz' was a stand out and one of the few tunes we often revisited live over the years. I got to do a reggae beat for the first time on the title track which I enjoyed as it was very rare I could deviate from the basic rock beats Mark wanted.

For the Curious show, the idea was to incorporate dance into the music. Mark's friend from Edinburgh, dancer Michael Clark, a student of the Royal Ballet School was to lead his ballet company. They had been dancing to Fall tracks independently and had worked with the band before on a TV appearance, the most I could remember about it was a couple of dancers wearing leotards with the arse cut out.

Michael was sent the new recordings as soon as they came out of the studio in order to choreograph the dancing in time for the opening on 21 June, so there was a bit of a rush to pull it all together in time. After a couple of days rehearsing the tunes, which included 'Kurious Oranj', as well as 'Deadbeat Descendent' and 'Cab it Up', the band along with Andrew Berry as hairdresser/vibesmaster, flew out to Amsterdam to meet up with Michael's dance company for a couple of days of production rehearsals in the theatre. Mark and Brix stayed in a hotel and the rest of us were put up in a canal-side rented house. To be honest though, although I'm obviously not against sex and drugs, I've always found Amsterdam a very seedy place. I wouldn't want to live there.

The Dutch audience seemed to enjoy the show immensely but like the

Hey! Luciani play before it, I found it hard to fathom what the hell was going on most of the time. There were dancers in green hooped Celtic football strips. Brix made her grand entrance sat atop a giant hamburger that was six feet across at least and wheeled around the stage while she played her Rickenbacker in a sparkly minidress. There was someone larking about inside a giant can of baked beans. I think Marcia was part of a pantomime horse at one point. There was a backdrop of the Houses of Parliament which I thought was good, but basically, I was baffled. Ed and Di had never seen anything like it either.

'Prancers,' Eddie called them, shaking his head.

It was a different kind of tour. We only did three cities with a few shows in each. It was nice to move to a different rhythm to a rock tour.

In August, the ballet moved up to the Edinburgh Festival for a five day run at the King's Hall. The festival wasn't as big back then. There certainly weren't as many celebrities as today. I remember we went to the opening night party, where I met the likes of 'thinking man's crumpet' Joan Bakewell in a hotel bar. I'm not overly intellectual, but I like to think I can hold a conversation with anybody, and I met some interesting people there, although I remember thinking it was a bit weird that everyone I met was from London.

The run went really well and even my parents drove up to see it. They took me and Andrew Berry (who I was sharing a flat with overlooking the city) out for lunch the next day and then we walked round Edinburgh Zoo for an hour or so. I remember it so fondly because soon after this my mum got diagnosed with breast cancer and it was one of the last times I got the chance to have a leisurely walk with her.

The Amsterdam and Edinburgh shows were good preparation for the two week run in London at the prestigious Sadler's Wells theatre. Mark and Brix stayed in a hotel whilst the rest of us, apart from Marcia who lived in London anyway, were given digs in a filthy mews townhouse in Earls Court, a suburb of Australia. I managed to find my own accommodation and shacked up with one of the ballet dancers who had invited me to stay at her place in Wood Green.

Though I like company and socialising, it was another instance of me putting a bit of distance between me and the band. I could stand back a bit.

Di was on hand to ferry us about London and to run us back to Manchester straight after the show on Saturday night, bringing us back on the Monday mornings. We all spent a lot of time in the afternoons running through the songs, this time with a click track - much to Mark's annoyance - so the dancers would be spot on every night. The place was near enough full for all the shows. Culture-vulture types filled the place and were nothing like the usual crowds we got, but they seemed to be genuinely enjoying themselves, especially when we performed a version of William Blake's hymn, 'Jerusalem'.

I remember going for a drink at the packed pub behind the theatre and spotted Kevin Rowland, singer from Dexys Midnight Runners, stood on his own at the bar wearing a miniskirt and stockings. Each to their own, I suppose.

That summer, I only met up with Ian and John a couple of times. It was difficult to see friends as I was away so much. One sunny evening I met up with Ian and went for a drive out to the airport, to watch the planes. I never did the full on plane-spotting, collecting the registration numbers and all that, but I used to like watching them. I like the sound of the engines and the smell.

I picked up Ian at his flat at Chatham Grove near the old picture house in Withington, where he proudly handed me a cassette of The Stone Roses' eponymous debut album. The copy was a prototype with just a bit of mastering left to do; I popped it in the stereo in my Golf GTI and headed off to the airport. I thought it sounded great. I played it every day in my car for ages and it grew and grew on me. I didn't think it would propel them to national stardom, but then, I don't have a great track record in predicting these things. Ian was full of praise for producer John Leckie and I could tell he was really excited about the album's forthcoming release.

I'd heard a bit of the Roses earlier output, but I was amazed how much they'd all come on. John's guitar lines had moved away from the punk sound and were more melodic, chiming and clean, like The Byrds. I was blown away by Reni's drums. He has a superb feel. When you watch him, his arms look like they're made out of rubber. And many a time in those days, he only used a three-piece kit.

There was a tinge of regret about not being in a band with my mates and producing songs as good as those, but I wasn't gutted about not being in the Roses. I was happy with my lot and I was happy for all of them. They had worked really hard for years to get this far.

More gigs.

At Barrowlands in Glasgow, someone threw a glass beer bottle towards the stage that ended up smashing me on the head, coincidentally, halfway through 'Wrong Place, Right Time'. It hurt like mad, so on the drive down to Liverpool for the next night's gig, I bought a packet of frozen peas, to help reduce the swelling.

After the last show, in London, on 21 December, we all went back to our hotel, The Columbia, opposite Hyde Park, to celebrate and to get our Christmas bonuses off the latest in a long line of tour managers, when we heard that Pan Am Flight 103 had exploded over Lockerbie, Scotland, killing all its passengers. It was a surreal moment. It was Christmas, we'd finished a tour and partied in the bar until dawn. But it was strange. This plane had just been blown out of the sky and I hoped there was nobody I knew on board.

15

Madchester

Meanwhile, back in Manchester, a renaissance of sorts was under way. 1989 was the year that the 'Madchester' phenomenon began to take full effect with both The Stone Roses and Happy Mondays appearing for the first time on *Top of the Pops*. And on the same show. You couldn't walk down the street in Manchester without bumping into people with flared jeans and Reni hats, which to be honest I thought looked a bit daft on your average punter.

With the success of my contemporaries, I was itching to get back in the studio or on the road with The Fall, to emulate our mates' success.

However, the first half of 1989 was a very quiet period, with just one concert at the start of the year. The only thing I remember us doing as a band was a bit of shopping.

Brix, always a bit of a fashionista, as her later career would bear out, took us all down to some trendy shop called Geese to get us kitted out in some new threads with a record company budget of 500 quid each. Amongst other things, we picked out short-sleeve silk shirts with intricate detailing over the shoulders and collars. Mine was red with black collar, trim and piping. A bit like The Clash used to wear. We stood around looking uncomfortable with Brix going, 'Yeah, you look great, that really suits you.'

We soon ditched the clobber when one of the roadies just started taking the piss out of us.

'You look like a fucking darts team,' he cackled. *'One Hundred and Eighty!'*

I didn't fancy being an Eric Bristow lookalike so I stuck to the clothes I was mostly buying from Richard Creme, a seven-foot bloke who ran a designer boutique off St Ann's Square. He wasn't cheap either.

Mark and Brix separated during this period and the couple would be divorced soon after. I felt it was a shame as she was a good laugh and the band would miss her once she had gone to pursue her solo career with her band The Adult Net. I wondered if the relatively stable ship would be rocked.

Mark, with his strong contrarian streak and suspicion of trends, wanted no part of the overhyped Madchester scene whatsoever, and in response, he decided to decamp to one of his favourite cities: Edinburgh.

There was a bit of conscious symbolism, I guess. Mark defiantly stayed true to his roots for much of his life, hardly ever moving from Salford and Prestwich. But as Manchester was on the rise he moved to beautiful, historic Edinburgh, The Athens of the North - the very antithesis of 24-hour gobshite Manchester.

I had no such cross to bear and so my response, with a love of partying and good music, was to move slap bang into the city centre and the maelstrom of Madchester. I rented a flat in India House on Whitworth Street, near the Palace Theatre.

Mark asked me if I would help him move in to his new flat so we set off on the train to Edinburgh in the New Year, with just a couple of suitcases, a couple of boxes and a load of carrier bags. He didn't seem to be that upset to be honest, and when we arrived at Waverley station, I found out why. Waiting for him there, was a stunning girl, who apparently worked for a record label in London and was the daughter of a well-known rock guitarist.

Mark was a member of the whisky society in Edinburgh, so we went to the club, not far from his smart new flat on a crescent of Georgian terraces and made a toast to his new home. Before we'd left England, he had invited me to stay over at his place for the night, so I was expecting that the two of us would be out on the town. But when this girl turned up, I didn't want to stay in the flat with them. Happily, when we walked over to the flat to deposit the cases, Mark said, with a wink, he had booked me a room for the night at the Hilton down the road. After a quick guided tour of the palatial flat, I bid my farewells, and left them to it. Before I went to check into my room, however, Mark said he had a present for me and opened up the antique chest in the lounge. He pulled out an expensive, heavy pair of navy-blue velvet curtains that were 10 feet in length at least. They weren't even his - he just took them out of this flat he was renting!

Very touching.

Anyway, they were perfect for the flat I had just moved into in Manchester.

A friend told me about India House, a former Edwardian packing warehouse, on the same road as the Haçienda and the Venue, two clubs that I often frequented, so it was ideal for the nightlife which seemed very exciting at the time. I went to have a look one day because my first flat in Levenshulme was damp and the underfloor heating was useless. As the India House flats were amongst the very first to offer city centre living in Manchester, they were cheap. They also came with underground parking for my Golf. The flat I ended up with was a belter too, situated on the quieter rear corner of the building on the second floor facing the south. It was a real novelty - it felt like I was living in a hotel. I put up the curtains Mark had kindly donated and became an urban dweller, partying endlessly for the next two years.

India House is famously where Noel Gallagher lived and wrote a number of tunes for Oasis but it wasn't just him, a host of future pop stars and actors lived there. The building was really big and had two reception areas, one at each end. Living next to me at number 93, was a researcher for John Peel's show. As it was a central location I'd get a few visitors popping in. Reni and Happy Monday's manager Nathan McGough, would often call round in the afternoon for a brew, whilst they were going about their business in town. Mandy, my girlfriend at the time, moved in with me, but she was out at work all day so I was grateful for the company. Pete Garner lived upstairs from me as well as an artist, Jeff 'The Pirate', whose name says it all, so there was never a dull moment.

Ian Brown lived at his mate's flat on the fourth floor for a time, so I went to see him for a chat one day and found him firing a Webley air pistol at some empty drinks cans, down on the deserted car park at the rear of the building. I watched as he fired off a few shots, cans tinkling across the cobbles.

After letting me have a few shots with the gun, he took hold of the weapon to show me how it was done. Suddenly, we heard a loud knocking on the door and as Ian went to answer it, the door burst open and four burly middle-aged blokes in Crombies and shiny shoes barged in and snatched the pistol out of Ian's hand. It was just like the time when Freak Party had been arrested at Decibelle Studios in 1981. But this time neither Ian nor I was arrested and as quickly as they had arrived, they disappeared with the gun. Ian reckoned they were cops, but I think they were mates of Frank, the ex-Green Beret, and caretaker in India House. He didn't take shit off anyone. They named the little road down the side of the building after him - McGinty Place.

It amazes me how many people I run into, to this day, who used to live in India House.

With the The Fall quiet, I went on the look out for another paid gig to build up my drumming CV, even though I was on a retainer and knew Mark wouldn't be happy if he found out I was moonlighting with another band.

The Smiths had split up in 1987 and Morrissey, who I hadn't spoken to since the sessions for their *Strangeways Here We Come* album, had released his cracking solo single, 'Suedehead', featuring Vini Reilly on guitar. I wondered if perhaps he needed a drummer for any future work and set about finding a way to contact him again. I had heard rumours about Morrissey buying his mother a big house in Hale Barns and it didn't take me long to establish exactly where it was after asking around a few locals I knew from my old stomping grounds.

I wrote Morrissey a short letter asking him if there was any chance of any session work with him. I then stuck the letter in an envelope and posted it through his mother's door under the cover of darkness, crossed my fingers, and waited to see if he would get in touch.

A month later as I opened my post box in India House, I found an envelope with the address written in Morrissey's immediately recognisable scrawl. I pulled out a postcard depicting a group of young lads in Smiths T-shirts and Morrissey's response on the reverse.

'Confused by your note - I thought your P45 was spoken for?' it said.

I had to laugh. He has a wicked sense of humour and I was amused even though my request had been rebuffed. There were plenty of reasons for him not to employ me, I suppose, and my current employer, Mark, had given The Smiths an early break when they were asked to support The Fall in the early eighties, though who knows if that was a reason.

He went on to say he'd get in touch if he needed me but I never got the call. I can't say I wasn't disappointed but I was having such a good time anyway. The Haçienda was my local - acid house and indie bands with comical swaggers. I slept most days until lunchtime and went out most nights. Just went with the flow.

One of the most memorable nights out that summer was at my good mate Andy Rourke's wedding reception, at The Four Seasons, near the airport. A lot of the faces from the Manchester indie scene were there. As the drugs started kicking in though it ended up getting shut down, just as the party was getting into full flow, after complaints from other hotel guests.

The Roses were taking off in a big way by now so I didn't see Ian and John much, except on TV, read about them in the press and got postcards from here and there. It was great to see them doing well and being credited with spearheading, alongside the Mondays, a new movement of Manchester music that was sweeping across the nation.

Although I'm not a big one for lyrics, I enjoyed the likes of Shaun Ryder, who I felt related to the man on the street. He seemed to me like a lowbrow Mark E Smith. He made me laugh.

In those days, there were talent scouts from record companies everywhere you went in Manchester, afraid to miss out on the next big thing.

Any time you turned the radio on - mainstream radio, there weren't that many options - there was a Manchester band playing: Inspiral Carpets, James, The Charlatans. Any band with a Manchester connection seemed to get some airtime; bands that had the odd good tune but fell by the wayside like so many others lumped in under the Madchester umbrella. Bands like World of Twist, New Fast Automatic Daffodils, and Intastella, whose earlier incarnation 'Sometimes' I had drummed with for a while.

Bands from further afield would pick up the 'baggy' vibe. The Soup Dragons, The Farm, early Blur, before the whole thing seemed to fizzle out just as quickly as it had begun and 'Grunge' took over.

For me, while it is something to be proud of and is much more diverse than the Madchester tag, Manchester has overhyped itself in terms of musical output. It's nothing on Detroit, LA, London, New York, any number of cities. But some of it really does stand up to this day and a whole new generation of fans recognise this twenty odd years later. I suppose the most obvious example of a band that has picked up the blueprint of fusing guitar and dance beats would be someone like Kasabian.

This was the backdrop to Fontana signing us back in 1989. Fontana was part of Phonogram Records Corporation and after The Fall's relatively successful run of singles, in conjunction with the Madchester bands signing frenzy, I think our new record company thought The Fall (from *Salford*, Mark would say to any journalist trying to lump us into Madchester) might be a good investment. But they didn't understand Mark.

As I say, Mark wanted no part of it. Personally, I hoped we'd get swept along on Madchester's coat tails. I felt we were being left behind again. Later, I came to admire Mark for sticking to his guns though. He deliberately avoided fads and marketing because he thought it was ridiculous and dated quickly, and he had a point.

We weren't ever going to be baggy.

We didn't look baggy. We didn't sound baggy. We were The Fall.

And Mark was right in seeing Madchester as a fleeting fad.

The zenith of the Madchester scene took place the next year, when the Roses played a gig to 30,000 at Spike Island. A great moment … but a shit gig. It started off on the wrong foot. Setting up in the days before, the crew were all buzzing on E and coming out with strange blisters - on a site acknowledged as the birthplace of the British chemical industry. White smoke belched out of nearby chimneys from Runcorn and Ellesmere Port. The PA wasn't up to it - it was just too windy and you couldn't hear the set well as it was blown across the Cheshire plain. There weren't enough bar staff or toilets. The complaints could go on and on, it simply wasn't well run. In the manager's defence, a gig of this size had never been attempted in this location, mainly chosen, I was told, because it was halfway between Liverpool and Manchester. And the lights were good too, actually.

The most striking memory for me was the *NME* helicopter buzzing overhead and Ian kicking a big inflatable globe out into the audience which became the defining photo opportunity. I thought they were going to take on the world.

The next Fall studio album, *Extricate*, was recorded with guitarist Martin Bramah replacing Brix. Martin had been in The Fall at the start of their career, before quitting in 1979 to start his own band, The Blue Orchids. Steve and Craig knew him well having been on the road with him with a support band for The Fall and were pleased to welcome him back on board.

We started off the bulk of recordings for *Extricate*, which had a much harder sound, at a studio in Buckinghamshire called The Mill, which used to belong to guitarist Jimmy Page. It was a residential studio, so as per normal when Steve, Craig, and I arrived there was a scramble to see who could get the biggest and best bedroom.

Whoever puts their bag down first claims the territory. That is the law.

Producer at The Mill sessions was a little Hispanic-looking guy with a goatee beard and an endearing Floridian accent, called Craig Leon, who had worked with American luminaries like Ramones and Blondie. He was suggested by Phonogram and assisted by his beautiful wife and solo artist Cassell Webb. She sang some backing for The Fall on this new record, and played some keyboards too, as well as giving the sessions a great calming vibe. I liked her a lot.

We were told on arrival at the studio that we might encounter some ghostly goings on in the night, such as unexplained bumps and heavy breathing sounds, but we weren't concerned as this was perfectly normal when the band were together. The main live room had a little stream that cut its way straight through the middle of the mansion, with coins tossed in for good luck. To get to the control room, you had to walk over a tiny little footbridge that looked like it belonged on a miniature golf course.

Scottish fiddle player Kenny Brady, who Mark joked looked like an out of work waiter, on account of his grubby white jacket, joined the recording session. Mark turned up with his carrier bag full of lyrics and his omnipresent Dictaphone. Mark had this thing where he would leave the Dictaphone in record mode whilst he left the room briefly, before retrieving shortly after, to see if we had been talking about him, which we usually had. He tried to catch us out all the time. We had gotten wise to this a long time ago and so we always made sure Mark hadn't left it lying around, if he exited unexpectedly.

After hammering a load of whizz, we got down to business with the opening track off the new album, called 'Sing! Harpy', which Martin co-wrote and was a favourite of mine. The single, 'Popcorn Double Feature', with Kenny Brady's fiddle work all across the intro, was next up, followed by 'I'm Frank', which a mate of mine said '… sounds like somebody putting a shed up'. The best track we did at The Mill for me was 'Bill Is Dead', which Mark actually sang rather than ranted.

A couple of days before the end of the recordings, I came into the studio and was told that Mark had had a seizure and been admitted to a hospital in High Wycombe.

It sounds callous but I don't remember us being especially concerned. We carried on working on songs regardless.

I couldn't say I was totally surprised by Mark's hospitalisation and thought maybe this would be a wake-up call for him to examine his lifestyle (though who am I to say). But it wasn't really and these episodes became a recurring feature.

He came back the next day, checking himself out against the advice of the doctors, and seemed to be OK, though he was a lot more subdued.

I returned to my Manchester bolthole, spending the summer nights clubbing away to Snap! 'The Power' and 808 State's 'Pacific State' and popping the odd Ecstasy tab along the way.

I knew some of the dealers who worked out of the Haçienda, where people were by now spending all their money on the tablets, which were coming down rapidly in price. At first they were more than £20 a go but they quickly came down to about £4 each. I dabbled with E but I never really went mad on it and didn't seem to get the same buzz that others seemed to be having. Maybe it was the other stuff I was taking. With the price coming down though, everyone was having a go, instead of the traditional alcoholic drinks, and then dancing the night away, gurning and hugging total strangers they had only met seconds ago.

Mark abhorred all this loving behaviour, and I was with him on that - all these sweaty strangers embracing you randomly saying how much they love you. He and I would still frequent the Haçienda though, on his return from his hiatus in Edinburgh.

It was really handy being right in town, especially in the early hours when it's only a five-minute walk home, though you can see that that would have its drawbacks.

Once, one of Mark's three sisters, after getting pissed at the Venue, rang my buzzer after closing time. I got up from a deep sleep to answer the intercom, thinking it was the fire brigade again.

'Simon, it's Caroline I need to use your phone to ring a taxi. I can't get one,' she shouted.

I told her to piss off and that she was out of order.

She shot back that she would be telling her brother about this and blah blah blah.

I hung up on her. Middle of the night for Christ's sake.

Mark never mentioned it to me but he wouldn't have been angry anyway - he'd probably have laughed.

After the session in The Mill, we relocated to The Town House studios near Shepherd's Bush, to record the tracks 'Arms Control Poseur' and 'British People in Hot Weather' with Adrian Sherwood. Adrian had engineered a lot of dub and reggae and was another producer who I admired and enjoyed working with.

To plug the gap before *Extricate*'s release in February 1990, Mark decided to release an album of live out-takes called *Seminal Live*. As I say: quantity. I thought it was crap at the time, apart from 'Deadbeat Descendent', and I hated the photo of myself on the cover wearing a purple jumper. For a while, Mark used to call me 'Cardi lad' on account of my taste for knitwear at the time. He'd ad-lib it into songs.

'I base myself on Simon Wolstencroft, he is a Cardi lad.'

But anyway, I didn't have much say in what got put out and regardless, I was still having a ball and getting paid for it. What's not to like?

We went out to Brazil for two dates, my favourite trip. After a couple of warm-up gigs for Martin and Kenny, we flew first class to Rio de Janeiro for our shows at the Toucan Arts Festival, just outside the city with Ed and Di our sound engineers.

Phil Jones, a Manchester based promoter, got us the gig and travelled with us, along with a new tour manager called Trevor Long from Birmingham, who had looked after Duran Duran for a while. I loved Rio immediately, not just the weather, the gorgeous girls and the cheap cocaine, but its vibrant colours and the topography of the place. It was nothing like Europe. I thought it looked prehistoric.

We checked into the Meridien Hotel, where we all found fantastic rooms waiting for us, looking out over Copacabana with the statue of Christ the Redeemer, over to the left. It was an awesome setting. Apart from Mark, who didn't like the oppressive heat, we all headed for the beach in our mostly black coloured clothes, even though it was in the high nineties. British people in hot weather. We must have looked ridiculous while we sat there, pasty white, watching the girls playing volleyball in their bikinis and the skilful beach footballers playing five-a-side in their bare feet. We rested up before the first gig the following night in a kind of open-air ballroom with covered seating all around the circumference.

On the day of the gig, I had a bit of time to kill before being picked up by the promoters, so I went on my own for a walk round the streets at the back of our hotel. I wanted to have a look at the real Brazil and within 200 yards I came across what was the start of one of the infamous *favelas*. They stretched back over the undulating hillside as far as the eye could see. There was all sorts of trouble in there. I was told some of the police would act as murder squads in their spare time, to keep control of the drug-dealing gangs, often shooting dead young Brazilian kids who were just running drugs for the big fish, who never got caught.

I approached a corner and a gang of about ten youths clocked me coming their way, eyeing me up like I was their next meal ticket. It was a bit daft really, just strolling into some foreign ghetto. The lads couldn't speak English, but they gestured that they were shoe shiners and wanted to clean my brand new shoes that were spotless. I said thanks, but no thanks, and started walking back towards the hotel quickly but they started following me, and persisted in their sales technique. One of them pointed at one of my shoes, which was now covered in a horrible sticky brown mud, even though it was nearly 90 degrees outside. I relented and after one of them had cleaned both shoes I offered him a wad of the local currency, which because of the enormous rate of inflation in the country was practically worthless. One of them hissed at me through his teeth in disgust. He made it clear he only wanted US dollars, of which I had none. I hurried back to the hotel before it kicked off, and went for a swim in the pool.

It can't help but give you a dose of reality and see how lucky you are. Here I was, swanning around in first class, staying in fancy hotels and being ferried around to fine dining restaurants. Meanwhile, these kids badgered people to shine shoes for a wad of worthless notes.

I did actually get some dollars from the promoters that night and I'd like to say I went to offer it to the shoe shiners, but what I actually did was chip in for a big bag of coke, which cost about $10 and lasted for the next two or three days. The shows passed without incident and I had enjoyed my time in Rio, drinking 'Brahmah' bottled beer with Martin Bramah, who had settled back into the group nicely, though he kept to himself, but it was his choice so that was fine.

Not long after we came home, we were invited to perform at John Peel's fiftieth birthday party, at a club called Subterranea under the Westway in London. I shook his hand and wished him all the best as the band had a photo taken with him. Mark, however, kept his distance from Peel most of the time, to keep up his air of mystique, possibly. Before our headline slot, we had to endure support band The House of Love, who had been hanging outside our tourbus all afternoon, holding scruffy mongrels on threadbare bits of rope. Mark had it in for them when he copped one of the dogs pissing up against the wheel of our gleaming tourbus.

Fortunately, Mark didn't have a pop at them and our forty-five minute set passed without incident.

Extricate was received with favourable reviews in the music press. They liked the Martin Bramah driven guitar sound, which on tracks like 'And Therein ...' added an almost rockabilly feel to the proceedings.

I needn't have worried about Brix leaving at the start of the year, Martin had changed the dynamic of the group and I thought *Extricate* was really good at the time.

The first single off the new album was 'Telephone Thing', and is one of my favourites from The Fall. It was produced by dance remixers Coldcut, who, not so long before, had scored a number one hit with Yazz's 'The Only Way is Up.' Jonathan and Matt were really cool and did a great job on the track they were given, which was quite rough when they received it. Mark was making references to phone-tapping and gossipy types. It's a pity it hadn't been released twenty years later when loads of newspaper journalists were exposed for using phone taps, to create news stories.

'Does the Home Secretary have the barest faintest inkling of what's going down?' Mark sang.

I thought it was the best chance we'd have of being included in the Madchester explosion, but it didn't happen.

'Sing! Harpy', 'Bill Is Dead', 'Telephone Thing', and 'Hilary' were my favourites from the album, though they don't all stand the test of time. In fact, some of it is badly (and probably purposely) out of tune. The cover 'Black Monk Theme' stands up well in hindsight.

In March, 'Popcorn Double Feature', a track written by Scott English, performed by the Searchers in the sixties, was released as the second single. I didn't like it. The singing was terrible and I just thought: what a *waste*. We had the backing of a major label, Madchester was at its peak, and this was what we gave them as a single.

It bombed.

16

On the Road 1990

Then followed the heaviest touring schedule that The Fall had ever undertaken - certainly whilst I had been in the line-up - running from March through to November, and taking us across four continents.

With Mark no longer married, he and I went out on the pull a fair bit until he settled down again. After a show in Switzerland, we made a long overnight drive over to what was Yugoslavia, first calling at Ljubljana in Slovenia. We chatted up two local girls, Barbara and Sylvia, in a restaurant over lunch in the middle of town and invited them to that night's show. They'd never heard of us. Still, after the gig we went out clubbing and we were invited back to Barbara's flat, across town.

Wingman Wolstencroft.

Though they played great hosts, the girls told us how scared they were at the prospect of an imminent Balkan war given the volatile situation in the region. In the morning, we invited Barbara and Sylvia along to the next show, at an ice rink in Zagreb, Croatia. They seemed troubled at the idea of crossing into Croatia, but they travelled with us anyway, over the long potholed roads, stopping only at a stall in the middle of nowhere selling just oranges. The girls wouldn't get out to stretch their legs, so I went and bought a bag of oranges off the surly guy minding the stall. He didn't seem very welcoming. Tense. The oranges were rotten too. Mark threw them off the bus, moaning he was already sick of carting all Marcia's vegetarian shit round, stinking the place out. The Zagreb show was strange. We played support to a prog rock outfit, with mullet haircuts, vests, Lycra pants, and white socks, in front of a very sparse crowd ... at this ice rink. They didn't think much of us.

There was more money in music back then, granted, but it didn't always seem to add up. The expense of visiting these places where there was so little interest baffled me. Not that I worried too much. I'm a happy tourist.

We carried on to Belgrade after sending the girls back to Slovenia on a train.

On the road, Mark and I were always watching CNN, the 24-hour rolling news channel that was the template for TV news stations. So many world-changing events were brought right to your hotel room. Tiananmen Square, the Berlin Wall, Nelson Mandela's release from jail. The world was changing without Madchester. That said, Manchester did get its slot on the news cycle, contributing the longest prison riots in British history from 1 - 25 April that year. We watched every day and bought the English papers for the latest updates. We couldn't get enough.

As the months passed, I watched on CNN as Yugoslavia tore itself apart in a bloody civil war rife with ethnic hatred. I kept wondering how the girls were and began to understand the stress they had been under. I never saw Sylvia again, but Barbara unexpectedly turned up at Mark's house later in the year, where Saffron was now living. Not ideal.

Prague was another beautiful place with a culture of payola. When we pulled into town and parked up, two armed policemen sauntered over, had a look around the bus and went to speak to Noel. They said it was illegal to park in the hotel car park, and there was a $50 fine, which was payable immediately. Noel started arguing the toss about parking in the hotel's own car park, but the copper, whose English extended to the phrase 'Fifty dollar', was having none of it. Mark told the tour manager to just pay them off before one or all of us were arrested and put in a cell. There were drugs on board, after all. The gig was hassle free though, and the crowd was more welcoming than the police.

After stopping at Vienna then Hanover, we did a show in a tiny club in Paris, where I thought Mark had finally lost his mind. After the gig he rushed at me with a huge red fire axe that he had taken down off the wall backstage. His face was contorted and he was foaming at the mouth as he burst into the dressing room where I sat minding my own business. He swung the axe down towards my head, whilst making a shrieking noise. At the last minute, he swung the axe away from me. He was only messing about, and everyone had a laugh, but for a second I thought he had snapped after being on the road for two solid months and finally going over the edge, here in Paris. He hated the French - he wouldn't even stay in Paris the night of the gig.

'They've always got to be different,' he said disdainfully.

A couple of weeks later, it was back over to the States for a couple of shows. Before leaving, a mate of mine gave me this AT&T password that he had gotten from a friend who worked for the company. It was some sort of engineer's code which allowed you to make free calls to anywhere in the world from their pay phones. It was about twenty digits long and it was a bit of messing about but I was really grateful for this with my mother now being diagnosed with cancer. I rang her every day for a chat.

Then, because I had this password, I started ringing any and everyone just for a natter, you know, see how they were getting on. People I didn't even ring while I was in England. After a while, I let Craig and Steve in on the scam because I thought it was a bit tight just watching them make calls while all their quarters got gobbled up. They started hammering it as well.

In New York, at the Ritz Theatre for the soundcheck, an attractive blonde called Suzie, from Idaho, and who I presumed worked for the record label, asked me if I needed her to do any shopping for me, whilst we were in the city. I did need some new Levis, so told her my size. Back in my hotel room, resting up before the show, there was a knock at the door. It was Suzie with the jeans, so I invited her in and when I asked her how much I owed her, she just said 'This' as she grabbed my crotch. Then followed what seemed like hours of grappling all over my hotel room, which continued all night after the gig and the next morning before we set off for the flight to LA, for the second and last gig on the trip.

It was only three weeks later, sitting on a 747, heading to Australia for a tour in the southern hemisphere that I started itching in the same spot that Idaho Suzie had first grabbed. When we stopped to refuel in Kuala Lumpur, I had a good look in the bathroom, but couldn't see anything untoward. After watching a snake charming competition on the TV in the transit lounge while scratching myself, we carried on with the flight, ending up in Brisbane, where the tour was to begin. I mentioned my irritation to Mark, who laughed and said, 'I bet you've got crabs off that bird in New York.'

On even closer inspection I found out he was correct.

Mark went on, still laughing, advising me to apply the area with urine, as his granddad's comrades had done in the Black Watch regiment. I decided against this treatment; modern medicine was at hand and I was not about to pour piss all over myself. Instead I bought some Bic razors and special powder from the nearest chemist.

The best thing about Australia was the weather. My favourite city was Melbourne. We did two shows there at the Old Greek Theatre, a really old place that had tons of character. It was along a strip of wooden fronted shops with verandas on the front. It reminded me of the Wild West.

Perth, the most isolated city in the world, was clean and modern, the air crisp. I spent a day on the beach at Scarborough, a magnificent stretch of clean white sand which was deserted. It was much nicer than the scruffy, touristy, Bondi Beach in Sydney, our next destination. We bumped into Nick Cave again.

When we weren't flying between gigs, our live sound man 'Acid Daze Dave', who had been the live engineer for the Sex Pistols, did most of the driving. We sat in the back of the station wagon, listening to Barry White and Abba cassettes on the way out to a gig in Coogee Bay, where there were cockroaches the size of saucers in my hotel room.

We did the usual tourist visits, taking in Sydney Harbour Bridge and the Opera House, before heading over to Canberra, which was as boring as advertised.

Meanwhile, Martin had been spending more and more time with Marcia, visiting museums and the like, whenever there was a spare moment. Once we were off stage we didn't see them. It was obvious to everyone that Martin wasn't sleeping in his own room and it didn't take a genius to work out where he was. This clearly annoyed Mark, though I don't really know why. Might have been jealousy, might have been that it was causing a division in the camp (though me, Steve and Craig didn't care), could even have been he was pissed off about a room going to waste, who knows, but he wasn't happy.

Marcia told me it had been all, I quit / you're fired / I quit / you're fired for a few months.

New Zealand reminded me of Wales mostly, lots of undulating, grass-covered hills, dotted with sheep and old Morris Minors pottering about everywhere, although I was staggered to discover that, with my new Natwest cash card, I could draw money out of my account *on the other side of the world*.

We played two sold-out shows at the Auckland Town Hall, where we

.ere given a rapturous reception. The show had to go on.

Our airline tickets, back to Australia before the onward journey to Japan, meant we would have to stop on the island for another four days in a small motel just outside the city limits. It rained cats and dogs for three days and three nights, during which time, Chris Waddle blasted the ball over the bar when he took his penalty in the World Cup in Italy, sending England spiralling out of the competition, as per usual.

I didn't leave my motel room and hardly spoke to anyone, until the torrential rain let up. There was nothing to do; we were stuck in the New Zealand countryside and I didn't have any drugs. It just felt isolated and as if I was going cold turkey. Well, I was. The day before we left, the rain finally did relent and the sun showed its face, so I drove with Marcia in one of the hire cars to see the geysers and hot mud pools of Rotorua, a couple of hours drive south.

Steve, Craig and I had tried to invite Marcia out a few times but she just wanted to stay in her room with Martin, so I was happy she finally decided to come out. It was also great just to see a little bit of the country, but I couldn't help thinking what must be going through Marcia's mind, with the camp's uncomfortable atmosphere. Elephants in rooms and all that.

Martin had been really excited about going to Japan, where we were due next, and where none of us had ever been.

Instead of going to Japan though, Martin and Marcia got a phone call off Trevor Long at 4 a.m. telling them they were on the next flight home. Trevor had a car booked for the airport at 6 a.m.

Mark sent our latest tour manager, Robbie Burns, a hard-drinking Glaswegian, to deliver the tickets. I didn't see Mark and Martin interact at all in this period so I never really got to the bottom of Mark's reason for axing him, although he did say once to me, '… that Martin, he's like a vampire. He sucks all the energy out of you just by standing next to you.'

The band awoke to the surprising but not entirely surprising news. It was The Fall all over. We just took it in our stride.

Finally, after what seemed like an eternity, we took off for Japan's Narita airport, landing on a very hot and humid day. Our leader had mixed feelings about Japan as he said he had issues with the way a family member of his had been treated as a prisoner of war by the Japanese.

We met a huge queue at immigration. Mark made his way to the front of the long line and barged his way in, nearly knocking a few little old

ove: Mum, sister Jane, and Emma,
e Dalmation.

Above: With my dad on holiday,
Southport, 1967.

ove: Class photo 1975. I am third from left on front row, next to Ian Brown.

Above: The Patrol, South Trafford College, Halloween, 1980.

Above: One of the many Clash shows I travelled to.

Left: With Johnny Marr, Marple Bridge, 1983.

Right: Mike Joyce, Andy Rourke, Melanie Morrison, London, 1984.

Left: Morrissey backstage, London, 1984.

Right: The Weeds photo shoot, 1985.

© Ian Tilt...

Below: Brix, Rocco, me, Lancaster University, 1986.

Below: Hacienda membership card, 1986.

FAC 51
THE HACIENDA

SIMON
N. WOLSTONE-
CROFT
No. HONORARY
Sig.
Exp date:-

Left: Mark E Smith and a gorilla, 1988.

Below: Steve Hanley, LA, 1987.

Above: Craig Scanlon - I'll get my coat, 1987.

Right: With Alan 'Reni' Wren, Ian Brown, India House, 1989.

Right/Below: Postcard from
Morrissey - Giz a job ...

POSTCARD   july 23 1989

Dear Si'
Confused by your note - I
thought your P45 was spoken
for? My hip-swivelling days
re "temporarily frozen". In the
vent of a thaw, I'll give you a
ing. best Wishes MORRISSEY

Above: Postcard from John Squire.

Left: The Fall
down to a four
piece, 1992.

Above: San Francisco, 1993.

Right: With Dad and my daughter Emily, 1996.

Below: On holiday in the Gamb with Dr Alban's percussionis

Above: Inder 'Goldfinger' Matharu, adding the final touches, 2000.

Above: The short-lived Intruda, 2003.

Above: Carpe Diem, 2009.

Below: The Family Bizarre.
With Keo Martin and Jez Kerr, 2011.

Below: With the Vistalite, 2014.

Above: Two Roses fans taking in the reunion, Barcelona, 2012.

Left: Catching up with Andy Rourke, 2014.

Below: The Mill Studios, Chadderton, 2014.

Below: Chewing the f[a] with Ian Brown, 2014

Below: With Emily, Anglesey, 2011.

Japanese ladies over, as he deliberately swung his hand baggage around, like a mace. I was hot and tired and followed right behind him. We met our minibus driver in the arrivals hall, and then set off on a two-hour journey to our hotel in the Roppongi district of Tokyo, where our first gig was booked.

A lot of western bands stayed at the hotel we were in and so there were always groups of girls about handing out small cuddly toys and trinkets but they were very shy and giggly when I smiled and thanked them.

Though I had expected it to be different, I was often surprised by the gulf in culture in Japan. In Tokyo the whole staff from an upmarket department store was doing stretches and touching their toes in unison at 7.30 a.m. outside the front door. I watched some schoolchildren, all wearing white surgeon masks. practising an earthquake drill. There were vending machines on the streets selling razors or nuts or drinks - basically anything. Shops selling samurai swords and armour. In an empty park, stage after stage had groups of Japanese youths dressed up in leather jackets and pointy shoes, with their hair done up in a quiff, belting out Elvis, Gene Vincent, and Eddie Cochran hits. A forest of neon lit up karaoke bars and sushi houses where I drank hot sake. You didn't see this sort of thing in Manchester.

After Tokyo, we boarded the Bullet Train, which shot across the countryside at high speed, visiting Kyoto, Osaka, Nagoya and Kobe. Some of these gigs were high up in tall tower blocks with shopping centres on their lower floors.

Like in New Zealand, the crowds here seemed to love us. The few punters that I tried to talk to after the gigs were grateful but also very respectful. In fact, after a while, all the bowing made me feel a bit uncomfortable to be honest. Still, it was better than people being rude to you, like in France.

After the tour, I stayed behind in Tokyo with Mark, who was scheduled to spend two days doing interviews at the record company's office, whilst the rest of the band flew home. Despite his reservations about Japan, Mark seemed to be in really good spirits. He was banging on about Public Enemy and rap music, saying how literate it was compared to most bands (The Fall excepted). He loved it.

'It's proper poetry,' he said to me.

His profile often seems to be about going off the rails, which he did a fair bit of, but it wasn't all like that.

17

Shiftwork

Meanwhile, my mum's dream of buying a cottage in nearby Dunham Massey to live out the rest of her years with my dad, who had planned to retire early, were put on hold after a course of chemotherapy began. Her health began to deteriorate dramatically. The house on Grove Lane had been sold, but unable now to move to the countryside, Dad rented a house in Hale.

He feared the worst for Mum. He had seen many of his patients with cancer go into a steep decline, just like Mum appeared to be doing now. I tried my best to visit her whenever possible to bring her some kind of comfort, though by now she was on morphine a lot of the time and it wasn't always easy to talk with her as she drifted in and out of consciousness. I mostly sat next to her as she lay in bed and held her hand, talking about holidays and happier times.

My dad was, naturally, devastated, though he still carried on running his practice in Sale Moor, for the time being. Jane would bring her six-month-old daughter, Hannah, to visit Mum nearly every day, which used to make Mum smile, as this was her first grandchild. I felt guilty about not visiting Mum more, but I knew that she was happy seeing me doing what I wanted to do and that made me feel a bit better.

I clocked back on.

Our next show was a late afternoon slot on that year's Reading Festival at the end of August, playing on the Sunday night before headliners Pixies, who I was a big fan of. I loved the big gigs, though Reading wasn't as big as it is today, with tons of corporate sponsors and campers and excitable TV presenters. It was a treat for me to play at a well-run set-up though because the next night we might be in a tiny club with a load of shit equipment.

As I stood around, Mick Jagger's chauffeur-driven car swept back-stage at high speed and Mick jumped out in a rush to see his new bass player's band, but he had missed the show.

Before we went on stage, Mark spotted a line of photographers snap-ping pictures for the daily press as well as the music magazines, and his body language picked up as he walked toward the stage.

'Is that alright for you gents?' he joked as he posed for photos. He was really enjoying himself.

By now, we were commanding much higher fees for this kind of gig than ever before. This suited us all fine. It all went into the pot, so to speak, to pay the band's monthly retainers, but we started receiving little bonuses now and again after gigs like this one.

The following week we were due in Tel Aviv for a one-off show, followed by two consecutive nights playing in Athens, Greece. I got Phil Powell, Johnny Marr's guitar tech, a job on the dates.

This was not long before the first Gulf War and Saddam Hussein was threatening to fire over scud missiles armed with poison gas into Israel. Mark sat us all down in the airport bar with a copy of the *Telegraph* which had a report stating that children and infants in Tel Aviv, were all being issued with gas masks in school, in case of a sudden attack by Iraq. He then asked us all if we were sure we still wanted to go, claiming he had some inside information from the MI6 that the situation could escalate. He once told me that MI6 had tried to recruit him, but I didn't really believe him. I thought it was some kind of *Walter Mitty* fantasy.

But regards Israel, nobody had any qualms. Of course we wanted to go, we said, we hadn't been before. I don't know if Mark was scared himself but we appreciated his concern for us - it was fair play as our employer.

The trip went without a hitch and I slept under the stars on the flat roof of a whitewashed villa, and woke to a sunlit morning and a flight to Athens. I've got to go. *Yes of course I'll write to you ...*

The same promoter, who had given us the acid the last time we were in the Greek capital, was there to greet us again. I didn't mention that the last time we were in town I had spent two days in bed, in agony, after he had given us the gift. In fact, I just ignored him and he made no effort to speak to me, he was only interested in talking to Mark. Anyway, it was my own fault for taking the tab in the first place and I had learnt from the experience. Beware Greeks bearing gifts or some such.

Instead of indulging, I made my way to the Acropolis in the baking midday sun.

I missed Marcia on the keyboards since her ousting in Australia. She had decided to begin studying for a new career in the medical profession. For the time being, Mark's new girlfriend, Saffron, stood in on the odd song on keyboards, though she could only play with one finger, which didn't sound very good. I didn't agree with her being in the band because I didn't think she was good enough, it was the same with Lucy who came next. Saffron was put to better use when she started running Mark's Cog Sinister record label from his house. She also did merchandising and things like counting the number of people coming into the gigs to make sure the band was getting its dues.

In November, Saffron's eventual replacement, Dave Bush, came with the band to Barcelona, as a roadie at first. He lived in a house just opposite the Greenhouse Rehearsal Studio, in Stockport.

Dave had a home studio set up in his back room and had mastered Cubase, one of the first available computer programmes for music. Like me, he wanted to make The Fall a well-known, commercially successful band. I think everyone in the band did, except Mark. We used to discuss the whys and wherefores of Mark's spoiler tactics, and all we could come up with was that maybe he was scared of success. Anyway, Dave would have a big influence on the sound of the band for the next two or three years. This suited me because I liked all of the samples and beats he was coming up with and his general *joie de vivre*.

Before he joined though, the band had slimmed down to a four-piece outfit, which went on the road for a couple of weeks in England in conjunction with the single 'High Tension Line', a brutal sounding rock track; great chorus though.

Being a four-piece limited the tracks we could play. For the first time, Mark decided to throw in a few older numbers that suited the line-up. Up until this point, it had always been new stuff that we'd recorded together so I'd never learned the back catalogue, even though the crowd often shouted for the early work.

This meant I had to learn a few songs on the spot. I'd be in the dressing room with either Steve or Craig going; right, it goes like this. And then I'd just get on stage and play it. I felt uncomfortable doing them unrehearsed. I was aware that some Fall stalwarts mostly preferred the pre-Brix material and I didn't know if I was doing them justice.

Back on the *Shift-Work* album we moved the recording to Sheffield, at FON studios, with a Rasta named Robert Gordon, who had a broad South Yorkshire accent, which reminded me of my family in Doncaster. Made me smile.

FON was a great studio, right in the heart of the vibrant city. We were put up in digs and went clubbing. I liked Sheffield. Good chippies. Good pubs. Mark loved it.

The first time we went there, we recorded 'So What About It?' which I had written most of the music for. It wasn't the first time I was credited on a Fall recording, Mark could be very generous when giving out songwriting credits, depending on if you were in his good books or not. However, 'So What About It?' was the first piece of music I'd written for the band that I was truly proud of. I had written the main bass line on an old Yamaha SY55, which Mark had given me the money to buy. I came up with the drum beat and then added in keyboards. I don't play much guitar, so that's how I write songs. Craig added his distinctive guitar.

Several months later, as I was watching a sports show on ITV, one Saturday morning, I heard the remix of 'So What About It?' that Robert Gordon had done, whilst they were showing some football footage. I was over the moon with the way it sounded and wanted to write more. Mark himself encouraged us to write music. It was his preference, actually, for everyone to bring at least one tune, to get us all involved.

I'd pass my tapes to Mark and if he thought it was shit, he just wouldn't say anything. But if he thought it was good, he'd make a point of working on it.

'Where's that tape you did Simon? I've got some lyrics for it.'

Grant Showbiz was also brought in on the album and did the production on 'Edinburgh Man', this being one of Mark's favourite cities, even more so after his self-enforced exile there. I did like the song because I felt he actually put some feeling into it, whereas on most tracks he didn't seem to bother.

The cable channel MTV also seemed to like it. MTV was the biggest music thing around in 1991. The Sunday night indie show, *120 Minutes*, started using the track 'Edinburgh Man' during the show. It was an example of the band's more accessible sound, which would surface from time to time.

Every time we checked into a hotel and put MTV on in Europe in those days, it seemed the Roses were on.

That was Mark's new one for me, now The Smiths weren't around, if he wanted to have a go at me, and felt I was too comfortable or whatever.

'You're not in The Stone Roses, Simon. You're in The Fall.'

It did piss me off a bit.

Steve, Craig, and I, began spending more and more time at Dave's home studio in Stockport, getting to grips with the new writing method, on a PC. If we had a couple of weeks off, we'd go round. Dave became an honorary member of the engine room and a good friend. We had some great times there. I think we'd all say that. Dave was really positive, good for the vibes, and energised us. I loved working on tracks before we actually went into the studio instead of just bashing it out on the day.

Craig, however, insisted that we also still record the 'organic way' - as a live band. I think some of the stuff we did at Dave's - 'Free Range' for example - was better when we'd demo'd it than at the final output. Still, at least we knew the songs beforehand. We got through a lot of tracks and I think it was a more productive way to work. Previous writing sessions were on tourbuses, hotel rooms, soundchecks, and pubs - impromptu.

Although Dave's sunny disposition could piss Mark off, he generally took to him as well. He was the obvious choice for the new keyboard player and it wouldn't be long before Mark asked him to join the band full-time, a move we completely endorsed.

18

Levenshulme Man

At the start of 1991, the rent at India House had almost doubled to £90 a week.

The fire alarms were deliberately being activated, at least a couple of times a week, usually in the middle of the night, when Mandy and I were fast asleep. It really started to get on my nerves after a while and because there were no cameras in the building, the culprit(s) kept on getting away with it.

It was becoming party central. More and more strangers visited the building, after all the nightclubs had shut, making a racket, being sick on the stairs and generally misbehaving.

One evening, I went down in the lift to the car park and found two men having sex, just outside the lift doors, in a little alcove. I felt shocked and wished I had a bucket of water to throw on them, as you would with a pair of dogs. I just carried on walking past them towards my car without saying a word.

In January 1991, the Haçienda closed its doors to clubbers for the first time after its licence was revoked, following months of escalating gang violence over the huge sums of money being made in the Ecstasy and cocaine trade.

Just before the closure, Mark and I had been there for a night out and as we tried to leave the building we noticed all the doormen were in a huddle discussing something with very concerned faces. The shutters were down, so I said to one of them, who I vaguely knew, that we wanted to leave. He turned to us with a terrified expression and said, 'No I can't let you out, it's too dangerous, there's a guy out there with a gun. You'll have to wait until the police arrive.'

You could tell it was a serious situation, because we had to stand there for about twenty minutes, until the coast was clear. The revellers carried on oblivious, dancing to Nomad's 'I Wanna Give You Devotion' and other dance floor classics, while we waited, and waited. Finally, we were let out and there were police everywhere, a chopper overhead.

For all these reasons, I'd had enough of city centre living. Madchester was over. Gunchester was taking over. I started looking for a small house to buy.

As I was trying to move out of Manchester, Mark was back and looking to base the band in town.

Before *Shift-Work*'s release in April, Mark decided to move the Cog Sinister office from his back room in Sedgley Park, to a suite of offices in central Manchester, at 23 New Mount Street, just to the north of the city centre. He rented another room there to store the band's equipment, including my new red Pearl drum kit and custom-made flight cases, now there was extra money sloshing about.

There was a Victorian pub with a beautiful sloping black and white tiled floor called The Marble Arch, about a hundred yards from the building, which was often used by Mark for business meetings.

The office and vicinity then became the central meeting point for the band.

We went to an impromptu Christmas party in the lobby one year, put together by the receptionists. Mince pies, cheap plonk, crackers, etc. Mark even got up and did a bit of karaoke, which surprised me. He must have been enjoying himself! I can't remember what he sang, though.

We used to have to go into the office and do stints manning the phone until Mark's mate John 'The Postman' got the gig full-time. When I did go in, the phone never rang so I used to bring a pillow and have a kip.

Mark seemed chuffed having the office, like a proper boss, rather than running the show from his dining room table.

He sent us for medicals and set up a pension for us all, so everyone would all be able to retire at the age of 50, if we kept up the payments. It sounded great and I admired Mark's concern for us, but after paying in for about five years, I couldn't afford it any more and stopped the contributions.

We rehearsed downstairs in Gilly's Rehearsal room. It was convenient, but it was the most uncomfortable rehearsal room I'd ever been in - with no natural light, in the bowels of the building. Loads of padding on the walls to soundproof it. Claustrophobic and baking hot. I suppose it was apt we were rehearsing in a padded cell.

Just up the corridor from us was Inspiral Carpets' office - another of the so-called leading lights of the Madchester scene that had passed its peak by now. Noel Gallagher was their roadie at the time, only a couple of years before he teamed up with his brother and conquered the world with Oasis. He was often hanging about the reception area where his then girlfriend worked behind the desk. He always took the time to say hello whenever I had to go into The Fall's office. In the same building were the offices of music promoters SJM, whose accountant, Karen, I had known from my drinking days back at The Vine in Sale. She had a younger sister, Sue, who I would later marry.

By the time we kicked off the European tour at Hamburg's The Docks, in mid-May, the sound was no longer being looked after by Ed and Di. Instead a rocker from Nottingham called Graham Lees had taken over; Mark used to wind him up about being part of a new breed of 'sensitive man'. Designer glasses, ponytail, mollycoddling their kids - Mark was not impressed. He was old school.

'Worst thing that can happen to a bloke is to have kids,' he said.

An old friend of Mark's from Prestwich, commonly known as 'JR', who had been checking up on Mark since his split with Brix, started to travel with us over the next couple of years. He sold Fall T-shirts at the back of all the venues we played. JR was another fun person who loved life and people. He had the gift of the gab, bit like a market stall owner, to get all the punters buying the gear. He was really funny JR, and Mark would feel more comfortable on tour, if he was around to have a drink and generally look after him, as Mark invariably got into scrapes, upsetting people. I remember a couple of times abroad we went to restaurants and JR marched straight into the kitchens. He started checking out the ovens, seeing how clean the place was, looking in the fridges, seeing how fresh the food was, and asking what they had on that evening.

'What's in 'ere mate?'

Mike 'The Haircut', also from Prestwich and an ex-hairdressing colleague of Weeds singer Andrew Berry, also came along for the ride for the next couple of years. It seems a bit odd now. For a band as studiously unfashionable as The Fall, it was strange that this was the second time we took a hairdresser on tour with us. But they were just Mark's mates really - for a while we were accompanied on UK tours by Charlie, a Cambridge University professor.

As Phonogram were subsidising the touring at this point, they also provided us with our own catering, travelling on another tourbus with our crew. Mark didn't like to be too familiar with the catering staff and would eat separately in his dressing room, while the rest of us ate together. Some of the caterers, he held in utter disdain, often taking the piss out of them when they weren't around. He couldn't believe that most of them were on more money than us and that some of them were as drug addled as the roadies (and the band). Plus, I think he thought it was all too cushy. If there'd been an option to take the money spent on the caterers, he'd have chosen that.

We started the usual trawl of German cities, where I sprained my hi-hat ankle playing football in the grounds of the magnificent Le Park hotel just outside Bremen. I just had to grimace and get on with it.

The following day on the trip to Rotterdam, Mark told us he had seen blood streaming down the wall of his hotel room, during another restless night's sleep. We were quite used to comments like this by now, especially when abroad, when we couldn't score speed as easily.

We did used to get deliveries of speed from Jan and Lydia, two ardent Dutch fans, who would also come to shows in Germany. When Mark couldn't get speed, he would go to the nearest chemist and buy packs and packs of Sudafed tablets and have a drink, which meant things could easily go tits up, very quickly.

In June, I bought my first house in Levenshulme. It was a bit further south-east of the International 2 club in Longsight, which had also seen a lot of gun violence in the previous year or so. The house was a two-up two-down end terrace on Audley Road that was within our budget.

Mandy had recently started working as a credit controller, just near to United's ground at Old Trafford and we thought it was a good idea to get on the property ladder, while we could.

Mark had a look round and wandered through the back to the small courtyard and ginnel.

'It looks just like *Coronation Street*,' he laughed.

I could tell it got his seal of approval. Living with 'real folk' and all that.

'Don't tell anyone you're in a band,' he counselled. 'You'll get your house robbed.'

It was great for a while, until we had some new neighbours the following year who played Shamen's 'Ebeneezer Goode' all day long at high volume. But I did enjoy living there all the same, and my mum, who later that summer would be admitted to St Ann's Hospice in Cheadle, as her illness got worse, seemed pleased that I appeared to be settling down with someone, in my own home at last.

I began to keep my ear to the ground for new opportunities.

During a break from The Fall, I went into Drone Studios in Chorlton to record a couple of tracks with a Salford girl called Eilidh Bradley, who I had met a few years earlier.

She had assembled a backing band at short notice for the project that was to include my mates, Andy Rourke, Primal Scream keyboard player, Martin Duffy, and Chris 'Geordie' Bridgett from Dubsex on guitar. The studio, in the basement of a large semi-detached property, was owned by a guy called Paul who liked a drink. Andy had been in there before, with the Smiths, recording 'The Boy With The Thorn in His Side'.

One of the tracks I recorded there with Eilidh and the band, 'I Need', was very commercial and a big departure from what I was used to doing in the day job. Eilidh had a folky but powerful voice, somewhere between Alanis Morissette and Florence Welch. It was a massive breath of fresh air for me, but for whatever reason, the project failed to progress further, probably because we were all so busy back then. It's just one of those things.

In early August, The Fall was asked to step in at the last moment for The Soup Dragons and The Beautiful South, who had both pulled out of the 'Cities in the Park' festival weekend at Heaton Park in Prestwich. The gig was put on in honour of Factory Records producer Martin Hannett, who had died in April. Though I never worked with him, I knew loads of people who had and most of them thought very highly of him indeed. I did meet him, however, only a couple of months before his death, in a pub near Cheadle, when I went with Eilidh Bradley to see if he would work on some of the tracks she was writing at the time. He was drunk, and was massively obese, and it was obvious that he wasn't interested in Eilidh's project, no matter how many times she fluttered her eyelashes at him.

The Fall played on the Saturday along with the Buzzcocks, whose drummer John Maher had been replaced by Mike Joyce, for the time being. The Sunday line-up was much better, made up with Factory artists, such as A Certain Ratio and Durutti Column.

Also on the bill was Johnny Marr and Bernard Sumner's new project, Electronic, which I thought was even more exciting than New Order. Later in the year, Johnny invited me down to play a session while they recorded their new album. I think he wanted to cheer me up because he knew about my mum. He also wanted me to drive him down to London in his new SL Mercedes as he wasn't keen on driving on the motorway. He'd had a bad accident in '86 in another powerful car. Johnny told me to pick a studio of my choice in London and stay with them for the weekend. I appreciated the gesture and said let's go to Olympic, where the Stones had done a lot of their work. I didn't stay the whole weekend though, and my work never ended up on the record. I was still smoking quite a bit of heroin at this point and started to feel shit when the session started. I was also paranoid about Mark finding out that I was moonlighting, so I made my excuses after one night and got the train home. Another wasted opportunity.

Highlight of the Cities in the Park weekend though, was the headline spot from the Happy Mondays, who were at the peak of their powers following the previous year's release, *Pills, Thrills and Bellyaches*. During their set a police helicopter hovered menacingly above them and the large crowd for what seemed like ages, filming the crowd, looking for trouble.

The rest of the year, there were only a couple of gigs, and so Steve, Craig, and I spent a lot of 1991 round at Dave Bush's house, writing music for *Code: Selfish*.

Code: Selfish was partly recorded in Ca Va studio in Kelvingrove, up in Glasgow, where the likes of Deacon Blue had recorded, with Simon Rogers producing. It was in an old church with a balcony around it, and still had a pulpit, mahogany panelling, and crimson velvet cushioning. It had a big live room, and great acoustics, comparable to Abbey Road. The programming skills that Dave had been learning since joining the band had started to shape The Fall's sound in a big way. Tracks like 'The Birmingham School of Business School' and 'So Called Dangerous', amongst others, were written as a result of the afternoons spent at Dave's.

Craig preferred the organic method as a live band. So we did still employ that approach on anything he wrote. Songs like 'Gentleman's Agreement', about the band members' unwritten rule, which stated that if one room-mate got lucky on tour, the other party had to sleep elsewhere; i.e. on the floor in someone else's room.

What gentlemen we were.

19

Selfish

During September, I went at every opportunity to visit my mum at the hospice in Cheadle which upset me a lot as it now seemed there was little hope left. She was being given huge doses of morphine to ease the pain but my dad felt that it wasn't right, the amount she was being administered. Jane was there every day and it seemed so sad that our family had become so close again in these circumstances.

Mum passed away at the beginning of October.

Dad was, naturally, deeply upset and complained bitterly that mum had been basically killed off with all of the drugs they were giving her.

I was devastated obviously, but felt it had been inevitable for some time and in a way there was an element of relief. She had suffered for a while and hadn't been the vibrant Pat that everyone knew and loved for a couple of years.

I didn't have much time to mourn.

Two days later The Fall had a couple of European gigs, including another visit to Athens.

At the soundcheck, I was more reserved than usual and must have looked upset – for which I don't apologise. Mark started shouting at me whilst I sat at my kit.

'Just cheer up you miserable bastard,' he said. 'Everyone dies. Get over it.'

To emphasise his point, he pushed over a cymbal stand and attached cymbal, which crashed down on top of me, as I sat there astonished.

And then I was in motion.

I flew into a rage, possessed, adrenaline coursing. I hurdled the drum kit and weighed angrily into Mark with a flurry of haymakers to his head.

Mark didn't fight back, but I couldn't stop. I didn't care about any consequences.

Steve jumped in and eventually pulled me off Mark in the middle of the stage as all the crew looked on gobsmacked.

'That's a sacking offence, isn't it Steve?' was all the startled Mark said as he staggered off in a daze with a bloody lip.

'You started it Mark,' Steve responded tersely.

Mark's dad had died about a year before so I don't know if he felt he had kept his grief away from the band and I should have kept more of a stiff upper lip, but whatever it was, I wasn't having it.

We did the gig and the next day I flew home in time for Mum's funeral at Dunham Massey crematorium near Altrincham, just along from the village hall where I had played with The Patrol all those years before.

Mark never apologised but things seemed to come back to an even keel before long.

Code: Selfish was released in January 1992. It was more forceful sounding than *Shift-Work* with tracks like 'Return' and 'Everything Hurtz', but it was the addition of Dave Bush that really shaped this record which scraped into the official Top 20 album releases in March 1992, if only for a week or so. Craig Leon and Cassell Webb were still around on production duties, which spoke volumes for Mark's opinion of them.

That same month, 'Free Range' became the first of my two tunes to enter the Top 40 - just - it was number 40. It is, so I'm led to believe, the only non-cover The Fall has had in the Top 40.

Trevor Long, from Halesowen, originally brought in by John Lennard as the latest in a long line of tour managers, was now full-time manager. He is the inspiration for the track 'The Birmingham School of Business School'. It wasn't long before Trevor, who I thought was a decent tour manager at the time, bought himself a new Audi to shuttle up and down the motorways between Manchester, Birmingham, and the Phonogram office in London.

Mark used to joke he looked like the former German Ministry of the Interior, with his little wire-rimmed glasses and beady eyes.

'Stand by your beds, here's Himmler.'

During the rehearsals for the tour while we were still in Manchester, I received a phone call from Sale Police station, informing me that my dad had been in a car crash and was now in Wythenshawe Hospital, where my mum had worked nights for all those years.

Dad had been on the way to his dentist (he hated going to the dentist) in Sale where he now lived and had suffered a stroke outside the surgery whilst at the wheel of his car. Jane and I rushed over to Wythenshawe to see him as soon as we could but I don't think he even knew we were there.

He had been travelling at low speed, fortunately, and though the doctors said it was only a minor stroke, they kept him in hospital for a few weeks. But he was never the same again and had to retire from his practice soon afterwards.

In March it was to be business as usual with another UK tour starting.

At a student ball at Queen Margaret's Union, Glasgow, Mark got a kicking.

When we arrived late at the gig, Buster Bloodvessel's band, our support act for the night, were waiting impatiently for us to finish our soundcheck as Mark had turned up half an hour late.

Buster's guitarist (or sax player depending who you ask), a giant black guy, had waited long enough and started plonking his equipment on the front of the stage as Mark was testing out his new wireless Shure radio mic.

'Get that fucking equipment off my stage,' Mark barked.

As Mark finally left the stage, before I had even realised what was happening, Buster's man had smacked Mark in the mouth, which began pouring with blood.

Mark curled up in the foetal position as the guy kept kicking him.

'You soft cunt!' Mark shouted.

The police were called as the scene degenerated, a knife was pulled and Buster's band were escorted off the premises and barred from playing the gig, with the guitarist accusing Mark of racism.

'Five hundred years we've been fighting against people like you.'

I don't think it was a racist issue, but we didn't bother running through any more songs after that and this wasn't the last time Mark was attacked after one of his ill-conceived outbursts.

Business as usual …

The next morning, I bumped into Robbie Coltrane, in the lift of the hotel in Glasgow, reeking of BO and cheap aftershave. Unsmiling, dressed all in black, huge, like a grizzly bear on his way to his black vintage Citroën. I told him I was a fan and had watched his interview with Jonathan Ross on television the night before. All he said was, 'Ooch, Jonathan Ross, he couldn't even run a sweetie shop.' He ambled out, poker-faced. I had a chuckle.

I enjoyed that aspect of life in the band. You'd never know who you'd run into.

Supporting The Fall at the City Hall in Glasgow that night were, an unsigned, Suede, who seemed scared to death of bumping into Mark backstage in case he had a go at them.

Backstage at Glastonbury Festival, the blonde, moustachioed JR spotted the late Lou Reed. JR was a big fan and interrupted him, wanting an autograph, as he talked to someone outside our dressing room.

'God dammit, can't you see I'm talking here?' Lou snapped.

JR laughed it off. He thought it was great Lou had just been rude to him. Couldn't wait to tell everyone.

At the Boddington's beer festival I ran into American comedian Bill Hicks, whose scathing social satire I found hilarious. I didn't chat to him much - he was keen to get to London and was just asking me how long it would take.

He passed away with cancer a couple of years later, sadly, but I was glad I got the opportunity to meet the comedy icon.

In Cologne, in June, Mark and I had another altercation.

Hanging about, waiting to do a soundcheck, I was chatting to a girl who'd just arrived to attend the cloakroom and Mark started going on at me to leave her alone. I was just making polite conversation so I told him to shut the fuck up. As I made my way across the lobby he threw a bottle of beer at me, which glanced off the back of my head. The red mist came down again - I ended up giving him a couple of slaps and he backed off.

Nobody made a move to stop me. The feeling was probably that it was warranted.

It was, again, quickly forgotten.

In hindsight, Mark's disdain for people was becoming worse. He drank more and charmed less.

Toward the end of the year, I received a letter from Mike Joyce's solicitor regarding a dispute over pay and royalties that Mike had brought against The Smiths. The letter asked about any financial arrangement that I'd had with the band. I spoke to the solicitor and told him there wasn't any arrangement. He then asked whether there were any plans to get rid of Mike in 1983, when I'd been rehearsing in the same space above Crazy Face jeans. That wasn't the case - I was just rehearsing there for the Terry Hall gig because I got the room free - I told him so and cut the call short.

Andy had wanted me in at one point, and I wouldn't have minded being in the band but it was never realistic - they already had a drummer. But that was after all that business above Crazy Face. Anyway, I didn't want to get involved. I was Johnny's mate as well.

Mike Joyce, though, kept fighting, went to court and would get a huge payout, years later, after a High Court settlement in which the judge had been particularly scathing about Morrissey. Considering Morrissey's lengthy retort in his book, this must have really rankled with him.

I did wonder what I'd have done had I had been in Mike's shoes, and, honestly, I don't think I would have fought as tenaciously as he did. Fair play to him though, I think he deserved the money.

Andy, sadly, didn't get his dues, in my opinion. He settled out of court, years earlier, for a fraction of what Mike won. He bought a new build house on an estate in Burnage and settled some debts. I'm biased, but I think he's one of the finest bass players around and I don't think people give him enough credit for his work in The Smiths.

Meanwhile. Back in The Fall. We were recording tracks in Rochdale again when Mark told us all that Phonogram wanted to hear the band's latest demos before they would pay for the recording of the next album. Mark was outraged at this suggestion and refused point blank to comply.

Phonogram, in response, terminated our contract.

20

What Goes Around, Comes Around

Out of the blue, Mark told us that he was going to bring back Karl Burns, who would be playing a second drum kit, for the *The Infotainment Scan* tour.

I didn't like the sound of this at all.

I didn't say anything, but I wasn't happy about it. I didn't have to say anything, it was clear. Karl is a great rock drummer, but we had moved on to a different sound since Dave Bush had joined the ranks. It transpired that Karl was dating Mark's youngest sister, Caroline, now he was back on the scene in Prestwich. Steve and Craig seemed delighted that Karl had been invited back into the fold, but tried not to show it for my sake.

With the situation as it was, I went to meet Karl, on my own, at a pub in Levenshulme, to discuss who was going to play what, and when, on the upcoming tour. I liked Karl a lot. He had a reputation for being wild, which he generally lived up to, but he was a big softie at heart.

Having said that, I had to prevent him from stabbing Andy Rourke years earlier, after he had seen his girlfriend, Carrie Lawson, through a gap in the curtains at his gran's flat in Prestwich, kissing Andy. Karl ended up grabbing a kitchen knife and chased Andy round and round my Datsun Laurel, like a bleeding cartoon, threatening to kill him. Andy couldn't stop laughing (nervously). I intervened because this nonsense probably would have carried on all night, so when I had a chance, I gripped him by the arms.

'Leave it out Karl!'

Though he looked like an outlaw, in his studded leather jacket, biker boots and leather kecks, I knew he'd never use the knife and I just had to stop the Keystone Cops farce.

After experimenting with the two drum kits set-up for a handful of gigs, it was agreed he would play percussion, instead, using an Octopad, timbale, and cowbells, acquired from Suite 16. On stage, two drum kits could add more power, but if it wasn't spot on, all the drums would be overlapping - flamming, as it's called - and it would sound shit. It is very difficult for two people to drive the band without being telepathic. We weren't, and I wanted to drive. Happily, the percussion set-up worked really well in rehearsals and in the shows. Anyway, if a two drum kit set-up is so good, how come all bands don't use it?

We nicknamed Karl, 'Mongo', after the dim-witted enforcer in *Blazing Saddles*. He was a good impressionist. He'd stand at the front of the bus as we boarded, directing us like a stereotypical sergeant major in the British army - a bit like the Windsor Davies character in *It Ain't Half Hot Mum*.

'H'officer's mess, to the *re-yaar*, sar!' he would shout, standing to attention and saluting me and Mark, the grammar school lads. Steve was a sergeant but wasn't allowed in the officer's mess in Karl's long running gag.

Mark quickly tired of Karl's daft antics but it lightened the mood.

I always thought he had a future in radio voiceovers, after hearing him do that voice, as well as the sad and abused character of Mongo himself.

If Mark had a go at Karl he'd sometimes just sort of slouch and go, dead miserably, 'Mongo no *haapppeey*…'

Other times, of course, it could just kick off.

Karl had been earning a crust as a motorcycle courier in the years since his absence from the band, a period he liked to call 'the desert years'. He seemed to spend all his wages on running his Moto Guzzi bike (which he nicknamed Gustav) and bags of speed and draw, which suited me fine as he would sell me chunks of Afghani Black, which was dynamite back then. He also took over as Mark's whipping boy, succeeding Dave, who had borne the brunt of Mark's verbal abuse, for the last year or so.

Trevor Long continued to manage the band at this point and found us the first of three new tour managers, who he thought might put up with Mark's temperament. A number of managers just walked away rather than take stick off Mark. They weren't being paid enough.

So, with Mongo in tow, we set off on tour, which was a lot more fun with the returning percussionist.

Mark asked me to fly over to New York with him for a week, at the start of July, to keep him company, and assist him with some interviews.

I did a couple of interviews myself, though it was mostly Mark. Mark took the piss out of me because in one interview I'd said how shocked I was to see the increased number of homeless people on the streets since I'd first visited.

'Like you give a shit!' he spluttered.

He had a point. I *was* concerned. But I wasn't doing anything about it.

We were promoting the album's release over there, as well as the accompanying tour in August, and fielded telephone interviews from all over the country from the boardroom of Atlantic Records, located high inside Rockefeller Plaza in the heart of Manhattan.

I always enjoyed Mark's interviews. He is an independent thinker, generally has a really sharp eye and I felt he captured the zeitgeist better in his interviews than in his lyrics. It helped that I could hear what he was saying as opposed to the records. I did wonder if the Americans could tell what he was going on about though.

As I was already going to be in the States, Mandy and I decided to get married in Las Vegas at the end of the week's trip. Mark kindly arranged with Matador Records to pick up the tab for Mandy's flights to New York.

I thought the time was right to settle down and perhaps start a family, as my mum would have wanted. I should have known better really. Mandy and I had been an item for six years by now, and this, surely, was tempting fate.

Mark flew home after the week of interviews which had been good fun on the whole, and I stayed an extra night on my own at the Gramercy Park Hotel on Lexington Avenue to wait for Mandy, arriving the following morning. I got locked in a park opposite the hotel - the Gramercy gave out keys for it. I tailgated someone in and then couldn't get out. I stood there for twenty minutes shouting through the tall wrought iron fence at nonplussed New Yorkers for assistance.

'Excuse me mate ... Mate? How do I get out of here?'

'Same way you got in,' a guy shot back, and just walked off.

When someone finally came into the park, I spirited out and went to a bar around the corner, alone, for my last night of 'freedom' with a wrap of coke that I had bought from someone at Matador. I remember chatting to a Scouse girl in the bar and then starting to drink vodka and oranges. I don't remember much after that and woke up with scratches and cuts all over my body. I can't explain it - I just need to be careful when I drink.

My fiancé arrived and we made our way to JFK and boarded the flight to San Francisco with me feeling like death warmed up. There had recently been an earthquake in San Francisco and we had to drive around a collapsed overhead section of a freeway. I thought about those kids in Japan. We checked into a nice little hotel on Powell Street right in the middle of town and went out clubbing at the I-Beam.

We got up early and went out sightseeing on, essentially, the same trip as the first time I'd been to San Francisco: Fisherman's Wharf, Alcatraz, the Golden Gate Bridge. The usual tourist traps. We went to see American band Jellyfish after I'd bumped into the lead singer walking around the Tenderloin district. After Mandy had gone to sleep, I went back to the Tenderloin to see what was going on, flitting about. I erm … I scored some crack. Don't know what I was thinking really, I was supposed to be getting married, settling down.

The following morning we hired a car and set off across the bay to the outskirts of Oakland, where New Order were performing at a huge open air bowl that night. We hadn't realised they were playing so we went looking for Eddie and Di, who were doing the sound, to sort out a spot on the guest list. The show was a belter and Mandy and I partied with the band and crew until midnight as we had an early start in the morning. It just so happened that in the motel room next to ours, there were a couple of lads I recognised from recent Fall shows in Europe, so I stayed up partying with them whilst Mandy slept.

After a quick dip in the swimming pool in the morning we finally started our journey through the desert to tie the knot in Las Vegas, arriving at dusk, the neon city coming to life as the mountains behind went from orange to purple to black, as the sun finally set. We checked into the Flamingo Hilton for a couple of nights and went down to the casino to place $50 worth of chips on 38 black on the roulette wheel for Johnny Marr. We lost that for him in a matter of seconds.

Having crossed ocean and desert, we nearly missed the wedding. We booked a limousine to take us first to the town hall to buy a wedding licence then on to the 'Little White Chapel' for the ceremony. However, there was a bit of confusion with all the entrances around the huge hotel and we couldn't find the driver at the allotted pick-up time as we walked round searching for him. When we eventually found him he was in a foul mood as he was now behind schedule. He sped towards the town hall at a ridiculous speed nearly crashing the white stretch Cadillac as we were tossed around in the back. The guy who married us had a big quiff and snakeskin cowboy boots and looked genuinely upset that Mandy and I were giggling all through the short ceremony, which was indeed as tacky as hell. Cheesy piped organ music in the background. It just seemed ridiculous. We went back to the Hilton for our first night together as a married couple.

We honeymooned in southern California in a beautiful place called Laguna Beach for three nights. We walked along the Pacific shore, or gazed out from our hotel balcony as the beautiful people lapped up the surf and the rays, while on MTV Radiohead's 'Creep' was constantly being aired. We spent our final night at a motel directly beneath the airport flight path, which I had read about, and couldn't resist.

In early August, we held a wedding reception at Old Trafford Cricket Club for family and friends.

Not long after, whilst I was away touring, Mandy started an affair with the brother of Phil Powell. I thought there was something wrong when I went to visit Phil. I remember he looked a bit shifty. When I asked him what was the matter, he just said 'oh, my head's in bits'. I happened across a rail ticket to Swansea in one of Mandy's coats. It wasn't somewhere Mandy had been before, and I knew Phil's brother was staying in a halfway house there, after being released from prison. So it clicked then why Phil had been so uptight and I confronted Mandy about it. She came clean straight away and though I wasn't happy, considering my track record, I couldn't be self-righteous about it.

What goes around comes around.

By November, she'd moved out.

Meanwhile, *The Infotainment Scan* tour was going as well as any tour we'd done.

Steve, Craig, and I, were invited over to Matador's offices, just off Broadway, one morning, to say hello to Gerard, the label's boss and to pick up some freebies. The boxes of CDs were kept in a locked room along the corridor from a neighbouring methadone clinic.

I say the tour was going well ...Karl was sacked again at the hotel in Detroit, after arguing with Mark about wages that he was owed. Unlike the rest of the band, who had their salaries paid by direct debit or cheque, Karl didn't even have a bank account. It was a shame because the dynamics would change straight away and we wouldn't sound as good on stage without his blistering percussion either.

After an overnight drive on the Karl-less bus we arrived in Cincinnati where ticket sales for our show had been very poor indeed. So poor in fact, that Mark told us we could have as many guests as we liked for the show at Bogart's. The club was in a small town in the suburbs of the city, where piped music could be heard emanating from tiny speakers, clamped to the lamp posts of the tree lined streets.

I went off trying to hand out tickets like a charity mugger. The only person who showed any interest was a willowy blonde called Allison who came shouting over that she was already coming to the gig.

Backstage in Chicago, a tall, long-haired, bearded geezer, about thirty years old, fangs, multiple face piercings, wearing a long black leather coat with a tail sticking out of the back, like a pantomime horse, walked in. He was followed by half a dozen young girls, similarly attired, who for all intents and purposes, looked like they were his followers in some sort of gothic cult. I did shake the big guy's hand as he told me how much he enjoyed the gig, but it was Dave Bush who really got chatting to him. He was engrossed in a conversation with the group for a good half an hour, whilst the rest of us packed up the bus with equipment, food, booze, and ice for the overnight drive to Madison.

On the way there, Dave told us that the 'cult leader' was a massive fan and had given him four medallions fashioned out of what looked like lead with a pentangle engraved on one side and some strange hieroglyphics on the other. A hole had been drilled into each one so it could be worn on a chain - something I wouldn't be doing with mine any time soon. Like most objects that I picked up on tour, such as hotel room keys and sewing kits, I just threw mine into the bottom of my suitcase underneath the bus. Craig quickly lost his medallion, but Dave kept his on the table at the front of the bus. Mark, who hadn't been travelling with us all the time, spotted it on the West Coast a few days later and told him to get rid of it straight away. Mark was visibly shaken when he saw the medallion as he claimed he knew a thing or two about the occult and he had a bad feeling about the gifts and the bloke who had gifted them to us. It was something he'd claim from time to time about having a bit of psychic power. There were times when I believed him.

When we had finished the gig at the Roxy on Sunset Strip in Los Angeles, everyone sat on the bus, waiting for the equipment to be stowed underneath before the long drive east to Dallas. Kurt Cobain and his wife Courtney Love were standing at the open front door and asked the driver if they could come on board to meet Mark and the band. We had played the same bill as Nirvana at Reading in 1991. I don't know if something had happened then - but when they asked Steve, the driver, or whoever, if they could come aboard, Mark's response was, 'No they fucking can't, don't let them on whatever you do', which was about standard. Dave Bush said they did manage to get on, though, in the end, although I had pottered off into the back lounge and missed the chance to meet them. It was around the height of the grunge phenomenon and Nirvana, the leading light of the scene, was probably the biggest band in the world.

Years later, Brix and Marcia told me that Nirvana had actually played support to The Fall on an early Sub Pop tour in the late eighties in Germany. I don't remember a thing about it, which tells you something of my sobriety at the time. They didn't have a pot to piss in and the girls said they took pity on them, giving them butties and booze off the rider because they looked so skinny and starving.

Then the next day we were told that The Fall had been offered a couple of support slots on Nirvana's European tour the following year, which Mark seemed to be really chuffed about. I was a bit surprised because I didn't think Mark would have wanted to be associated with the grunge scene, but he seemed genuinely excited about the prospect. It was, however, not to be. Kurt took an overdose of the sedative Rohypnol whilst he was in Rome before the dates we were due to play and then went into rehab back home in America. Not long after came his sad and well-documented suicide.

Having had a bit of experience with heroin, I could see how, with plenty of money and other users enabling the habit, it could easily slip into a debilitating full-blown addiction. I couldn't say I was surprised when Kurt died, but it was obviously a waste of a great talent.

The show went on. We had two gigs lined up in Texas, first in Dallas, then Austin. The day before the Dallas concert we were in town with nothing to do, so I went to stand on the grassy knoll near the book depositary, where Lee Harvey Oswald was said to have taken the fatal shots that killed President Kennedy. I had watched the infamous amateur cine film footage dozens of times before on television and it was quite a surreal moment for me - I was finally at the scene of the assassination that had occurred in the year of my birth, 1963. It looked exactly the same as it had done in the clips from thirty years earlier, as if nobody had the heart to change it.

At breakfast in the hotel restaurant in Austin I tried eating grits, but wasn't impressed at all.

On the reclaimed swampland of Washington DC, dozens of rats were running about in the back alley behind the 9:30 club, while the local crew shot at them with an air rifle.

In Atlanta, we couldn't get enough rooms and Dave had to sleep on a cot in a room with me, Steve, and Craig, because there was a big rap convention in town. This was in the middle of the golden age of rap. I was a big fan. EPMD, De La Soul, Wu-Tang Clan, Snoop Dogg, were all on the scene, before it all went a bit murderous a few years later. We stuck out like sore thumbs, though. We got in a lift with Professor Griff and the S1W from Public Enemy. He looked sneeringly at Dave with his nose piercing.

'You some kind of faggot?'

It all went a bit quiet. I didn't feel threatened - I was stoned, but it was surreal.

We covered a lot of miles on the tour and listened to a lot of music. I think, which may surprise fans and observers of the band, that the most played CD on the tour was En Vogue's *Funky Divas* LP. Well, at least when Mark wasn't on board.

When we arrived at the check-in desk at JFK airport for the flight home, we were all gobsmacked but happy to see Karl Burns stood there at the counter, smiling his head off. We hadn't seen or heard of him since his sacking in Detroit three weeks earlier and wondered what he had been doing since. There he was, wearing the same clothes, no baggage, just his passport and a grin. It turned out that he had been shacked up with a girl he had met the first couple of days into the tour as he couldn't change his return airline ticket, or didn't know how to. My thoughts were, 'Good on you, Karl.'

Following a week's rest back at home we set off for Europe again. After the first night's gig in Vienna, as I sat in the rear lounge of the bus outside our hotel waiting to go, I heard a huge commotion from the front. It was Mark spitting and screaming at Dave, who was trapped in his bunk bed half-asleep, before throwing a hot cup of tea over him as he cowered under his duvet. It transpired that Dave had kept hold of the pentangle medallion given to him back in Chicago, despite Mark urging us all to throw them away immediately because they would put a curse on the band. Dave had foolishly left his medallion in plain view on the table at the front of the bus and Mark had seen it as he boarded. He totally lost it.

1993 had been a productive year for The Fall, what with *The Infotainment Scan* entering the Top 10 in the album charts - the highest The Fall had achieved - and, give or take the odd sacking, successful tours of America and Europe.

The album, which was released in April 1993, was considered to be the most accessible Fall album to date and stands out as my favourite during my time in the band. Our cover of Sister Sledge's 'Lost In Music' sounded great. As I loved the original so much I always enjoyed performing the song live. 'A Past Gone Mad' was another favourite of mine, as was 'Paranoia Man in Cheap Shit Room'.

Once again, Dave Bush's pre-production at his house in Stockport, during those long winter afternoons, had paid off.

We had bounced back from Phonogram's early termination of our contract - in fact, they had to pay the band compensation, which helped fund the recording sessions for the *Infotainment Scan*. We were then signed by on/off manager John Lennard to his new record label, Permanent Records. He also secured us the deal in America with Matador Records, part of Atlantic Records, which led to the US tour.

It was another high point for me. There had been a few ups and downs in the band's popularity since I'd joined, back in 1986, and for the most part I'd had a brilliant time, touring a lot of countries that most people would never have the chance to visit, and playing some huge gigs like the Pyramid Stage at Glastonbury and Elland Road. And I had been paid to do it. You can't say fairer than that. Many drummers, who were much better players than me, would never get to experience what I had. I never took it for granted. Every time I got on a plane, I thought how lucky I was, and treated it as if it was my last. It could easily have been.

I had been a member of The Fall during the period that Mark liked to call 'The Glory Years', but while I thought we had turned a corner in 1993, after the dawn of 1994, things started to go downhill for the band. Gradually at first, then, in an accelerating downward spiral, very quickly indeed.

The Glory Years were over.

21

Revolt

Now Mandy and I had divorced, I rented the house in Levenshulme out to a young couple who would stay there for the next ten years. For a while, I stayed over at my dad's new house in Sale, where I could keep an eye on him. He had daily visits from an ex-patient of his called Pamela and also from Jane whenever I was away.

Even though the doctors at Wythenshawe Hospital had told my sister and me the stroke he had suffered was only a minor one, there was a noticeable difference in his memory, and it appeared to be getting worse by the month.

While previously we'd had a bit of a frosty relationship, Dad and I now became closer than ever. When I went to see him, he was always very pleased to see me. We'd go for lunches in country pubs. He was really missing mum, his lifelong companion - and she had done everything for him. He was adamant he wasn't going into a nursing home, though, but he enjoyed company, and I was happy to oblige.

In January, he decided that we both deserved a holiday and as the studio for the next Fall album hadn't been booked yet, and there were no upcoming tour commitments, I agreed. We booked seven nights in Tunisia, at a resort we had been to as a family, in the seventies, Sousse.

When we arrived it was raining and would do so every morning, all week. So we spent a lot of time in the bar, chatting or reading books and magazines. By now, he was finding walking anywhere difficult and would lose his breath very quickly.

In the evenings, he would have a big measure of Johnny Walker, after which we went down to the restaurant for dinner. We sat watching the cabaret and genuinely had a good time. It didn't feel forced; it felt like we were making up for lost time.

On returning to Manchester, I thought I had better ring Steve to see if the studio for the next record had been booked yet. I rang his home in Chorlton, where his wife Heather answered.

To my horror she told me he was already with the band at a studio near Wrexham called The Windings.

'Didn't you know?'

After writing down the address and phone number of the place, I got in my Golf GTI and roared off down the M56 in the direction of North Wales as fast as I could go. There was snow on the ground. Still, it didn't take me long to find the place: a rustic looking, residential set-up, at the end of a long single-track road, hidden in some woodland.

What was all this about? Had Mark started without me as punishment for going on holiday? Did he want me out?

As soon as I crunched to a halt on the gravel driveway outside, I heard someone playing drums, through a partly open set of French doors. I knew it was Karl straight away, as I recognised his style. I wasn't too surprised either, if I'm honest, as he had been in Mark's good books for a while and had been reinstated again after his sacking at the start of the previous year's American tour.

I was annoyed, not with Karl so much, but with Mark, as I had told him I was going away for a week and would have cancelled the holiday. Studio time had been loosely discussed but had not been booked. As I walked in through the French doors I saw Karl sat at my red Pearl drum kit. He immediately stood up and backed away from the kit after quickly putting down the drumsticks on the floor tom. He looked like a naughty child who had been caught with his hands in the biscuit tin, and mumbled some kind of apology. I was just glad I'd arrived in the nick of time, and before he had recorded the whole of the next album which was to be called *The Middle Class Revolt*.

It turned out that Karl had recorded just one song before my unannounced arrival at The Windings - the song 'Hey! Student', a reworking of a vintage Fall track, 'Hey! Fascist', that made number two in John Peel's Festive 50 that year. As it happened, I thought it was one of the better tracks on the album, but it felt like a step backwards, musically.

Maybe Mark had been listening to the criticism we had received from some fans that we had become too electronic. Tellingly, Dave and I didn't receive any credits on the album.

Middle Class Revolt, which wasn't released until May, only reached number 48 in the charts, for one week only. There were moments on a few of the tracks, but apart from 'City Dweller' and 'Behind the Counter' (which Karl played on), I thought the album was a botched job with three scrappy cover versions that nobody had ever heard of.

I particularly hated the title track 'Middle Class Revolt', a song that the band and I hadn't had the chance to learn properly.

'Just get on with it - *one-two-three-four*!' Mark demanded, before railing at the pretentious aspiration that seemed to be in the air.

In the meantime, Mark had appeared on *Top of the Pops* for the first time, guesting with our old office mates Inspiral Carpets.

Typical, I thought, we had this shit album and Mark was lending his hand to a more commercial sound for another band.

Mark had separated from his second wife Saffron by now and started bringing his new girlfriend, Lucy, along to gigs and recordings.

To me, it felt like he had no guiding hand.

That said, I wasn't socialising with him as much now, so didn't know exactly where his head was. I'd get a call now and then on tour when Mark had sent Saffron, or Lucy, or whoever home after another row.

He'd invite me over to his room for a line where he had the shower running for the dual purpose of foiling bugging devices and getting the creases out of his shirts hung over the bath.

The next tour didn't start until May, so I had a lot of free time on my hands.

When I wasn't round at my dad's keeping him company, watching war documentaries, I would call round to Johnny Marr's house, next to my old school, Altrincham Grammar, and just hang out, sometimes staying overnight in one of the guest bedrooms or sat in his basement studio, called 'Clear'. He was working on new stuff for Electronic so I'd listen and chat with his resident engineer Owen Morris.

One night Ian McCulloch from Echo and the Bunnymen came round and introduced himself to me with the air of a man talking to a lackey, 'Can yer gerrus some coke or wha'?'

Charm? Offensive? I ignored him and went home.

In the spring, I got a call off John Squire, inviting me down to Rockfield Studios in Monmouthshire for a couple of days, where The Stone Roses, now on Geffen Records, were recording their second album, *The Second Coming*. They had been bogged down in legal wranglings, trying to extract themselves from their first contract, but were now free to record.

I was telling John I was thinking of going over to America to see Allison from Cincinnati, who had invited me to the Kentucky Derby, but was skint. He offered to lend me some money for flights, but as we carried on chatting, he mentioned that he was in touch with Sue Williams, who I had seen briefly, years earlier. Sue, and John's partner at the time, Helen, had recently set up a business called Funni, designing and selling trendy kids clothing, with John as a backer. He offered to reunite me with Sue, so instead of borrowing money off him, I asked for Sue's number.

I drove down to Rockfield for the weekend, where the Roses had been camped for at least a couple of years. Mainly what appeared to be happening while I was there was nothing.

Ian wasn't feeling too well, so spent most of the time in his bedroom. I went across to the other side of the farmhouse and popped my head round his door to say hello. He was huddled under his duvet.

'I'm not getting up just yet. Soz mate.'

'How's the album going?'

'OK, OK,' he said. 'The cheques just keep on coming Si,' he added, with a bemused grin.

John and I sat down to watch a video about American fighter jets which he had bought for me, but I didn't generally see much of him. He kept disappearing to his room saying he had to make a phone call.

Reni wasn't even there. I didn't pick up on the fact that the band was slowly growing apart amidst musical and drug differences, but looking back the signs were there.

Happily, Mani bowled in, rubbing his hands together.

'Aye aye. Here's the Woolly.'

He was as jubilant as ever - at least someone was having a laugh. He played me a couple of tracks they were working on. 'Begging You' was one of them. I thought it sounded immense. That and 'Love Spreads' were the only ones I really liked off the album.

I don't know precisely where they were up to with the recording, but it seemed at total odds to a Fall session where we'd get in and just bang out half a dozen songs in a couple of hours. There must be some kind of happy medium.

With John and Ian lying low, Mani took me to the pub in Monmouth for an evening's drinking with the locals, who appeared to have deified him. You couldn't buy a drink in there - they just kept being presented at the altar of Mani.

The next day we all had a kick about, using the side of a barn as a goal, and then I went back to the pub with Mani, for my second and last night where I was now famous by association.

I rang Sue on my return home and started seeing her again shortly afterwards.

In the summer, with The Fall, we found ourselves at an odd date in Lithuania, at the Vilnius Rock Festival. Pete Nash, the band's agent from Fair Warning, had secured the slots again. Because he was such a fan, he booked us on dates we didn't warrant and which they must have lost money on, for years.

We flew into the country in a clapped-out Lithuanian Air, Boeing 737, which made all sorts of groaning noises during the flight, leaving Dave Bush fearing for his life. On the coach to the hotel, the interpreter gave us a potted history of Vilnius. Just as we arrived outside the hotel, the hapless translator asked if anybody had any questions. Mark, who had been drinking miniature bottles of whisky all morning said, 'Yes I've got one. What about all the shootings that you did for the Nazis?'

The middle-aged interpreter looked stunned. We all were. Someone at the back of the bus shouted to Mark, 'Why don't you just shut your mouth and leave the poor woman alone.'

I couldn't have put it better myself.

We visited the grim KGB museum and the local market stalls where they were selling Nazi lapel badges. Mark was back on his MI6 thing, warning us not to use the avocado-green phones in the hotel rooms because they were bugged.

The morning after the gig, there was a bit of a scene, when checking out of the youth hostel-type hotel where all the bands at the festival had been billeted. The receptionist, a severe-looking woman who someone likened to a shot put champion, was shouting her head off about something or other. It turned out that Mark had broken all the slats of his single bed, in one of the drab, cell-like rooms that we had been given. Don't ask me how. The interpreter was no longer with us, after enduring Mark's outburst the day before, so it was left to Pete Nash to try and sort out the mess, handing over his credit card to the irate woman.

In July, we got a slot on a new festival held in Stratford-upon-Avon (at the Long Marsten Airfield) called the Phoenix Festival, just before headliners The Wonder Stuff and Carter the Unstoppable Sex Machine. Vic Reeves, comedian, and fan of The Fall, had recently taken The Wonder Stuff to the top of the charts with the song 'Dizzy'. He turned up to watch the band many times when we played in London.

August, surprisingly, brought the return of Brix, about five years after her split with Mark and with her solo efforts unnoticed by the world. She had been dating classical violinist Nigel Kennedy and hanging out with the likes of ex-England star Gary Lineker and his wife, after moving down to London.

I was glad Brix had rejoined and hoped she would bring a little bit more stability to a volatile Mark, who showed no signs of slowing down, but it didn't make any difference. Mark and Karl had another bout of handbags in the dressing room of the same gig.

A couple of nights later, under a marquee at Calton Hill, Edinburgh, Mark spent much of the gig berating monitor man Rex Sargeant. After about twenty-five minutes, Mark snapped. He marched over the top of the mixing desk, breaking off the knobs, as he screamed at Rex. The PA's owner pulled the plug and chased Mark off with a mic stand. Rex left.

Thankfully, we had a bit of a break to let things cool off.

Sue and I went on holiday for two weeks to the Gambia, a sliver of a country flanking the river of the same name in West Africa. The decision was largely based on pictures in a travel brochure, so imagine our surprise when, three or four days after our arrival, there was a military coup. It was, thankfully, a bloodless coup with new upstart, Lieutenant Jammeh, promising 'a coup with a difference'.

Jammeh installed a curfew at sundown and the tour operators moved all the tourists to one hotel. It had better security than all the other hotels as its grounds were surrounded by a high wall.

There were no more flights coming into Banjul airport and holiday-makers left in droves on whatever flights out they could get. All the remaining tourists were advised not to leave the hotel grounds, and its private beach, after dark. It poured hot rain and we sat watching the downpour as six-foot monitor lizards roamed the gardens. You had to keep your door shut in case you found yourself with an unwanted guest.

Apart from the odd surly checkpoint soldier, the only trouble I had out there was with a local youth who had supplied me with a bag of bush on the beach upon our arrival.

He offered to take us to see his village - a community of corrugated iron huts - if I bought them a big bag of rice for $25. I agreed and set off in our hire car.

We had a few shots of the local brew and a couple of spliffs. I was introduced to a guy who claimed to have played percussion on Dr Alban's 'It's My Life'.

Hmmmm.

Later, when I refused to buy a sarong for Sue, our guide, who was openly flirting with her, threatened to tell the police I was smoking weed, so I chased him down the beach and he never bothered us again. He was rapid though, I didn't get near him, even with his arms full of sarongs, flapping in the sea breeze.

Sue and I both had a great time in the Gambia, despite the political situation, which never spilled over into violence. I'd certainly go back.

There wasn't much time to rest at Sue's flat in Fallowfield, where I was now living, before the next US tour.

It began in Providence, Rhode Island, where I was asked for ID when trying to enter the club we were playing in, even though I was 31 years of age by now.

It was an especially madcap tour, even by Fall standards.

Mark picked up a stalker in Boston from Salem who had the look of a witch - black clothes, long straggly black hair, a vacant stare. She followed us through the tour and turned up later at Mark's house in Prestwich.

The next night in Boston's Axis club, Mark sacked the American tour manager, for the crime of wearing shorts and a baseball cap, as well as spending too much time hunched over a laptop instead of getting his hands dirty. Mark replaced him with a local crew member, also called Mark, who couldn't believe his luck, especially when he was issued with a record company credit card.

At 2 a.m. on the overnight drive back to New York, where we were based for the East Coast gigs, Mark (our singer not the tour manager) suddenly got up to speak to the driver.

'Can you stop the bus here?'

The driver pulled over but groused about getting back to New York and only being able to work so many hours. Meanwhile, Colin and Mark got off and spent a good couple of hours searching lonely dark fields for the grave of horror author HP Lovecraft. There was no sign of life in any direction. The rest of us sat there growing grumpier by the minute, wanting to get back to the hotel for some sleep.

Dave Bush told me later that they actually found the grave, somehow.

Within a week, Mark had started to have a pop at his mates from Manchester who had come along to act as road crew for us. He put a strip of white Gaffa tape across the middle of the bus, stating that they weren't allowed into the band's half of the bus anymore, which made it difficult if they needed a piss, as the toilet was in our half. I thought this was a bit of fun, but the crew didn't think so and the very next day they flew home in disgust, leaving the band to lug all the gear ourselves, which pissed us all off. Steve, Craig, and I, took it in turns to help Dave Bush pack the equipment away, well, me and Steve anyway.

We played Washington, New York, and Philadelphia, all the while shuttling back to New York, the Vietnam-vet driver, laid back, arms behind his head, steering with his feet.

In New York, Karl fell asleep in his hotel room sometime during the late afternoon after taking a snort of 'China White' we'd scored together in the Lower East Side. He not only didn't make the soundcheck, but also missed the gig completely, despite me, and several others, rapping on his door for ages and repeatedly ringing his hotel room.

After Philadelphia, we returned to New York to play at The Grand, just off Times Square, to a packed appreciative audience, peppered with the usual ex-pats and friends of the band. The atmosphere was always electric in New York. The Big Apple was my favourite by now.

I still couldn't believe I was getting paid for this.

Mark and I went to Barry White's fiftieth birthday party in a club downtown. I looked on, star-struck, thinking, fucking hell: I'm at Barry White's party. The walrus of love himself played a white grand piano.

'**Awwhh yeaahh**. This one is for all the *ladies* out there...'

Rochdale crooner Lisa Stansfield wandered over, pissed, and without a word shoved her tongue down Mark's throat - like one of those Gambian lizards, she was. Mark seemed delighted, although me being a puritan, as you know, I thought I was going to be sick.

When the new tour manager started banging on to anyone who would listen about how he couldn't help lift any equipment because of his bad back, I smelled a rat. I didn't particularly like this guy. A roadie who wouldn't carry any gear? What's that about?

'Has anybody got any pain killers?' he kept asking.

Why hadn't he replaced the mutinying road crew?

I ran into him in the hotel corridor, his pupils like pin pricks. I had been round long enough by now to know that the new tour manager was an addict - I knew what kind of prescription he wanted - and that if the record company weren't careful, he would be off into the sunset after using their credit card to withdraw thousands.

We were then told by this Mark, that he might have a problem crossing the Canadian border for the gig in Toronto because of his dubious past, which didn't instil any confidence in us whatsoever, though they let him in anyway.

Returning to the US we played in Ann Arbor, then Bogart's in Cincinnati. There was definitely a feeling of déjà vu about this stop on the tour. It was dead again. Allison came again. I was allocated the same hotel room as on my previous visit.

After shows in Chicago and Minneapolis it was a 38-hour drive over to Vancouver in British Columbia. Alighting from the bus, upon arrival at our hotel, in a seedy part of town, Mark was attacked by a stranger who had some kind of grudge against our singer. It was quickly broken up by Steve and the tour manager. Mark was visibly shaken by this incident. I'd never seen him like that and I'd seen him in some scrapes. He could have been stabbed or anything. It was proper stalker stuff.

Despite the incident, Dave, Steve, Craig, and I, went out that night to watch dance band Deelite at The Starfish Rooms - the same venue we were playing the next night.

My feeling about the tour manager proved correct. Steve and Karl caught him openly 'Chasing the Dragon' off a large strip of tin foil in the rear lounge of the bus - a complete no no.

No stranger to heroin, myself, I hankered after a hit but I knew there was a time and a place.

The next day he was gone.

After receiving instructions from Mark over the phone from a hotel near Seattle airport, the tour manager was thrown off the bus in the middle of downtown by Steve and Karl. He cut a sad figure as he trudged off to catch a bus back to his native Boston.

With a complete lack of management or crew, Steve was asked to take control of the tour. But it had been chaos.

Worse, the gigs were only half-full, if we were lucky.

The final gig on the tour was in LA.

I was taken out for the night by one of the guys from Matador Records to a club on Sunset Strip called the Viper Rooms, which had made headlines the previous year when actor River Phoenix had collapsed and died on the pavement outside, after taking an overdose in the VIP area.

I was introduced to Anthony Kiedis, singer from the Red Hot Chili Peppers. I told him we'd been listening to *Blood Sugar Sex Magik* on the tourbus and asked him who sang the ethereal backing vocals on my favourite track, 'Under the Bridge'.

'Yeah, it's my mom,' he said proudly. We had a chat. He was really down to earth.

The night before we flew home to England was spent at the Hyatt on Sunset again. Dave, Steve, Craig, and I - basically, those of us who had not been sacked or left the tour in protest - went down in the lift for a final night's drinking in the bar. The lift stopped on the floor below and in stepped Noel Gallagher and guitarist Paul 'Bonehead' Arthurs, which took us by surprise.

After the thing about *fancy meeting you here*, Noel said to me in the lift, 'You don't fancy joining our band do you?'

I didn't really know how to deal with this unexpected question, as I wasn't sure if he was joking. Also, I was surrounded by my own band-mates in the lift, so I just nervously laughed off the proposition as the lift doors opened in the lobby and we all made for the bar.

I chatted to Noel a little in the bar but he didn't bring it up again. He seemed a bit stressed out. As the days wore on, Noel briefly left Oasis and a few months later drummer Tony McCarroll would be fired from the band. It made me wonder.

Only Noel can say if it was a serious offer - he had a lot on his mind as it transpired as Oasis were in a Fall-like turmoil. Now, I wish I'd just said yes straight away and waited to see what his reply was, but I was used to missed opportunities by then.

If I could have one wish, it would be to know which fork to take in the road. Or maybe a chain of American diners.

22

Caustic

Mark took our ex-manager, Trevor Long, to court, because he believed that Trevor had been helping himself to the band's funds.

On the night before the court case at Wolverhampton Magistrates Court, I had a really heavy night out, watching one of my favourite live bands, Primal Scream, who were playing at the Academy in Manchester. I hung out with Bobby Gillespie and Johnny Marr backstage into the early hours and rolled home in a right state. I only managed to snatch a couple of hours' kip before I had to pick up Mark at seven o'clock and then drive him down to Wolverhampton Court for nine o'clock, for the Smith v Long case.

I woke up at seven, still half an hour away from Mark's house. I raced downstairs into the car park panicking, bleary-eyed and with the worst hangover ever, only to discover my car had been broken into. My Alpine stereo and speakers were gone and the passenger window was completely smashed in with glass all over. I reported the incident to the police and then set off for Mark's.

He looked really pissed off when I turned up at his place, nearly an hour late, as you could imagine. He got straight in and I drove like a madman at top speed down the M6 with the two of us freezing to death because of the missing window on the cold winter's day. Tiny shards of glass kept blowing back into the car. We hardly said a word all the way down.

We arrived, just in the nick of time - literally as the court usher was calling out Mark's name at nine o'clock. Mark was representing himself so I feared the worst. I left him to it and went for a lie down in the car at the back of the courthouse. The case was thrown out due to lack of evidence and we drove back to Manchester in the afternoon, with Mark sullen and frozen.

Just before Christmas, after a quiet autumn, with only a smattering of dates, we went to a studio in West London called The Pavilion. Mike Bennett, a production man who had experience in the theatre, and who we had never worked with before, was at the controls.

We were working on songs for our next offering, *Cerebral Caustic*. It would be the last time that Dave Bush and Craig Scanlon worked on a Fall record, though we didn't know it at the time. The whole thing was written and recorded in twelve days.

Brix had a big input on some of the better tunes such as 'Feeling Numb' and 'Don't Call Me Darling' and an oddity called 'Bonkers in Phoenix'. Brix was now accompanied by a minder called Mike Faux who drove her around in a silver Porsche 911. Mike was a member of The Stockport Shooting Centre and showed me and Steve how to shoot his 9 mm Ruger.

Karl, who was still in favour with Mark, also played guitar on several tracks, but as per normal there was a lot of shouting and bawling between the two of them - he was sacked again after three days.

At the end of the sessions at The Pavilion, Brix asked me to play drums on a couple of tracks she was recording for her solo album. One of them, David Bowie's 'Space Oddity', was really fun to play and didn't sound that bad either. Brix had booked the studio for a couple of days and on the second day a big-shot publisher wearing a fedora, who was a mate of Brix's muse, wafted in. We got talking and I mentioned how pissed off I was with the chaos in the band and wanted another gig. He said he could get me session work in London anytime I wanted.

'I can't read music though,' I said.

'It's up to you, if you learn how to, I'll get you a job.'

Next time I saw him - a couple of months later at a Fall gig - he asked, 'Well, did you learn to read?'

'No not yet.'

He walked off without saying a word and I never saw him again. I wish I had taken the time out to learn. What had I been doing in my time off? Just scoring the odd 10-bag and sitting around. I do wonder if I'd been clean, whether I'd have pulled myself together and followed up the offer.

Another missed opportunity. And I've had a few.

As far as I was concerned though, I was keeping the habit under control. I was eating. I looked normal. I was spending small amounts on the drug and nothing had been said by anyone. Until, one day, sat on a coach with Mark. Coming down.

'Do you want a line, cock?'

'No thanks.'

'What's the matter with you? Why you so miserable all the time?' Mark asked. He started rubbing my forehead as if he was trying to massage the frown lines out. I batted his hands away.

'Get off!'

'Have you been taking heroin, Simon?'

I was taken aback.

'What's it got to do with you? Is this the Spanish Inquisition or something?'

He turned away, cackling to himself.

I tried to wrack my brains for any careless moments, but the only time I could remember coming close was years earlier in the Dry Bar when the typically indiscreet Shaun Ryder saw me and Mark come in and started shouting the place down. 'Oooh look Gen-tle-Men. It's Funky Si,' he said in a faux Cheshire accent, and then: *HAVE YOU GOT ANY GEAR? GET YOUR GEAR OUT!*' I just quickly told him no and moved on.

I was becoming jaded. I liked Mark, but perhaps all this time together had worn on us. We weren't teenagers anymore and me and the rest of the band were less willing to put up with Mark's antics. We had our own problems - plus we were a ridiculous seven or sometimes eight-piece outfit by now, with Julia Nagle joining the fold and Lucy or the odd session player on board.

Mark seemed to be hinting at a clear out.

'You look like a load of old men,' he'd say as we lugged gear. 'Look at you.'

Dave Bush was the first to go. He stopped getting paid regularly and with Julia being encouraged to play keyboards as well as guitar, he saw the writing on the wall. Dave couldn't be arsed with all the mood swings and abuse and after a lot of his keyboards had been wiped off *Cerebral Caustic*, he'd had enough. Perhaps he sensed the band was on the way down. He bought a van and started selling a load of hippy gear, joss sticks and the like on Stockport market, before he joined

Britpop group Elastica.

Though Mark was still with his latest partner, Lucy, who did some backing vocals for us, I didn't feel at the time it was all business with Julia. So it was no surprise when Julia unknowingly edged out Dave. I was gutted that he'd left.

As long as the money was coming in, I stuck with it, and as I was living with Sue in her flat and had the rent coming in from my house in Levenshulme, things were okay financially, so I stayed as I was.

Until the gigs promoting the album started in March, most days I lazed about in the flat in Fallowfield and visited my dad in the afternoons, while Sue was at work.

Cerebral Caustic, released at the end of February, fared even worse in the charts than any of the albums I had worked on, reaching a lowly number 67, which surprised even me.

The whole Britpop phenomenon was really entering its stride by now and we were being pushed to the margins again. And again Mark was wary of the fad. I wasn't really concerned about being Britpop, either. This was a new generation and we stood even less chance of being absorbed into the latest scene.

Mark was convinced that he was partly responsible for Pulp frontman Jarvis Cocker's image, though. He had said it about a few acts now - the last one had been Pavement - and it seemed like a bit of a regular rant, but I think there was some truth in what he said.

Julia's first gig was in March at the Forum in London and Brix would do her best to make her feel comfortable on the road, while she herself kept her head down and avoided any confrontations with Mark. Brix had now split up with violin virtuoso Nigel Kennedy, and was dating, and before long, marrying, Philip Start, multi-millionaire rag trade king, who started turning up at one or two gigs. Brix seemed very happy to be with him. I liked him, I was glad for her.

Later that month, we hired a 52-seater coach instead of the usual sleeper and made the long journey from Manchester to the Saint-Lo Festival in Normandy, France. There was no longer money for flash tourbuses. The bus driver looked at us with a mix of bewilderment and disdain and didn't really know how to take us. He looked like he was used to ferrying pensioners on day trips to Cleethorpes.

The following week, we flew to Lisbon for a couple of shows. On the flight down there I got talking to a teenager from Manchester who excitedly told me he was on his way to the festival. He had brought a Brazilian 'Gope' drum that he intended to play at the gig. Mark took an instant dislike to him and when he bumped into him just before we took to the stage, he snatched the drum and stuck a ballpoint pen right through the middle of the skin, then tore it to shreds. The lad didn't seem arsed - like when JR met Lou Reed. Good story to tell round a dinner table.

Craig had taken to inviting a girlfriend, who he had met on the last tour of America, to a few of the festival dates in Europe. Mark either didn't like her or didn't like seeing Craig happy, or taking his focus off the band. The love struck duo did their very best to keep out of Mark's firing line. Craig would be at the front of the bus listening to Crosby, Stills and Nash, while Mark glowered incredulously at the back. There were no bunks to hide away and Mark could see your every move, so we'd all be ducking or slouching down below the headrests, trying to stay out of sight.

We moved on to Salzburg in Austria, playing in an old mental hospital. Mark claimed he could smell the stench of madness inside the wood-panelled venue. He said he knew what he was talking about, because he had known a few patients over the years, on day release from Prestwich mental hospital, just down the road from his house. I remember a number of times sat in The George with Mark on Bury New Road and people would nod at him and Mark would say, yeah, he's from the hospital, he's from the hospital, he's from the hospital. Karl had a drug counsellor mate who worked there at the time, a small, rotund, guy with John Lennon glasses and a mass of unkempt curly hair who lived up in the hills near Rawtenstall. He looked a bit a poacher turned gamekeeper. He wrote out prescriptions for his mates, no questions asked, it seemed.

At some point on this mini-tour, Steve and Craig started coming to my room asking if I had any draw. This was a first.

'You what?'

'Have you got any hash?'

It was like Dylan going electric.

I skinned up and we had a smoke together. It became a new ritual after every gig, along with the vodka. I don't know why they started, maybe because good speed was becoming scarce. It was being cut with milk powder and besides, everyone was dealing Es now. Maybe they just wanted to sedate themselves, escape.

By October, it was Craig's turn for the push, which was just as sudden as Dave's sacking earlier in the year. This may have been something to do with his girlfriend and his newfound penchant for marijuana, but I think it was mainly Craig's ditching his trusty Vox AC30 amplifier. It was the only amp I'd known him to use and had given him his signature raw sound. He then replaced it with a Roland Jazz Chorus amplifier, which has a totally different sound. Mark said to me at one point that Craig's American girlfriend had turned him on to jazz and Bob Dylan and had made him soft. It was a real shame that Craig was treated so poorly after putting up with Mark for 16 years. Not to mention the amount of songwriting he did. And for me, I never forgot Craig looking after me when I had first joined the band.

Still, I saw Craig recently, and he doesn't seem to be too cut up about it.

'It was my time, Si,' he said, quite adamant on the point. 'I'd had enough.'

The night after we had played at the Astoria in London again, Karl had brought yet another bumper pack of air bomb repeaters and a bunch of rockets as Guy Fawkes Night approached. We were staying at the Columbia Hotel, a bit of a dive back then, situated opposite Hyde Park. Karl's room was at the back of the hotel overlooking the old headquarters of the Football Association. He pulled up the wooden sash windows and proceeded to fire a couple of rockets at the FA's front door, which was closed, just for something to do. He liked explosions, Karl. Then he started firing the air bombs as well, setting the net curtains of his room alight in the process. Soon there was a knock at the door. It was security and they wanted him off the premises, immediately, banning him for life. Mark had already been banned from the same hotel several years earlier for completely flooding out his room, after leaving the bath taps running and falling fast asleep one night.

Mark invited the surviving members of the group, minus Brix, who was now living comfortably in Holland Park, to a bonfire night party at his house. Karl doused the stack of wooden planks in Mark's tiny back garden with way too much neat petrol just prior to it being lit, with predictable results. A huge fireball roared upwards and sideways singeing everybody's hair and eyebrows and setting fire to the fencing panels at the foot of the garden. Mark went into a seizure and an ambulance was called. He was wheeled away with an oxygen mask pinned to his face and taken to a nearby hospital.

Mark sat with a blanket wrapped around him in his wheelchair as he waited to be taken away. He was blaming his seizure on the two fights he and I had had years earlier.

'It's your fault this,' he's going. '*He* keeps hitting me,' he said to anyone who would listen, jabbing his finger in my direction.

But nobody took that seriously. Mark was always getting into scrapes and besides, it was more likely down to the amount of booze and speed he was taking.

Mark was soon discharged and back on stage for a one-off gig on New Year's Eve 1995 at the Volksbuehne, an old theatre in Berlin.

For all the chaos, it is only fair to Mark, to point out his continued generosity.

In the New Year, he took me and Sue, along with Lucy and himself, for a few days break in Venice. After landing at the airport, we boarded a mahogany-lined Riva motorboat that took the four of us to a little jetty right outside our swish hotel, near St Mark's Square, which was bathed in fog. Mark had been here many times over the years so knew the place well and took us to good restaurants he knew. We spent an afternoon in the Peggy Guggenheim museum where I had a look at their collection of Picassos. We walked past the Bridge of Sighs along the near empty streets. Mark said he'd taken a photo on the bridge on a previous visit and when the picture was developed there was a girl in a red coat who he swore wasn't there when he took the shot.

The thick fog did not lift all the time we were there.

I enjoyed looking at the glassware shops. Mark bought a ceramic face mask. We drank espressos. Me and Sue hired a gondola for half an hour, but it was freezing out on the canals. We got soaked by spray as we headed out towards the lagoon. Mark preferred Venice in the winter to the summer, when he said it stank of sewage and was overcrowded with fat American tourists in shorts.

Couldn't stand shorts, for some reason, Mark.

Once back home, the single 'The Chiselers' was released. I thought it was notable only in that we spent more time working on this one track than any other Fall song I can remember. I'm not really sure why Mark wanted to keep throwing money at it, because I didn't think it had much promise to start with, compared with some of the stuff we'd done. We spent hours and hours and hours on it. The end result? Hardly anyone bought it.

Shortly after, I went on a fly-drive holiday with my old man to Florida.

As we drove across the state, it seemed as if Oasis' 'Wonderwall' came on every radio station I tuned into. I felt quite proud that a band from Manchester seemed to be big in the country. Noel had come a long way since the days in the office on New Mount Street. My mind wandered back to our encounter in the lift.

A couple of weeks after the break, Mark rang me to ask if I would come over to his house later that afternoon to witness the signing of the band's new record contract with Jet Records, a name I was familiar with from my sister's ELO collection. As Mark was putting the kettle on, our new record label boss pulled up outside the house in a huge blue Mercedes (referenced in the song 'Cheetham Hill'), and on entering he introduced himself. His name was Frank Lea, he was briefly a second drummer in glam rock band Slade and had once run Trojan Records. After a bit of chit-chat in the kitchen, the three of us sat round Mark's dining room table in the back room, where I had first thrashed out my 'contract' in 1986.

Frank opened his briefcase and pulled out the contract which was about an inch thick. Half an hour later, after Mark and I had signed the papers, the three of us clinked our glasses of Glenfiddich and Mark put on some records from the early seventies, including The Move. Call me a Philistine, but I'd never heard of them. I thought Mark had put it on to make Frank feel at home! Thirty minutes later, the label boss had gone, so Mark and I went to The Woodthorpe up the road to have another drink. By now, the surly Fred had moved on to running a pub in Blackpool, but The Woodthorpe was never the same without him.

It had been ten years and things seemed to be drawing to a close. Would things turn round for the band now we were on a new label? I was always optimistic that the band's fortunes might improve. I certainly hoped so.

Sue was pregnant.

23

The Frightening World of The Fall

The latest line-up was told to report to 'The Dairy Studios' in Brixton to begin work on the next album. Apparently, there was a drug squad stationed on the roof of The Dairy, staking out another building. Meanwhile there was enough speed on the premises to get someone sent down for supplying.

The Light User Syndrome was recorded with Mike Bennett again at the helm. For the best part of the first week, Mark didn't even bother to show up, which was ominous. He turned up in the middle of a run through of a backing track, shouting and bawling.

Craig and Dave were gone and it felt like a new band. Not as good.

Karl had been reinstated again, and was his usual boisterous self. He seemed to go into his shell a bit when Mark was around though. In Craig's absence, he ended up playing a lot of guitar and even took lead vocal on a song called 'Stay Away (Ol' White Train)'. I'd never heard him sing before. I thought it was a waste of recording time.

If I'm honest I didn't think Julia was a suitable replacement for Dave, though she did bring an enthusiasm which was perhaps lacking in the rest of us. She wasn't confident enough, though. Mark tried to encourage her creativity, while not giving the rest of us an inch.

Steve and I were generally keeping quiet and trying to make things work as smoothly as possible.

Brix brought some song ideas and her presence helped move the sessions along but I got the impression she was grinning and bearing it, a bit like I was doing. She felt that Mark had aged a lot and become moodier since her first stint. He probably had, but it wasn't as obvious to me as I had been amongst it.

Mark was drinking more heavily than normal though. He admitted that himself, later. In the middle of the night at the residential Far Heath studio in rural Northamptonshire, he ran out of drink and went wandering into the private quarters in the main farmhouse. He stumbled into the studio owner's parents' bedroom.

'Where's the booze, cock?'

As Mark retreated to the studio, the startled farmer came downstairs, shotgun in hand, to find out who the intruder was. Angus, his son, who ran the studio, diffused the situation.

It probably goes without saying by now that I thought the album was patchy. I thought 'Spinetrak', 'Powder Keg', 'He Pep!', and 'Cheetham Hill' were good tracks though.

Sue and I moved to a beautiful rented flat in rural Ashley in preparation for the arrival of our daughter.

Emily Patricia was born on 9 June at Wythenshawe Hospital, where mum had worked all those years. We brought her back to our new home and I went for a drink and a cigar at the village pub called The Greyhound with one of our neighbours.

I have fond memories of long summer evenings slumped in a deck chair, reading magazines, in the back garden on Cow Lane. I rocked Emily to sleep in her pram, as huge green and blue dragonflies and bumble bees hovered above the honeysuckle flowers all around.

My dad would call over to see his granddaughter sometimes, as he was still able to drive safely at this point. Within a year my sister Jane and I had to take his car keys off him, because he had started to lose his faculties. He wasn't happy.

The idyllic living was soon interrupted.

The Light User Syndrome was released the day after Emily's birth to a non-interested public, who were buying Oasis and Blur products by the truck load. Two weeks later I was back on the road with the new line-up. First London at the Astoria, then flying out to Denmark for the Roskilde Festival, one of the best in Europe in my opinion.

Mark got a hiding from a huge black rapper, from a band called The Brotherhood, who were also on the bill with us. On arrival at the airport, we boarded a minibus waiting outside to take us to the festival site and The Brotherhood, who were entitled to be on the same transport as us, started boarding. Mark didn't want them on the bus and said to one of them, 'Get off the bus, boy, it's reserved for The Fall. Fuck off.'

Mark is no racist but it was a very poor choice of words. Considering his appreciation of rap music, I was surprised he was so hostile to the group. But then, he was hostile to pretty much anyone he didn't like the look of.

The guy went for him and got in a flurry of crushing hooks as our wiry singer was cowering in his seat.

I didn't move. I just thought, fuck it, you can't keep talking to people like that. I thought it would teach him a lesson.

Steve jumped in between Mark and the guy from The Brotherhood but by now Mark's face was bloodied.

When we arrived at our hotel, someone in our party made a complaint against The Brotherhood at the police station, which was right next door. The Danish copper, who reminded me of one of the pot smoking Dutch policemen in *Harry Enfield and Chums*, asked if Mark wanted to press charges, but he decided against it.

'Good. Letsh not fight, letsh all be friendz, huh?' the incongruous copper counselled.

Despite Mark's condition, we went on to play a stormer early that same evening. It was the first time I'd seen people waving long poles with flags on, like you see at most festivals now. They were letting off flares at dusk. They looked like an army of battle ready Vikings.

When we got home, Mark set up a meeting in the Ostrich pub in Prestwich, as he had some news for me and Steve. Not long after Craig's dismissal, we had been made partners in the business. He pulled out a demand from HM Customs and Excise for an unpaid VAT bill amounting to about £32,000 which shocked me to the core.

After getting a round of drinks in, Mark explained that as partners in the company, Steve and I were both liable for the bill, but not to worry as he would come to a financial arrangement himself with Customs and Excise, paying the bill by monthly instalments.

I felt sick to the stomach and angry with myself for getting into this mess, as I knew the band weren't selling anything like the amount of records that we had been doing. The live bookings were getting fewer and fewer as people's interest in the band was waning and Mark's reputation for being unreliable and cancelling shows at the last minute was increasing. As a partner, I was expecting my wage would go up, not down.

I buried my head in the sand again.

When Emily was just three months old, I took her and Sue down to the Phoenix Festival. It was a scorching hot day. Not that she'd remember, but it was Emily's first gig. I drove the three of us down in the early afternoon and as I was coming off the motorway, south of Birmingham, I noticed a coach parked on the hard shoulder with a flat tyre, with half a dozen people surrounding the driver, at the back of the vehicle. As I got a bit nearer, I realised it was my bandmates. Mark was haranguing the poor driver about something or other. I put my foot down. When they eventually turned up a couple of hours later, Mark was still having a go at the driver for making him late.

The Sex Pistols, who had reformed for the first time in eighteen years for a series of summer festivals, were headlining that night, just after our spot. They still had it. I managed to get a chat with Glen Matlock, original bass player of the Pistols over some tea in the catering tent. The Pistols' road crew were dead cool too - they couldn't do enough for us.

In October, sixty people turned up to our show at the Town Hall in Motherwell, Scotland. The band were saying Mark was on some OCD thing. Washing his hands constantly - speed psychosis - claiming he'd caught a skin disease after shaking hands with a young girl in a wheelchair. He had welts on his arms, trying to bite away the sores.

During the soundcheck, Mark threw a mic stand at an engineer and Brix got into a massive row with him, threatening to smash his head in with her 12-string Rickenbacker. After the set-to was quelled, Brix fled. She was really upset, crying, refusing to play. Despite me and Steve trying our best to comfort her, it was obvious that she had reached her tipping point for the second time. She went back to London first thing in the morning, missing that night's gig at the South Shields Arts Theatre.

That show was a disaster from the start as Mark was an hour and a half late and the impatient crowd turned nasty, throwing anything they could towards the stage, beer bottles mostly. The police were called and turned up in riot gear in a couple of vans. Things got uglier.

A few days later in London, at the Forum, Brix played her last gig with the decaying band and I was sad to see her go. It felt like a swan song. I knew she wouldn't be back again.

There were times when I was lounging about the flat in Ashley when I expected to see my BMW being towed away, at the behest of Customs and Excise.

I was really worried. I think it was making me physically ill.

The payments from the band were no longer regular. Mark would just give us bits and bobs of what he could afford, as and when. We were, in theory, still on 300 quid a week, which hadn't changed since 1986, which still wasn't bad. But, you know, it doesn't matter what your wage is if you don't receive it. Mark has said himself that he is not really any good with finance. He said that he'd once been told, 'As long as you've got a fiver in your pocket, you'll be alright.' I needed more than a fiver.

As I only had six O levels and a City and Guilds in catering, I bit the bullet and drove to the local taxi firm, to see if they'd give me a job. The boss, Ray, said he would take me on once I had gone to get a taxi badge from Trafford Council, which I duly did, after taking a medical and passing their version of 'The Knowledge'.

A couple of weeks later, I began working the night shift at the cab firm in a four-door saloon, after trading in the coupe, which broke my heart. I told Steve about my moonlighting, but thought it best not to mention anything to Mark, who I hardly saw at all, socially, now. He had started hanging out and writing new songs with Julia, round at her place in Stockport.

The final show of the year for the rapidly disintegrating band was on Christmas Eve at the Volksbuehne in Berlin, where we had played on the previous New Year's Eve, with Brix's replacement, Adrian Flanagan, a young guitarist from Salford who was Mark's sister Caroline's latest muse.

Tired, skint and fraying, Karl and I returned to our hotel and started tearing slabs off a huge gingerbread house on show, hungrily stuffing our faces in the deserted lobby.

I sat on the Lufthansa jet to Manchester happy to be eating a Christmas dinner and going home, but I couldn't help wonder just how much longer I could take all this stress.

It wasn't much longer.

I would have liked to bail out from the turmoil there and then and step into another group, and as it happened a glimmer of an opportunity came my way.

I was invited by Britpop band Elastica, who Dave Bush had joined a

few months previously, to fill in for their regular drummer at a recording session, at Mayfair Studios in London. Elastica, who were writing
new material, also seemed to be in the doldrums, laboriously crafting new
material as well as having internal problems of their own. Their regular
drummer, Justin, was in rehab and Dave put my name forward.

That session was aborted with me making a quick exit - Justin had
left rehab and come to the studio to find me sat in his chair ... It can be
a mercenary game.

I finally left The Fall in 1997, after more than ten years of ups and downs,
but mostly ups. Karl had been sacked yet again. Another new guitarist
called Tommy Crooks was brought in to replace Adrian Flanagan, who'd
had enough.

It felt as if every man and his dog was now having a stint at being a
Fall band member for a while and as a result, the chemistry between band
members just wasn't working as it had done in previous years.

At the end of January, The Fall struggled along with the latest line-
up, playing the Bristol Bierkeller and, for the first and last time, I told
Mark that people were taking the piss out of his performances. He was
affronted and defiantly responded, 'If I fart into the microphone, people
will buy it, alright Simon?'

At the sparsely attended shows, I felt people were more interested to
see Mark in meltdown than in listening to the songs.

There were hecklers, goading him. You could almost see the expec-
tancy on their faces.

Meanwhile, Mark hadn't been keeping up with the payments to
Customs and Excise. I was contacted by a bailiff from the VAT and went
to meet him in a car park behind a Kwik Save in Eccles as I didn't want
him in the flat with Sue and Emily. He handed me a summons to appear
in court in London. I was now seriously worried about my immediate
financial situation; the summons had come as a massive shock.

In the meantime, I got on with the taxi driving. I worked for Anytime
cabs in Altrincham. That was a bit of a gag among the locals with Anytime
- they could turn up any fucking time.

Still, it felt great to be earning regular money again and to no longer
have to depend solely on the band, financially.

As no reputable promoters would touch The Fall with a barge pole
anymore, there was very little to do during the day, which meant I could

visit my dad at his house during the afternoons.

We would often go for pub lunches together and to Tesco in Baguley for a weekly shop. He was a bit of a celebrity in there with ex-patients stopping him in the aisles all the time, to see how he was. I was the doctor's son again.

Though I didn't know it at the time, in May, I performed my final two shows with The Fall, in Manchester at a small club on Oxford Road called Jilly's.

In mid-summer, Steve picked me up in a battered old blue VW Transporter Mark had bought, as nobody would extend any credit to even rent a van. Steve was taking more and more responsibility now and I admired his commitment, even if I was unwilling to do the same. We were on our way down to West Heath Studios in London (owned by Orange Juice singer Edwyn Collins) that had a load of vintage analogue equipment which Mark preferred. We had been picked up yet again by John Lennard on his new label, Artful Records, after being dumped by Jet following the poor sales of *The Light User Syndrome*.

While Mark and Julia stayed in a flat near Lords Cricket Ground, Steve and I checked into a flea-bitten bed and breakfast in West Hampstead, a short distance away. We went over to the studio to find two more collaborators in the ever-changing line-up. It was Keir Stewart and Simon Spencer. The electronic duo had a side project with Mark called D.O.S.E., releasing a song called 'Plug Myself In' the previous year, which was excellent. I wish I'd been involved in it.

Keir and I had actually tried to work up a song once, previously. I had been round at Keir's one day when he started showing me some equipment he had to make phone conversations clearer which he sometimes did for the police.

'Why don't you ring Mark now, get him talking?' I said, 'we can sample it and put it over some beats.'

Keir made the call straight away and we put this track together but when Keir sent it to Mark, Mark went beserk. So much for, *if I fart into a microphone...*

They must have made-up anyway because here he was, in the studio. Steve and I weren't expecting them to be involved with The Fall's new album. Maybe it would be a good thing.

We set up our gear and put down a couple of backing tracks that we had been working on, then waited a few days, working on more tracks, for Mark to show.

One morning, Julia swept into the studio and announced to me and Steve, 'Mark says to forget what you are doing and to start recording all my songs instead.'

This was now the final straw.

Mark walked in pissed and started rubbishing everything, per usual. I was out of money and patience.

I said to Steve, 'I've had enough, I'm going home', and with that I walked out of the session back to the flea pit and packed my suitcase. Steve followed me and did his best to persuade me to stay, but I had finally made my mind up. I told him I would be back in the morning to pick up my drum kit as my car was parked outside the flat in Ashley.

As I talked things over with Sue I realised that I now urgently needed to resign from the partnership, before Customs and Excise cleaned us out.

When I returned to London the following afternoon to collect my kit, Steve practically begged me to stay, asking me to give it one more chance. But I had already drafted a letter of resignation and was waiting for the right time to present it to Mark.

At a meeting in a receiver's office in Manchester, I told Mark I was resigning. Mark was livid.

'That's fuckin' great that intit?' he said, contemptuously, 'I take you round the world and this is how you repay me.'

Mark had done a lot for me, and I am proud of being in The Fall, but I didn't feel guilty. He said he would sort the tax bill out and he hadn't. Plus, he was probably the last person who should be playing the loyalty card.

I had my daughter to think about and I'd had enough of it all. I walked out of the meeting and didn't see Mark again for fourteen years.

As it turned out, I had extracted myself from the liability of the VAT bill in the nick of time.

ACT III

24

Crew Filth

Back in the real world for the first time in eleven years, I actually enjoyed the taxi driving. It wasn't completely alien as I was forever at the front of tourbuses, navigating, and driving was one of the few things I was qualified to do. Plus I was working when it suited me. I could listen to music, and I'd meet all sorts of characters.

It was mostly trips to the airport and ferrying revellers to and from town. With the taxi business being based in Altrincham, I was sometimes driving footballers from clubs and pubs back to their nearby mansions.

One rainy Thursday night in Hale Barns, I had to turn down a fare from Teddy Sheringham, the England and United ace, as I already had a better job going to Liverpool. With me being a United fan, I felt sorry for him as he walked off, soaking in the rain. But I reckoned he was doing alright for himself so I wasn't that sorry.

While the taxi driving was bringing a steady income, the drums were never far from my thoughts.

Performing in a band is the most powerful drug I have known and I soon started to develop withdrawal symptoms. For the first time, I started looking in the 'Musicians Wanted' section of the *NME* to see if I could find myself a new band to join.

One of the adverts took my eye: 'Drummer wanted for new band with deal, due to record album in new year.' I rang the phone number and spoke to a Scouser who lived in London where the band was based and ran through my drumming CV. He told me the name of his band was Airbourne or Airplay - I can't really remember - and that they had a record deal with London Records. Did I want him to post me a CD of their music to see if I would be interested? The auditions would be held at a rehearsal studio in London in February - 1998. Yes, go on then, why not.

I listened to the songs over Christmas with the audition in mind. It sounded a bit like New Order but with more guitars - I decided to give it a go.

Meanwhile, as I drove around Manchester, I started seeing exaggerated simian-like impressions of Ian's face on the back of buses promoting his new album *Unfinished Monkey Business*. I was glad he was back up and running after the sad demise of the Roses - and, for me, the much publicised split with John. Although I hadn't particularly been in touch with Ian and John, the rift seemed a shame, when you consider how close they'd been from an early age. John also had a band going, having set up The Seahorses.

Not long after, I heard on the news that Ian had been arrested for threatening an air stewardess. I was surprised - it didn't sound like him.

In preparation for my audition with Airway, I booked a small room at The Greenhouse rehearsal studios in Stockport where I had spent many hours with The Fall over the years. After a couple of hours of practising along to the CD, I went to make a brew in the kitchenette and was surprised to hear the instrumental sound of 'My Star', a song from Ian's first solo album, coming from the main room. It sounded too polished to be anyone other than Ian's band.

It was.

I bumped into Noel Walters, Ian's manager at the time, outside in the car park on a fag break. I knew Noel from my Weeds days as a face about town. He told me Ian would be in the next day.

Noel introduced me to the band: Aziz Ibrahim and Sylvan Richardson, both ex-Simply Red guitarists; Simon Moore, a red hot young drummer from Moss Side; and percussionist Inder 'Goldfinger' Mathura, who I made an instant connection with.

When Ian arrived, he was pleased to see me - I hadn't seen him in more than a year. It was great to see him again. He told me about the incident on the British Airways flight and said he felt the flight attendant had it in for him, treating him like some pissed-up thug who was going to be trouble. Ian didn't even drink, having stopped a few years before, and didn't seemed unduly worried about the charges against him. He was mainly just buzzing about his new album and band.

Ian suggested we go for a brew and asked me if I wanted some roadie work, starting in a month or so. I would have preferred to be the drummer, but that seat was taken, and it was a good offer so I said yes. It was better than the taxi driving.

Still looking for my own seat, I went to the Airwolf audition in the East End of London and was offered the gig straight away. Max, the band's manager, took us all out to a trendy club in Shoreditch to celebrate. He plied us with free drinks all night in the VIP area and then brought out a bottle of vodka from his man bag which was gone in about half an hour. I don't really remember what happened after that. Though it isn't very often, I can get a bit out of control if I drink too much. I woke up alone at dawn, in the back seat of my Audi near Fleet Street, with one shoe missing. Head mashed. God knows what happened. I must have said something that upset them because I never heard from them again.

I was in the band for about six hours, my shortest ever tenure.

If I offended anyone in Airmaster, I apologise unreservedly.

With that, I took Ian up on his offer of some Scandinavian dates he had coming up. I'd never been a roadie before, apart from when I'd helped push the Clash's flight cases from their truck outside the Manchester Apollo as a teenager. Still, I'd been around roadies enough and lugged my own gear enough times to know the gist. Mark's throwaway song 'Crew Filth' went round my head a couple of times - I imagine he'd have had a laugh at my expense.

All your friends might turn out to be: Crew Filth!

I actually got a credit on that song, but I don't know why, it was Mark just handing them out. It's an awful song anyway.

It was a top gig though, the roadie work. It felt like I was being paid to hang around with my mate. I also got to go travelling again for the first time in a year - we went to the north-western coast of Norway, which, at that time of year, never went dark.

My main job was to set up Simon Moore's drum kit suspended from a newfangled scaffolding system which I'd never used before.

Tabla master Inder 'Goldfinger', who I had taken a shine to at the rehearsal room, was a real calming influence on me. I'd hang out with him and Ian most of the time. I think it was his Yorkshire accent too. Although from a different part of Yorkshire, and some years younger than me, he'd say things that reminded me of my grandfather back in Doncaster.

The tour was no stress whatsoever and ran like clockwork. It was brilliant just to be on the road again.

Elsewhere, I heard that The Fall were still in chaos. Steve, who copped for half of the tax bill when I resigned, quit the band after yet another massive bust up, this time in New York. Mark and Karl had a scrap on stage during the gig and Mark was arrested after the gig on suspicion of assaulting Julia, though no charges were pressed. I have to admit to watching the Mark and Karl bust up on YouTube, and knowing the two of them, found the carry-on hilarious. Karl looked like the leather-clad biker, with the peaked cap, out of The Village People.

I felt relieved that I was no longer part of the madness. It makes for great copy and notoriety but it is no fun to be around after a while. I did feel for Mark though, and worried the booze and drugs and stress would impact his health irreparably. I went round to see him not long after this, after finding a load of old two-inch tapes from a recording session that he had asked me to hang on to, years earlier. Stuff as far back as *Kurious Oranj*. I took them up to his house but there was no answer, so I just left the tapes in the shed with a note, but I didn't hear back from him. He probably wasn't very happy with me still.

After a stint back on the taxis, my next job was at the Glastonbury Festival where Ian was performing to a huge adoring crowd, who by now were chanting his name again and again, before coming on stage, football crowd style.

Ian's band was super tight.

That summer, the weather was atrocious and the backstage area became a quagmire, but I was still having a blast. I met Joe Strummer again, who was camped in a RV vehicle, sat round a camp fire with loads of mates. Someone had used a motorbike exhaust to make a pipe, though I didn't have a go myself. I have smoked through some odd things in my time. I used a pop can a few times as a makeshift pipe - it was actually Mark who showed me that. He also pointed out you could use the blank pages of hotel room bibles to skin up if you ran out of papers. Lord don't strike me down … Still, I didn't bother with the motorbike pipe. There was plenty of weed-smoking going on during that tour though, as you could probably have guessed.

The work with Ian kept coming. We went to the Shetlands where someone pinched Ian's tambourine off the stage but it was handed in after the local radio put out an appeal to return it. Quaint.

We went to Ireland, to do a big festival in Galway, supporting the

Beastie Boys, on their *Intergalactic* tour.

It was a great day until Simon Moore's drum kit started collapsing halfway through the gig, after I neglected to tighten his framework properly. I was mortified - one job to do ... Hugh, the tour manager, ran on stage and averted disaster. The young drummer was pissed off with me about that one, but it was soon forgotten.

We flew out to the Fuji Festival in Japan, which had been relocated to Tokyo harbour because of heavy rains. It was a great bill: Beck and The Prodigy were on among others, and played awesome shows. I was a massive fan of both, particularly The Prodigy - I hadn't been as excited about a band since The Clash.

Afterwards, I went out with a few of the crew to the Lexington Queen, a club I had been to with The Fall, where I nearly got into a scrap with Keith Flint, singer/dancer with The Prodigy.

Keith was sitting on his own in a red-velvet upholstered booth in the VIP area of the club. I didn't really want to talk to him, as much as I liked his band, so went to take a seat. On entering the roped off area Keith snorted at me.

'You carnt sit ere, s'reserved for the lay-deez.'

'You what?'

I didn't see any signs saying reserved for Keith Flint's fucking ladies.

'You 'eard.'

I told him to fuck off and started to advance towards the rude, pierced fucker. Hughie, who knew Flint from the circuit, saw what was about to happen, came running over, got in between us and defused the situation, but I wasn't happy. You can't talk to people like that. No wonder he was sitting on his own.

25

Golden Days

One evening, back on the taxis, I heard on the radio that Ian had been banged up. My heart sank. *Behind bars?* He was convicted of using threatening behaviour towards the stewardess on the British Airways flight and sentenced to four months. I think the government wanted to make an example of him. At the time, pre-9/11, air rage incidents were becoming more and more common, with lairy Brits on their way abroad. Still, I hadn't seen this coming and a prison sentence was a shock.

I sent Ian a letter offering support, asking if I could visit, but he didn't want anybody to have to suffer the indignity of being searched just to say hello. I sent him some of his favourite Embassy cigarettes instead. I felt really bad for him, and thought there was no way he would endanger the lives of other passengers on a flight - he said he had gone to knock on the captain's door to complain about the stewardess but they took this as some sort of terrorist threat. Maybe it wasn't the smartest move on Ian's part, but it all seemed overblown. I do remember feeling he would be looked after by the other inmates because of his reputation as a man of the people around Manchester and he could handle himself. I hoped that if he kept his nose clean, he would be out in eight weeks, which he was.

In the meantime, after moving the family from the country to a new build in Broadheath, I got a call from a guy called John Barrett from Stockport, who had managed a band called Easterhouse in the eighties. He wanted to see if I would be interested in joining a new band he was putting together called Foreign Bodies. Front man Mush was the ex-vocalist from a band called Kaleef and brought along Paul his DJ in the same outfit (they had released a fairly successful version of 'Golden Brown' by the Stranglers). He wanted to start writing tracks straight away. I agreed as soon as I heard Andy Rourke was on bass.

Before my night shift, I would pick up Andy and the pair of us would drive over to a pub in Ashton-Under-Lyne called The Witchwood, for an afternoon of songwriting in the rehearsal room upstairs. I thought the band was great with Pakistani frontman Mush bopping about energetically whilst he rapped over grooves and dance beats supplied by me, Andy, and Paul.

On Christmas Eve, Ian was released early from Strangeways for good behaviour.

He got his Embassies and walked to the train station with a black bin bag and didn't look back.

A few days later, he rang me up and asked if I'd take him to Heathrow as he was going to visit his future wife, who was living in New York.

On the way down he offered me the drumming job in his band. He'd seen me drumming a few times round at his new house in Lymm, when I'd been visiting. Though I didn't want to let the lads in Foreign Bodies down, it was another offer I couldn't refuse.

I don't really know why all of a sudden I was in and Simon Moore was out, but I do remember reading an interview in the *Manchester Evening News* where he was going on about how he didn't have any Christmas presents for his kids, now Ian was in the big house. Anyway, I didn't ask any questions. I wanted in.

Two weeks of rehearsals for a Japanese tour began in mid-March, running through most of the songs off *Unfinished Monkey Business*. Bass player Sylvan was so good he would read the *TV Times* and plan his weekly viewing while playing the songs. His playing was top notch - I used to just grin at some of the things he came up with. That's what music should do to you. Me and Ian used to argue who was the best: Andy Rourke or Sylvan? Ian used to say Sylvan, but I couldn't make my mind up.

One night after rehearsals, I drove Ian over to Reni's house in Whalley Range, where the two of them had some sort of business to sort out. When I walked in the kitchen, Reni asked Ian, 'What have you brought that bum with you for?'

I couldn't believe it. I turned straight back round and left.

'I'm leaving E.'

I think Reni was still pissed off at me for saying there were only a couple of good tracks on *The Second Coming*, years before in *Select* magazine, when The Fall were asked if the album was worth the wait. Maybe it was because he knew I had been taking gear for years. It's a small place, Manchester.

I was happy at the way my life seemed to be turning around. Through a couple of debacles, I had fallen on my feet. You never know what's around the corner.

The only thing troubling me was a conversation me and Ian had about some guy he had met in the nick.

'Says he knows you, Si,' Ian said. 'Deals brown. How do you know him?'

I was on the spot and I'm a terrible liar.

'I know him from my Wilmslow days,' I said, quickly changing the subject.

'Right.'

I knew full well that Ian was totally against heroin and that I had scored off this guy in the nick in the past.

The Roses had played in Japan a few times and I had seen how popular Ian was over there the previous summer at the Fuji festival, so it was no surprise when we arrived at the hotel to find dozens of excited fans. Out came the cameras and cuddly toys and the autograph books, whilst we waited to be checked in. It was like when The Fall had played there nearly ten years before, but on a much bigger scale. The next day we set off on the impressive bullet train for two shows in Nagoya, then Osaka, returning to Tokyo for four shows.

Most nights after the gigs we were taken to the Lexington Queen again, the club where I always seemed to end up in Tokyo. It was run by a tall blond Russian guy who wore a white suit. The place was full of European models and musicians and had walls covered by pictures of bands, past and present, who had visited. 'Ghetto Supastar (That is What You Are)' was on heavy rotation.

I did the usual browsing for electrical gadgets and sitting barefoot on the floor over traditional Japanese meals and Saki. I was mostly hanging out in Inder's room though. He showed me how to fold and wrap his white turban.

The gigs themselves were packed every night, which I hadn't seen for a good few years now. This was on a different scale to my previous employer's tours, even at their peak - having always wanted The Fall to go the next level, it felt great to be playing on bigger stages.

In May, we played Cork, Dublin, then two nights in Belfast at the Limelight. As we were travelling up the M1 to Northern Ireland, a burning truck tyre rolled down from the top of the embankment towards the path of our speeding bus, with its London telephone number emblazoned down the side. By the time the flaming tyre careered onto the road, we were about 150 yards past, but I was shocked. There was less military presence than when I had visited Ireland with The Fall. Naively, I thought the troubles were basically over and differences were being sorted around a table.

Our ex-army driver pulled up, grabbed a baseball bat and ran off up the embankment in the dead of night looking for the 'terrorist', like some kind of action hero. When we reached the gig, he refused to leave the bus for two days in case anyone planted a bomb underneath. There had been a big explosion around the corner from our hotel on the Falls Road not long before. Our driver reckoned he had seen a circling BMW with two guys in hoodies inside, watching us.

Before the gig, Inder came into my room while I was watching Man United complete the treble, supersub Solskjaer snatching the unlikely victory in the dying seconds. Even Inder, who is no football fan, and from Leeds, celebrated the magical moment. Ian went on the stage singing a Georgie Best terrace anthem, and the good people of Belfast lapped it up.

We played a one-off show supporting Catatonia in Margam Park, Wales, before starting work on Ian's second solo album *Golden Greats* in London.

I flew down to Heathrow on my own - on a British Midland flight, following Ian's trouble with British Airways - and headed to the Halcyon Hotel in Holland Park which was ten minutes' walk from the studio. Ian was living in a nearby flat, opposite Hyde Park.

Me and Inder spent a lot of time in London hotels over the next eighteen months. We used to smoke and drink tea, and watch *Ready Steady Cook*, and sit there laughing at the camp and clumsy double entendres from presenter Ainsley Harriott. One morning as Inder and I went for breakfast, we were hit by a fug of cigar smoke and an extremely loud voice that I instantly recognised. It was the late great Sir David Frost, sat reading the papers, talking loudly to someone on his mobile. He gave us both a smile and boomed 'Good *Morning* Gentlemen', as if he was introducing a TV chat show.

Ian was already at Sarm West Studio at 11 a.m. when I arrived on the first day - he's a real stickler for punctuality - and introduced me to the programmer on the session, Dave McCracken. Hailing from Maryport in the northern Lakes, he had worked with the likes of the Spice Girls and Elton John and it was easy to see why. He could generate a pastiche of cool sonic soundscapes, underpinned by massive synth bass lines and samples like no one else I'd ever worked with. He did it lightning quick too. He would sit at his laptop set up just behind the huge mixing desk, manned by engineer Tim Wills, whilst his assistant Danny would scuttle around making brews and changing the tapes. Ian reckoned Dave looked like a miner at the coalface as he sat hunched over his screen. I knew what he meant - Dave just got stuck in.

There were no dramas or shouting matches either, as I'd been used to in the past. It was all really good-natured. Ian was well aware of the cost of Sarm West so kept things moving but I didn't feel it was rushed.

I got my first (and last!) full endorsement. Premier drums had sent over a brand new kit and a new set of Zildjian cymbals arrived which I had chosen the week before at their showroom in Windsor. All I had to do was use them on TV appearances. A load of gear used to go missing, though, and would just get replaced. Me and Inder used to laugh - we were sure someone from Ian's crew was flogging it off - but we never got to the bottom of it.

I got straight to work on 'Dolphins Were Monkeys' and 'Love Like a Fountain' for the first couple of days. We spent about a day just laying down drums on each track.

It felt good to be able to spend more time getting a quality recording of the drums on their own rather than the whole band playing at the same time and hoping for the best, like in The Fall.

Ian then said he wanted to work on a demo I'd given to him. Me and ex-Fall producer Mike Bennett had written the music the previous month at another studio in Warwickshire. This became the song 'Golden Gaze'.

I was knocked out when I heard how Dave had developed the song and with what Ian had come up with on vocals. It turned out to be one of the crowd's favourites during the gigs. I was really proud to be part of it.

Ian never used to show us any lyrics or have them sitting around in notebooks. In fact, I never saw him with any lyrics written down but he'd obviously been away working on them. This was in contrast to Mark who'd leave lyrics all over the studio. He used to have the tour manager carry around this heavy mahogany lectern so he could have his notes in front of his mic. Sometimes, when he went off to the pub, Steve, Craig, and I would sneak a look at them and try to figure out who they were about. It was like deciphering some kind of code.

On the second week down there, Sylvan was brought in to put his slinky bass down. Sylvan would sit in the studio lounge, waiting his turn, chatting to a girl he had invited along, pouring out fine wine and talking on his mobile in his suave plum tones.

I remember watching him sat on a couch in the control room, struggling for about ten minutes with the bass line for 'Love Like a Fountain'. Ian was perched on the arm of the settee, and started humming in Sylvan's ear.

'It goes like *this* ... then change to *this*.'

Sylvan picked it up straight away, nodding, playing more or less the finished article on the first pass. It all came together. It suddenly made sense. It's moments like this you live for as a musician.

Inder was brought in to put on his percussion parts after Sylvan was done. He had an array of Indian drums in addition to the usual percussionist's set-up. He showed me how to play the tabla, though I wasn't really a natural.

After the sessions, I used to eat down in the studio's restaurant in the evenings with Dave and Tim who introduced me to Baby Spice of the Spice Girls. Even though she was very young, she had a wise look about her. She was recording a cover of Edie Brickell's 'What I Am' at the time with producer Tin Tin Out. Dave and Baby Spice sat reminiscing about a previous session he'd done with the Spice Girls.

At midnightish, we all knocked it on the head until starting at 11 a.m. again. I would saunter back to my hotel for a nightcap or sometimes finish early and go to the pub on Portobello Road with Tim and Danny. Ian would always go back to his pad ready for the next day's work.

My dad's memory was really fading by now and he would ring me several times a day during the recordings to see when I was coming to visit. He couldn't understand why I hadn't been round that day.

'I'm in London, Dad, I won't be back until next week.'

'Oh I see,' he'd say. Then continue, confused, 'So what time will you be around? Have you had something to eat? What do you want for tea?'

'No,' I'd say, patiently, 'I'm in London. Jane will be round.'

In August, Sue, Emily, and I, took Dad on holiday to Cyprus for a week which was where he'd had one of his favourite holidays with Mum. Whilst we were there, there was a solar eclipse. I was listening to some rough mixes of album tracks and went outside to watch in anticipation, but it wasn't very spectacular in Cyprus. It can be, so I'm told, but this was just like the sun going behind the clouds for twenty minutes.

Apart from Dad's health, things seemed to be going great back then, watching Emily grow up, and I was never happier.

On the August Bank Holiday I went back to London to listen to mixes and in the evening we hung out at the Notting Hill Carnival which was a first for me. The place has always been iconic to me since The Clash days. It was really good fun.

The album *Golden Greats* was released soon after and got good reviews generally, and though I had only played on a few tracks (the rest were drum samples and loops), I was made up with the results. Of the albums I've worked on, it's the one that I'm most proud of being a part of.

26

Top of the Pops

September brought the start of a deluge of TV appearances in London to promote the first single 'Love like a Fountain.' I was finally on the kind of circuit I had wanted The Fall to rise to - credible pop shows.

We had a TV liaison officer, Jackie from Didsbury, who left nothing to chance. It was a bit like having a schoolteacher around though. *Where you going? What do you want to eat? You're on in 10 minutes* …you do know that? A bit corporate.

The label would arrange for me to get the shuttle from Manchester and be picked up by a chauffeur with my name on a placard at Heathrow. You know, me and all the other executives… I'd get taken straight to a hotel in the West End and meet up with Inder, who came in from Leeds, ready for the live broadcast the next day.

Much better than worrying about the tour manager getting sacked, or the crew refusing to work with the band or anything like that.

In November, I made my first appearance on *Top of the Pops*, which was a real milestone for me personally. By that time, *Top of The Pops* was on the decline, but it was a childhood ambition realised.

We later played live on the show, which I hadn't expected. We had to get down dead early to do the soundcheck.

'Bet Tina Turner doesn't have to do her own sound check,' Ian joked. The run through was important to Ian though because he'd copped a load of stick about his singing over the years with the Roses, especially since Reading in 1996.

The show was shot at Elstree Studios, next to the set of TV soap *East-Enders*, so Inder and I went for a nosey round Albert Square whilst we were waiting to be filmed. I've never watched *EastEnders* though to be honest, I'm more of a *Coronation Street* man.

After doing *Top of the Pops*, I just went back and sat in my hotel room on my own. It wasn't quite what I expected. With The Fall there would always be someone to go out with.

The whole experience wasn't rock 'n' roll, really. Everyone had families and lives to attend to each night. Ian started calling us the Papa Trio - 'Ian Brown and the Papa Trio' - because we all had young children.

But I couldn't complain - I wasn't a kid anymore. I was staying in nice hotels and doing the job I always wanted to do.

I went down to the bar. I got chatting to the guitarist and bass player from Wet Wet Wet who was looking pretty glum. Their singer, Marti Pellow, had just gone into rehab for alcohol and heroin problems. I didn't ask.

I went home and scored a couple of bags ...

The following week, the band appeared on the Jools Holland show at the BBC TV Centre. We had a new line-up of me, Dave, and Inder, now that Sylvan had moved on. It was an unusual set-up for a band, with just keyboards, percussion, me and Ian.

All the bass lines were now generated by Dave from his laptop on stage where he would also do bits of guitar.

Dave, for all his wizardry, didn't seem comfortable in the spotlight, playing live. He would go really quiet half an hour before we were due on and say he was sick with nerves, really uncomfortable. But once he got going, he was fine and it worked a treat.

More rehearsals in London followed before embarking on the UK leg of the *Golden Greats* tour, which took us well into December.

We looked like a football team when alighting from our tourbus at each stop in Adidas trainers and tracksuit tops. This was alright with me as I was a fan of the trainers ever since watching the World Cup in the early seventies. I was always wearing Sambas and Gazelles.

Gary, the Adidas rep, brought down boxes and boxes of free clobber and trainers to wear. The boxes would be dumped in the middle of the rehearsal room and we'd all jostle like hyenas over a carcass, ripping the boxes open to get the best stuff. I ended up with some dodgy gear in hindsight. I got this silver tracksuit which I looked ridiculous in ... I gave it to Aziz.

My drum roadie for the tour was an ex-Fall roadie called JT, who claimed he was related to the Duke of Wellington. I was dead pleased to see him - I hadn't seen him since the early nineties and I knew I could trust him. Plus, I had a mate to go out with again.

We did two gigs at the Manchester Apollo, where Sue, Emily, Ian, and I, drove down to the soundcheck together. It was the first time I'd played the Apollo. I'd been going since I was 15 and had so many great memories there. Now I was going to be on stage, under the lights, I was made up. At the soundcheck, Inder gave all the band members' kids a little shaker each to rattle as we practised. It didn't get much better than this.

The home crowd gave Ian a hero's welcome. He was well and truly back after his difficult period since the Roses' split. I was buzzing - I had just bought a house, I had a young daughter, I was on stage with my mate at the Apollo.

Later, I ran into Reni and his kids, taking Emily to a picture house in Stockport.

'Si! Saw your gig at the Apollo,' he said. 'Never seen you live before. Really good mate! I'm glad for you.'

I was happy to hear it after our last encounter, and from someone whose opinion on drumming I value.

Just before Christmas, I flew down to London again to record Michael Jackson's 'Billie Jean' as a b-side at The Town House studios. It was a great version of the classic song that could so easily have sounded crap, but the crowds loved it on the few occasions we played it. The only problem was, when I started it, the punters thought/hoped we were launching into 'I Am The Resurrection'.

The final night of the twentieth century was spent playing an outdoor arena in Manchester called the Castlefield basin where I had an argument with Ian's new manager, Steve, who just didn't seem to get along with me. You can't please everyone, I suppose.

We all retired to a hotel next to Granada Studios for a night of revelry and Sue was stunned when a bottle of champagne she was about to open, which we had salvaged off the abandoned rider, was snatched out of her hand by Ian's wife as we sat drinking in the lobby. It was a sour note to end a great year.

February brought the next single 'Dolphins Were Monkeys', which made it to number five in the charts. I was vaguely aware that the Internet had begun eating into music sales, so maybe it didn't mean as much, but I didn't even own a computer and was obliviously happy.

'Dolphins' was a real buzz to perform live. Ian had been inspired to write it after a visit to the Natural History Museum and the lyrics always made me chuckle. He used to get the crowd singing along and clapping and waving their hands to 'Dolphins' and I'd look over from the kit, with a wry smile. He was the same kid in front of the blackboard back at school.

More TV.

The Priory. Then back to the Riverside Theatre where *TFI Friday* was filmed, this time with our mate Paul Ryder from the Happy Mondays featured, miming bass guitar.

It was my turn to be self-conscious, miming the drums. A mate of mine had slagged me off something rotten after a mimed appearance doing 'Hit The North' years earlier.

The Pepsi Chart Show. All Saints were on the bill, performing 'Pure Shores'. It was another song that defined that time in my mind. Hardly the most rock and roll thing to admit, but what can I say, I'm a sucker for a pop song. William Orbit. Musically, it seemed that producers were now more important than the band.

And thinking about it, of the new music on the scene, I was mainly into heavily produced electronic stuff - Moby, Groove Armada, and the like.

More TV.

On *T4*, presenter Dermot O'Leary introduced Ian as 'King Scally'. Ian was shocked - he considered himself a family man, running a business. Sure, he prided himself on keeping the common touch, but you could tell he was fuming on the run through and made his feelings known to Dermot, who reappeared on air with a sheepish apology.

Ian was no longer the flared-jean, spray-painting agitator who had emerged from Hulme's early eighties bohemia, inspiring council estate hopefuls up and down the land to have a go. He was still an idealist and was still outspoken, but he was wiser through experience. He had been through bum contracts and band breakdown and now Polydor were re-creating him as a brand in his own right, he was determined that, this time, he was going keep what he had.

More gigs.

April, and a return to another iconic venue for me: the Hammersmith Palais - a venue well known for reggae nights and where, aged 17,

I nearly had my head kicked in by local security at a Clash gig, only to be saved by Topper Headon's drum roadie, Baker Glare.

Ian hired a reggae DJ for the gig, called Budgie, who span some great cuts, but he kept talking over all of them, toasting, which became comical after a while.

'*Respect* to Ian Brown.'

'Ian Brown: *respect*.'

'Big up! Ian Brown in the place…'

'*RrreESPECT!*'

He was having a ball anyway, old Budgie - he was about 60 - grinning ear to ear, five hundred quid richer, shouting like the battery had gone in his hearing aid.

In a club in Norwich, I left Ian holding court with his entourage as fans fawned over him, and wandered over to a bar on the other side of the club. A girl whose eye I kept seeming to catch, sauntered off the dance floor and slid beside me at the bar. The next thing I know, she starts chatting to me about how she'd just been to the Ian Brown gig.

Well. Funny you should say that …

I know I was wrong and selfish and it sounds pathetic but I just enjoyed having some female company, rather than sitting in the hotel, wishing there was a party somewhere.

It was the first and last time I cheated on Sue.

I got sussed when I bought two bottles of perfume - one for Sue and one for my new friend - in a Heathrow duty-free shop, lured in by a saleswoman who I recognised from the BBC fly-on-the-wall documentary *Airport*. I was meaning to give one bottle to Inder to mind for me until the next time I was in London but forgot and left them both in my luggage.

Back at home, I smoothly gave Sue a bottle of the perfume, but I quickly got found out when Sue went through my gear and found the other bottle.

'And whose is *this*?' she asked, accusingly, holding up the other perfume.

I was caught on the hop. She knew me too well. I crumbled and confessed to the affair - it was a fair cop. I promised it wouldn't happen again (and it didn't), but, as you can imagine, she never let me forget.

The next single was 'Golden Gaze'.

'You better hope it gets to number one, Si,' Ian said, as I was credited on it.

It didn't, but I am still proud of it.

And on with the tour.

Soon after, I got to go to Iceland for the first time, at a festival supporting Bloodhound Gang. We drove over the lunar-like landscape to visit popular tourist destination, the Blue Lagoon, a hot thermal lake that reeked of bad eggs in the cold afternoon air. Everybody jumped in except me and Martell, Ian's minder, as we didn't have our own trunks. We didn't fancy wearing the trunks they were hiring out.

As we watched our party from the little bar at the side of the lagoon, Martell was telling me he was nicknamed 'Parker' at school, after the shifty *Thunderbirds* character who chauffeured the sophisticated Lady Penelope. I burst out laughing. If you imagine a not so efficient Parker with dreadlocks and a Manc accent, that was Martell.

Later in June we did a date in New York at The Bowery Ballroom. Dennis and Lois, a couple who lived in Brooklyn and at that time were both about 60, came over for a chat. Dennis is a towering bloke and Lois is tiny. They used to watch all the British bands and were immortalised in a Happy Mondays track named after them. I was really glad to see them again. They asked, as usual, if there was anything they could do for us. They lent The Fall (after I'd left) a load of money to replace a vanload of stolen equipment - that's the sort of people they were. Great. Never grown up. Like me, I suppose.

Ian is a terrible driver.

While we were in LA, I hired a white Mustang convertible for a few days. Ian jumped behind the wheel outside the El Rey Theatre, going *yeah, let's have it, Si*, put his foot down … and slammed into the car behind. Loitering fans pissed themselves laughing as we drove off, trying our best to look cool, with the rear fender scraping along the road, Biggie Smalls blasting out of the system.

After the show at the El Rey, I took Martell to a lap-dancing bar on the Strip one night.

His eyes nearly popped out of his head.

Lap dance?

Yes m'lady.

The next day, me and Inder went shopping and ended up staying out a few hours. When we got back, Ian was nowhere to be found. He'd woken up and, as we had already left with the car, decided to go walkabout in shorts and a singlet in the searing heat. Eventually, in the evening, he walked in. He was badly sunburnt and none too pleased with the two of us for leaving him behind.

That night, I got smashed, alone, in a bar on the Strip and staggered back, stumbled into Inder's room and flopped on the bed like a starfish. Teetotal Ian stood looking over me, shaking his head at the state I was in.

I was probably overdoing it, and though it would have been about par for the course in The Fall, it didn't seem to sit well with Ian.

At the Quart Festival, we played support to a Noel-free Oasis, by the sea at Kristiansand in Norway, where I met Liam Gallagher for the first time.

Years before, me and Steve Hanley nearly ran him over in Burnage, just as Oasis was about to hit the big time. He was slowly bowling over the road, cocksure, as if daring us to hit him, come and have a go if you think you're hard enough. Liking our odds in this game of chicken, we sped up, nearly hitting him as he turned round shouting and screaming, offering us out. We were 100 yards up the road laughing our heads off.

Liam didn't seem bothered by the songsmith's absence. It was really hot and I spent a couple of hours chatting to him on a sun lounger on the wooden decking backstage. He was this larger than life character, some penniless kid straight out of Burnage, swaggering round with riches beyond his wildest dreams. He sat there holding court, mad for it, twizzling a gold ring around his finger with the letters TCB on it, like the ones Elvis used to have commissioned for his entourage.

'Yeah Si!' he's going, 'TCB! Taking Care of Business! Hey mate! Three more over here, please! Alright, love? What's that book yer reading there?'

I liked his love of life straight away, fed off his energy, and he had me in stitches the whole time. He was telling me about his problems back home with Patsy Kensit, but was in great spirits. Surprisingly, he remembered me from pictures in the *NME* from my days in The Fall. As I got up to leave, he stood up too, bowing repeatedly, shuffling backwards and rotating his hand as he doffed his imaginary cap.

Off we went to another festival on the global circuit. It was all change from the punk days.

At the Fuji Festival, I ran into Johnny Marr who was with his latest band The Healers. It was the first time I'd seen Johnny singing lead vocals. He seemed to be relishing the moment and I was glad for him.

It was perhaps the biggest gig I ever played, but not one of my best experiences.

During the huge gig on the main stage, Dave's computers crashed and didn't come back on for ten minutes. In the interim, Ian did his best to entertain the crowd, twirling a bamboo cane lantern around his head and assuming martial arts stances, the odd phrase in pidgin Japanese. Fair play to him - I disappeared. I found it embarrassing that we couldn't play without the aid of a computer. It was the longest ten minutes I can remember. I should have done a drum solo or something. *Coulda-woulda-shoulda.* I sat in the dressing room and waited until the fault was sorted out. It put a bit of a downer on the gig for me.

Elastica was on the same bill so I spent an afternoon catching up with Dave Bush and singer Justine.

The next day, me and Justine went around watching a few of the bands, checking out the stalls. Ian didn't seem too happy I was flitting in and out of the dressing room with her, doing coke, and drinking all the Moët from the rider.

In fact, Ian, who had steadily been making efforts to live a cleaner life-style over the years, was dead set against cocaine use and railed against it in the press.

Things came to a head in Spain.

At the soundcheck at the Benicassim festival during August, Ian started having a go at me, telling me to hit the drums harder as he couldn't hear me. There wasn't anything wrong with my drumming - it was like always, so I snapped back 'turn the fuckin' monitors up then'. This seemed to shock a lot of the crew who looked aghast that I had talked to Ian like that. But the thing was, I went to school with Ian, and it was the first time he'd ever shouted at me, I felt he was in the wrong.

I went back to my hotel room to cool off.

'Easy tiger,' whispered an on-looking Liam Gallagher as I passed by.

I watched a pre-season friendly between Man Utd and Real Madrid and, later that night, went to Primal Scream keyboard ace Martin Duffy's room and partied until the scorching sun came up.

Things seemed to get more and more frosty between me and Ian after this. That manager I didn't like started making dark mutterings about getting some mate on drums from a band called Menswear.

Little things seemed to get on Ian's nerves. One morning in London, waiting for a taxi from the hotel to Heathrow, the cab that the record company had sorted out didn't turn up, so the concierge flagged me one and put it on the hotel bill. I didn't think any more of it but the next time I saw Ian he wasn't happy.

It didn't help that we weren't socialising much when not on the road. Ian and Dave were in London and I was up in Manchester. Inder was in Leeds. All of us had young families, so when I went down to London, I was mainly just at a loose end, sat in the hotel bar striking up conversation with whoever was there, or watching TV in my room.

I went back home and to being a father. Sue worked part-time doing market research and I'd take care of Emily after nursery. The week after playing the Reading/Leeds festival, Emily started school at Altrincham CE behind St George's Church, a great little school. Her teachers said she was quiet but thoughtful towards others. I remember one week when she kept asking me to buy a birthday card for a dinner lady she would chat with - really sweet.

Mike Joyce's kids went to the same school, so we often had a chat, a couple of house husbands, about what we were up to at the school gates. One morning, Mike invited me to a recording session at Bonehead's house up in Bowdon where he was recording with ex-Oasis axeman's new band 'The Dogs', but nothing much came of it.

There weren't any more gigs or recordings going on with Ian until the end of November in Ireland, and on New Year's Eve at the Alexandra Palace in London, where he was headlining his own show, so I wondered what I was going to do for a while.

Earlier in the year, at the Homelands festival, we had been driven by a chauffeur named Roger, who owned his own limousine company. We got chatting whilst we waited for Martell to buy a book and I asked him if he had any work for me. He said yes he might do, so I gave him my number, and the next day he rang and asked if I would do a bit driving during the In The City music seminar. The event, held at The Midland Hotel in Manchester, paid good money and I might make some good contacts there for other drum work, so, as it was quiet with Ian, I said, OK, I'm in.

I had to hang around the reception area in the evenings, waiting to ferry the guest speakers such as producer, Arthur Baker, whose talk I went to hear, to the airport or train station. On the last night, I had to take Brian Eno and the late Factory supremo, Tony Wilson, to Piccadilly station as Brian was running late for the last train to London. Trying to break an awkward silence, I asked Tony if he remembered me. He said 'I remember your voice', which impressed me - I don't think I'd been in the same room as him since The Fall appeared on *The Other Side of Midnight* in 1988.

I did a couple more jobs but then it came to an end as quickly as it began. I was asked to drive actors from *Hollyoaks*, over to the club, Space, in Leeds, and then bring them back home. I waited outside for them all night despite them inviting me in, but when we arrived back in Cheshire, I broke the chauffeur's golden rule and socialised with them inside the house. I was only there for an hour but Roger never rang me again.

The taxi badge was up for renewal by now, so I thought I might make a change and be a van driver. I bought myself a little white van and started ringing courier firms for work.

Apart from a couple of gigs at the tail end of November, I hardly spoke to Ian at all for a couple of months. He was mainly in London with his new wife who didn't want to live in Ian's house in Lymm as it was too quiet.

The 'Papa Trio' reconvened in London for rehearsals for the final commitment of the *Golden Greats* tour on New Year's Eve at the Alexandra Palace, where Dave started playing the keyboard riff from a future release of Ian's 'The Fear'. I thought it sounded amazing and I really wanted to play on it, but it was not to be.

On the night of what would be my final gig with Ian, I didn't really feel like celebrating at all. I had a bad case of the end of tour blues - there were no plans to do anything after this gig. Or, at least, none I was privy to.

I was surprised to hear from Hughie our tour manager that my old employer, Mark E Smith, had been in touch and wanted to be put on the guest list for that night's show, as he obviously knew me. The gig came and went without incident, then, expecting Mark to enter the dressing room to say hello, I found out that Ian had scrubbed his name off the list. I don't think he had forgotten the incident back in 1987, when he had rudely been snubbed. Ian doesn't forget anything.

I would have liked to have spoken to Mark again, despite everything. We had spent an awful long time together, some really good times, and that night I needed an ally. Occasionally, I even missed a bit of the mayhem.

I had a glass of champagne but I didn't stay around for long as all our party vanished as soon as the gig was wrapped up. Inder was going to Leeds. Ian got off sharpish with his wife Fabiola - I had the impression she didn't like me at all. She wouldn't even look at me, let alone wish me a Happy New Year. I boarded the tourbus with John Ward, Ian's PA, and a couple of other crew members, lay down on my bunk and thought, 'was it something I said?' As we hit the M1, I fell asleep to the whirring prop shaft.

I was deposited with my suitcase on the main road running through Altrincham at breakfast time.

27

Ceremonies

There seemed to be an air of finality in regard to working with Ian again. No further gigs or studio sessions had been booked as far as I was aware. The blow up in Spain and the increasing distance between the two of us weighed on my mind, but neither Ian nor I was going to be the first to get in touch. We are both pretty stubborn people when we want to be. So for time being, I went back home to Sue and Emily, whilst visiting my dad most days, even if it was for only an hour or two.

It wasn't until a few months later whilst watching *Top of the Pops* at home that the fact I had definitely lost the gig was confirmed. A young girl appeared on the show sitting at the drum kit miming to 'The Fear' with a small string section in tow. It's one of my favourite songs of Ian's. It raised him to another level.

That same evening, I got a call off Chris Bridgett to see if I would drum for a girl called Jane Parker who was writing an album behind The Blue Cat bar in Stockport.

I was missing the drums and I suppose I had lost a bit of confidence, so grasped at the first opportunity that came along. Jane had a good voice and we rehearsed a couple of times a week for months, eventually doing a weekly residency in the bar every Wednesday for a month, but I soon lost interest in the project and jacked it in.

It seems in this pop game, one minute you're living like a king and the next minute you're down and out, Simon.

I married Sue on the last day of August. I just thought it was the right thing to do; we had a daughter and had been together for seven years. Maybe I'm a bit old fashioned like that. The wedding was not as manic as my first. We were wed at a simple ceremony at the registry office in Sale with a handful of guests.

Throughout that year I had thrown myself into the driving work. I had to put dreams about pop stardom aside.

By the time of the attack on the Twin Towers in New York, I was working for a company in Sharston, driving vanloads of mobile phones over to Milan and Copenhagen via the Channel Tunnel, twice a week. I didn't have the time or money to spend in rehearsal rooms looking for the next big thing.

The attack on the World Trade Center and the ripple effect on the global economy brought the end of that gig as freight sat in warehouses around the world, undelivered. I was last in and first out but soon found other work.

My dad was increasingly in the grip of Alzheimer's. The previous ten years, since my mum's death, he had slowly been in decline, though it was during this period I spent the most time with him. In the end, he seemed to come round to the idea of my drumming. He even offered to pay for studio sessions to record my own project, though I never got around to it.

One evening in February 2002, my sister rang me to say my dad had been admitted to Trafford General Hospital with breathing problems. It didn't sound good. I rushed over there as quick as I could to find Jane, who told me that she would stay the night on a sofa bed just off the ward, as she had been told by doctors he might not make it through the night. He had gone into an even steeper decline over the last six months and had appeared to give in to his battle with health some time ago. When I arrived, he was almost comatose on the bed with an oxygen mask on. Jane and I took turns sitting with him. He did open his eyes a few times and looked at us both, but there was nothing behind his gaze anymore and sadly he passed away aged 74, in the early hours of the morning, as Jane and I looked on.

I just thought how sad it was that Dad had lost my mum, whom he adored, just as he was about to retire. Then, after suffering a couple of minor strokes, he'd lived alone for the next ten years, making it quite clear that he would never want to be looked after in a nursing home under any circumstances.

I did at least feel good about the times we spent together in the last few years of his life, visiting with Emily, taking trips abroad, the drives out to country pubs or to see the in-laws in Anglesey. He was happy to be with me.

His last journey, to the crematorium, was in a burgundy-coloured Rolls Royce hearse, which I think he would have liked. There was a good turnout at the funeral, which pleased me, though it didn't surprise me - he was well liked as a doctor. His ashes were buried with my mother's in the garden of remembrance there, under an ash tree we had planted after she had gone in 1991.

After my dad's affairs had been sorted by Jane, his estate was divided up between me and my sister.

With that money and the sale of the house in Broadheath, Sue, Emily, and I, had enough cash to buy a terraced house in the middle of Altrincham. We moved there in the summer months after going to view the property on Osborne Road and buying it on the spot after falling in love with the place. The only regret I have is that I didn't insist on buying the place outright at the time.

I would stay here for the next ten years and made great friends with neighbours along the way, especially the tree surgeon over the road, Joe, who was a big music fan.

Despite my recent loss, it was a good life. Everything was on an even keel during this period. We went on holiday two or three times a year. I enjoyed walking with Emily down near the River Bollin, where I used to go as a kid, as well as the usual stuff: feeding the ducks, pushing her on the swings, watching the planes, going to the pictures.

I helped out chaperoning on a couple of school trips - museums and the like. One sports day I was defeated by Mike Joyce in the egg and spoon race.

Emily was doing well at school; she was already an avid reader in junior school.

Sue kept at me about starting up drum clinics or lessons in the local schools, where she had some contacts, but I never really went with it. Nothing seemed broken so I didn't try to fix it - just carried on as I was. I suppose I've always been one for an easy life.

While I was mainly working and being a family man, I did still cast about for drumming gigs.

During the summer of 2003, Adrian Flanagan, who I had bumped into whilst at a seminar, called round to Osborne Road and showed me how to write music on a computer I had just bought. Drum beat, fat squelchy synth bass, that sort of thing.

I hadn't seen Adrian since my final tour with The Fall, when he had been brought in on guitar. I hadn't realised the extent of his talents. He stayed over in the spare bedroom occasionally and would accompany me on some long road trips as the courier work kept coming. Adrian turned me on to a lot of great new sounds as we drove, including his mate Dean Honer's band, I Monster, who I had heard on the radio with 'Daydream in Blue', a great summery record, an adaptation of The Wallace Collection's 'Daydream'.

Adrian and I used my first PC to make beats and bass lines. They sounded really good. We got Martin Duffy down on a couple of tracks and later called on Happy Mondays' singer Rowetta to belt out some of her distinctive vocals, which I'd always been fond of.

We came up with a few songs with me playing live drums over what was on the computer. Rowetta sang on a tune called 'Stand Up (Be Counted)' which we rehearsed up at a Moolah Rouge in Stockport along with three or four others.

We played a short live set at the Night and Day Cafe on Oldham Street in Manchester. I put my new Ludwig Vistalite drum kit, which I'd just bought off John Rose Drums in Sale, through its paces. I had always wanted one of the see-through orange drum kits that were common on *Top of the Pops* in the seventies. John Bonham had one. Nobody turned up to the gig. It didn't matter to me though. I thought we sounded great.

We intended to do more with Rowetta and the band we had named 'Intruda' but she went onto *The X Factor* with Simon Cowell and scuppered my plans. She tends to split people down the middle, Rowetta, but I've always liked her and paid her to sing on another project I did with Mike Bennett called Spudgun. Her gospel vocals were the best thing on the song. She was well worth her fee, a real pro.

She told Mike once that Simon Cowell had said, weeks before the final, that the highest he could get her to place on the show was third. It confirmed for me that it was all a fix and most of the contestants on all these talent shows were here today, gone tomorrow, anyway.

There was a definite change in the music scene then. There didn't seem to be anyone coming through that I really liked, except maybe Just Jack.

Internet file sharing sites continued to eat into record sales and bands seemed to have to make their money from touring.

I felt left behind because I still wasn't Internet savvy, and plus I wasn't getting any younger. Not that that's completely a hindrance. They say music is a young man's game, but on the other hand, all this file sharing made for more live music than ever before. And this obviously favours established acts. It seems harder and harder for new bands to break through and have any sort of longevity.

I think it's carried though to today. There doesn't seem to be anyone saying anything. It's all very corporate, very safe, you know, lawyers, accountants.

I have been lucky to work with a few maverick frontmen. All very different. As I've said, I'm not really one for lyrics, but in hindsight, I took these songwriters for granted. I thought that was their job. The singer was going to have an original point of view, say something thought provoking and believe in it, even though it might upset people. Surely there must someone out there now, but I haven't heard them yet. They're being drowned out by all the celebrity bollocks.

28

I Monster

So. Erm, you know.

Smoking heroin.

When I had the time and the money and wasn't touring, I was still scoring. Mostly on my own. I never injected it, if that's any defence, which it isn't, but tell people you take that shit and they look at you as if you're the devil. Coke and MDMA and booze, it's all good time charlies. But heroin - people look at you differently. They stop calling.

Sue knew that I was doing it on the sly. She knew by my moods. She blamed the drug for me not drumming with Ian any more, given his stance on Class As. She may have been right. Not that I ever brought it up with Ian. I don't like confrontation or heart to hearts, and if I can avoid a difficult conversation, I will.

Eventually though, you have to have face facts. You can't bury your head forever.

You can drum, but you can't hide.

I suppose I could make all kinds of psychological explanations about my reasons for doing it: missing out on opportunities, missing the buzz of performing, or whatever. But I don't think any of that is really to blame. The thing is: *I just liked doing it*. I'd been dabbling in it since I was 19 - it was my medicine. Heroin's addictive qualities are well known, and the drug did call me back like a siren for another hit. It's a selfish drug in that regard. It does take good chunks of your life away.

Short bouts of calming euphoria and inspiration; where it felt as if everything was right with the world. Heightened sensory perception. It would give way to disturbing dreams as the drugs left your body and then feeling like shit the next day.

I was buying ten-quid bags, sometimes three or four times a week. That's not a lot for a heroin addiction, but it's still too much. I should have been putting the money away, for Emily, or virtually anything else.

Whilst I should never have started in the first place, I certainly carried on for too long, I know that. I was lucky or unlucky enough never to get caught. The thing is, I never thought it was that serious. We were never destitute and I believed I could get stop at any time. I suppose I sound like an addict. Anyway, that seemed to make it OK in my mind.

Finally, I just grew out of it. Not before time. I just thought; *this is ridiculous, I'm in my forties*. It began to trail off. Ironically, the dealers helped me out. The quality of the drug had been worsening as it was cut with 'bash' (a violin string resin, supposedly) and became less and less potent, helping to ween me off the drug.

The final nail in the coffin was when Sue told Emily that I was a heroin addict. She was 11 years old. My heart sank. I had actually all but stopped at that time, but I couldn't deny my past and the damage was done.

I wish Sue hadn't said that but maybe it was the wake-up call I needed.

I worry about the effect all of this has had on my mind. I don't remember some things like mates of mine seem to. It must have killed off some brain cells.

Maybe the drug created an illusion, but, despite my habit, it was a happy time with the family. I honestly feel that. We were still doing all the usual family things and I proudly watched Emily growing up.

In fact, the only real problem we seemed to have in those days was our next-door neighbours. A middle-aged couple moved in and proved to be genuine neighbours from hell.

One of the first the things they said when I met them, as I stood watching Emily playing with a friend down the street,was that they didn't like kids. I thought it wasn't the best decision to move into a cul-de-sac with a primary school at the bottom of it.

Sue and the woman next door really hated each other and would be having screaming matches on the doorstep. There was an incident with voodoo dolls being stuck to the fence, an attempted stabbing with an umbrella, a threat of assault with a frozen chicken ...

It was like being in The Fall.

For a couple of weeks, I was drumming down in the cellar, practising for an upcoming audition. I didn't think I was taking the piss - I was only playing for half an hour in the afternoon, dampening the skins with bed sheets and playing as quietly as I could. I thought I was being quite considerate. However, our neighbours got in touch with the council who planted noise level meters in her adjoining cellar so I had to stop.

Things escalated one Bonfire Night after we'd left Emily with a babysitter, for the first time ever. We both came back merry and I could see the woman next door staring at us through her bedroom window.

I shouted, ill-advised, admittedly, 'Piss off you nosey cow.' Twenty minutes later, a police riot van pulled up and four coppers started banging on our door.

'We've had a complaint from next door, we want a word with you Mr Wolstencroft, and we'd like to come in.'

'What complaint?'

'Threatening and abusive behaviour towards your neighbours and leaving a child unattended whilst you've been out drinking.'

I remonstrated with them that this was far from the case. I felt really pissed off, swore maybe once too often, and was arrested and taken away for the night.

As I lay there fuming in the cells at Altrincham a couple of hours later, I heard my wife protesting to someone at the duty sergeant's desk. Sue had been arrested too! Jane had been contacted to come round and look after Emily - god knows what must have been going through Emily's head. Sue was put in the cell next to mine, until we were both released in the morning without charge.

Thankfully, our neighbours moved out after two unpleasant years.

It wouldn't be the last dealings we had with the police whilst at Osborne Road, however.

I was still looking out for a gig through all this.

Adrian told me that I Monster were after a new drummer for a tour of France to promote their second album entitled *Neveroddoreven*. He set up a meeting at singer Dean's place in Sheffield with a view to me joining. I loved the new record and liked Dean straight away, so agreed to an audition a couple of weeks later, again in Sheffield.

I breezed through it and made the daily commute to south Yorkshire along the sunlit Snake Pass, for a couple of weeks to join Dean, Jarrod, the bass player, as well as French couple Fred and Marion from the band The Lovers, on guitar and vocals respectively.

The money wasn't brilliant but I thought there might be some legs in the gig.

The song 'Hey Mrs' was featured on a car advert in France, so I thought we might do alright. I was expecting full houses every night because the band's sophisticated sound was 'popular' over there, so Jarrod told me.

He was wrong. The TV advert hadn't provided much exposure for the band. People pay for cars, not music - not anymore anyway. It's sad to say, but some of the best sounds I hear these days are on TV adverts. And there's actually money in it.

Back to the tour.

Even though we were booked into small clubs every night, the thirty or so punters turning up just didn't get any larger as the tour progressed. This can be soul destroying, especially when you play a big city like Paris, but I was grateful to be on the payroll.

The promoter had the usual excuses.

'There'll probably be a big walk up ...'

'Oh, the students aren't back until next week, that'll be why.'

In a classic reaction to a poor-selling show, the promoter had put up posters on every lamp post between the hotel and the venue. It's an ongoing joke in the music game. Oh look, there's another poster - we must be *really* popular here. If you steered off the route, you wouldn't see one.

People think you're daft.

I kept to myself mostly on days off, though Marion was great company at dinner before each gig. I had never really travelled much in France and Marion would enthusiastically answer my questions about the country.

The best place was Marseilles. It felt different from the rest of France with its large North African immigrant community, its heat, and its Mediterranean feel. I love the sea. It stank a bit though - there was dog shit everywhere - but I liked the edginess of the place and the street food was amazing. But still hardly anyone turned up for the gig.

Back on Radio 2 in England, 'Hey Mrs' had been placed on the C-list for daytime play, but that's as good as it got. They may have been ahead of their time, with their electronica and ELO-tinged radio-friendly pop. 'Hey Mrs' sounded like something pop band The Hoosiers might do, but ten years earlier. Shame really.

As I Monster's new LP sank without a trace I had to decide what to do next. I didn't want to pack the music in, but I didn't know what else to do with it. Perhaps I was just too old, and I thought if this lot can't make it, what chance has anyone else got? I got a bit disillusioned with the whole thing to be honest. I've had my disappointments with the drumming, but this was the closest I came to hanging up my sticks.

I got an offer from Bez of the Happy Mondays to go in with him on a business venture opening a pie shop in town. Just pies. Manchester Pies, it was going to be called.

He already had a laundrette/dry cleaner called White Peg in the up and coming Northern Quarter on Tib Street, reckoned he was going to make a killing with all the yuppies moving in.

'Yeah Si,' he's going, 'get your clothes back wrapped up in the *proper tracing paper* and all that.'

I wasn't convinced and didn't want to sink twenty grand into a venture I wasn't sure about, so I declined the offer. Lou, the manager, told me years later that the laundry was a rock and roll hangout that ended up going bust, as most of the white powder in there didn't go in washing machines. It was more of a social thing than a commercial enterprise - even my old mate Eddie, the monitor engineer, got a job there, doing the ironing, and all I ever saw him wear was jeans, a rumpled T-shirt and a combat jacket.

So, for now, I went back to the van and got back in with the company who had laid me off shortly after 9/11. I began delivering mobile phones in Europe again.

I liked being back on the road. It was about as near as I was going to get to touring. I worked with some good lads as well, local tearaways. The drivers were mostly a great laugh. These vanloads of high value goods meant I had to share the driving with another guy and deliver the phones asap, passing through bandit country near the border in Italy, before we could book into a motel on the return journey and get some sleep.

It was non-stop. After driving home and resting in our own beds for a night, we'd be off somewhere else the next day and be halfway along the Channel tunnel by midnight.

The money was OK too, but one day when I'd returned to the office in Wythenshawe, another driver tipped me off about a pile of piss-sample bottles outside the boss's door. One of the other drivers had bubbled us for smoking a bit of hash whilst abroad.

When the boss asked me 'is it true, Simon?' I held my hands up, to which he replied, 'regrettably I'm going to have to let you go Simon, but I admire your honesty.'

Within six months he was back on the phone asking, 'How would you like to come back working for us?'

He was offering more money than the last time, but I didn't fancy going back for a third time.

Instead, I went to work for Clive who ran a small courier company, literally a stone's throw away from my back-garden gate. I had made deliveries for him when I was freelancing and we had got talking about music. He has been really good in accommodating my drumming around work over the years.

I began to play regularly with his covers band on the pub circuit round Sale and Altrincham under the name Intermittent Signal. The rehearsals took place in the warehouse next to the office and, as I didn't have a gig, I said yes, why not.

A lot of my mates said it was beneath me and whatever, but I didn't think so. I was glad I was doing something. At least I was still playing and keeping my hand in. If I don't play drums even for a couple of weeks I start to get the urge.

Inder kept in touch with me all through this period and whenever he was on tour with Ian in the UK, he would invite me along to shows. As I mentioned, with 'The Fear', Ian's profile seemed to go up a notch and I was really pleased for them both. I tried to go to as many shows as possible and say hello to Ian. As I went to more shows, we became good mates again. Time is a great healer etc.

29

Best Laid Plans

Meanwhile, things at home were about to change.

Four years on, and I'd hardly been out - working long hours on the courier job, looking after Emily, and playing the odd covers gig. Andy Rourke's Saturday night XFM radio show was the highlight of my week.

Emily had started at Altrincham Grammar School for Girls and Sue was now working as a special needs classroom assistant in Trafford.

One day, Sue brought home a CD from her colleague's son, Tom. Sue was quite insistent that I listened to the CD so she could report back to her workmate.

Johnny the guitarist, and Tom, had put together a three-track demo in their bedrooms. I liked what I heard. They sounded like a Californian rock band circa 1970, something like Quicksilver Messenger Service. I particularly liked Johnny's guitar work.

I told Sue to tell her friend that I was interested in the group and would do a session with them if they wanted. I didn't want to play covers, so it seemed as good an opportunity as any to try original material. I arranged to meet Tom, Johnny, and Matt the bass player, at a rehearsal room in Wythenshawe. After the session they asked me if I fancied being a permanent member of their band.

I agreed to give it a go. We worked on a thirty-minute set and did a few gigs in Manchester under the name Carpe Diem, which I didn't want to use as it is a well-used name, but it was their band, so I went with it. A mate of mine, Colin McGrath, had set up a recording studio, Swag-mantle, in his house and he told us to come over any time and record, no charge, he just liked doing it. It was a great offer and I advised the lads that they should not pass this up.

However, in hindsight, I think this was the beginning of the end of my marriage.

I'm not blaming the lads - it was my decision - but I spent more and more time recording, rehearsing, and playing after work. Having stopped the drugs, this was my new rush. It felt like I was coming out of hibernation. Sue, though, began to see this as a midlife crisis. But if that's the case, my whole life has been one long midlife crisis.

In addition to the band, to earn a few extra quid, I started to drive for Andy Rourke, who was now doing DJ gigs all around the country at small clubs and universities. It was only a couple of times a month but Andy was always great company. We treated it more like a night out than work. Rourky only had to do a couple of hours work, plug in his laptop and press play. Money for old rope I'd say.

Obviously, though, this meant more nights away from home.

After a couple of years, however, Andy suddenly told me he was moving lock, stock and barrel to New York to start a new life for himself. I was gutted to see him go but he got married over there and appears to be happy with his lot. I took the Carpe Diem lads to his farewell party to expose them to the wider Manchester scene, but as it ended up, I was unable to hold my drink again and they ended up looking after me and putting me in a taxi home.

Carpe Diem brought out the single 'How d'ya wanna do it?' and played a few gigs. The gigs were mainly attended by people the lads knew and we didn't stir much interest.

We did manage to get a break when Ian offered us a support slot for a couple of gigs he was doing at the 02 arenas in Sheffield and Leeds. The lads were over the moon and we got a reasonable reception with the crowd applauding enthusiastically - for a support band.

Once again, however, we were finding it very difficult to progress, just like so many new bands. I went to the In The City music conference in Manchester again, where there were companies offering services to get more downloads at a really cheap price. There was a talk on the so-called 'Pay to Play' culture and what could be done about it. I couldn't believe promoters were demanding that bands sell dozens of tickets before they would even let them play. Scandalous.

I just didn't get it.

I went and had a couple of pints in the bar with Pete Hook. It just seemed like a load of smooth-talking American guys after money to put you on their list for what didn't seem like much return. I naively still think that if the music's good enough it will find a way through. They were talking about digital marketing and whatever. I wasn't computer savvy. I still had to ask Emily to download tunes from her laptop and burn them onto CDs for me. She did her best to show me how to do it, but I always took too long and I'd end up asking Emily if she could just do it for me.

With the band often at our home, Emily showed an interest in playing drums, so I gave her a few lessons on an electronic kit at Clive's office. She was good - she could play simple beats like Michael Jackson's 'PYT' - if you can play that, you've got the funk. You're up and running. But I was too pushy and impatient to be a teacher. Unintentionally, I twice managed to make my daughter cry as I tried to show her how to play. Still, she had a good sense of timing, and I was proud of her. I hope I got that across.

Instead of the drums, and taking a leaf out my dad's book, I bought a kayak and took Emily out on the canal by Ye Olde No. 3, which was far more convivial than my tutoring sessions. Sometimes she'd just take a book along and read while I paddled.

Recessions, they say, make good business for divorce lawyers, and as the world lurched into its financial crisis, Sue and I were running out of money. Over the course of a few years, we had gradually eaten into the savings we had from the proceeds of my dad's estate and the property I had in Levenshulme. Sue now began nagging me to find a better paid job to keep us in the lifestyle we were accustomed to and stop messing around with bands that were going nowhere. And stop going out all the time.

I have been guilty, many times in my life, of burying my head in the sand, and hoping for the best. This was probably another. The thing was, I wasn't unhappy with my lot. It wasn't like there was no food on the table. For a number of years though, we had, like a lot of people, lived beyond our means. I just thought it was a simple matter of adjusting our budgeting.

But then, strange demands for money started to come in for loans I knew nothing about. Sue started to drink more heavily. She was increasingly annoyed at my very presence.

I again hoped things would sort themselves out, even though Sue was now calling the police to arrest me and accusing me of all sorts - using hard drugs, shagging around with groupies, assaulting her. No such thing was going on.

I had spent a couple of nights in the cells on the strength of Sue's accusations. I felt she was almost trying to goad me into hitting her.

The real loser in all of this, of course, was Emily, who retreated to her bedroom, and came downstairs less and less, as I set up camp on the sofa in the living room, for a year. I couldn't afford to move.

Things just got worse.

The final straw was one night when Sue started another fight with me.

I rang the police and Sue, seeing me ring them, said, well, she was going to call the cops too. So there we were, both ringing the police. Farcical.

I didn't want to do it, but I saw no other solution.

The police had been no strangers to our household in the previous years but, for the first time, they believed *my* side of the story. Sue was taken to the cells for the night. I hadn't wanted to see her locked up, but I felt I had run out of options.

As soon as Sue was taken away, I tried to have a discussion with Emily about what had happened, but she was having none of it. She went to her room and refused to speak to me.

She hardly spoke to me for two years.

The house was put up for sale and divorce proceedings began.

Despite this terrible home environment, I heard through my sister that Emily had passed all her GCSEs and decided to go to college. She had done summer work at a TV station, and was very into her music; she'd even had a gig review published. I was happy to hear it, but missed her terribly of course.

30

Full Circle

In 2011, as my marriage broke down, my past seemed to keep coming back to me.

A mate of mine rang me up one night out of the blue and said I had just been mentioned on *Mastermind*, with the question about who had played drums on the first Smiths recording - me!

It strengthened my resolve to try and write a memoir, though I'm sure, in fact I know, that I will have missed loads of stories along the way. A lot of things I remember vividly, but others seemed to have passed me by. Memory is a fickle thing. I'm 50 at the time of writing this and even if I had a good memory, a lot of these stories happened when I was as high as a kite.

A couple of months later, I got a tip that Mark E Smith was in the dressing room at the pub, Gullivers, in town, so I went to see him after a rehearsal. It had been fourteen years, I just wanted to say hello, see how he was doing.

It turned out that Mark was a fan of the band who were playing down-stairs, though it wasn't apparent, with him sitting alone in the dressing room, smoking, at a table with a pile of cans on it. He was a bit cagey at first and I remembered reading an article by Mark, where he said all ex-band members eventually want to see him again, it was just a matter of time.

He didn't disappoint.

'What do you want?'

The Fall were on something of an upturn in their popularity. I suppose they have never really gone away. They were playing small venues but to an appreciative crowd with a new generation of fans. They remain near the top of lists citing 'cult' and 'influential' bands.

I had no agenda with the visit.

'I've just come to see you Mark,' I said.

His mood lightened. He seemed to be okay with this and handed me, and my friend Sue Dean, a beer each from the huge pile. He seemed intrigued as to why I was with Karl Burn's ex.

'Where's your wife,' he continued, 'have you locked her in the shed?' He started cackling uncontrollably.

I told him no, Sue Dean was a good mate; she'd given me a settee to sleep on when my wife kicked me out. He was pleased to see me though, and I was pleased to see him. He'd not lost his sense of humour.

He asked me if I fancied going for a pint. I really wanted to, but I'd been to this rehearsal and I had a gig to go to early the next morning.

'What gig?' he said.

'In London, with Jez Kerr.'

'Jez who?' he replied. I explained that Jez was from A Certain Ratio, but he wasn't listening at this point. He gave me a look as if to say, why aren't you coming out you soft twat?

I wish I'd had more time to speak to him but said I was getting off. He pretended he hadn't heard me say I was leaving so I just had to walk off.

I saw Mark again the following year at the Frankfest gig in Manchester too, but only to nod at each other as we passed like ships in the night. He was on really good form that night with his latest band. I felt good about that. I'm amazed at how he's managed to keep it going

The gig with Jez had begun a couple of years earlier.

At a Carpe Diem gig, my mate Marc Hough aka Tin Tin, who I had invited along to see us, had come over and asked if he could have a word. Tin Tin, who DJs for New Order, tends to say precisely what he thinks.

His opening statement was, 'You're wasting your time with that lot.'

He asked if I'd be interested in joining a new band with Jez Kerr from A Certain Ratio. I was a fan of the band in the early eighties. I knew of Jez though I'd never met him before, despite The Fall and ACR having shared the same stage a few times over the years.

I agreed to meet up and give it a go.

As it transpired, Carpe Diem began to wind down anyway. Everyone just slowly lost interest.

So, gradually, I committed to Jez Kerr's project more and more.

We did a number of gigs and a couple of radio sessions with *BBC6 Music*. I really enjoyed the shows. The crowds were small, but we had a core of supporters from the off.

Jez is a great musician and has paid his dues over the years, and I respect what he does. He had quit his job with the post office and been on a course to learn the production side of things. I was glad to meet someone like me, who had stuck at it all these years; still enthusiastic and playing for the love even though he'd never had a big payday out of it either. As we were all seasoned players, the sessions went easily.

We approached a booking agent about getting more gigs but basically they said we were all too fucking old. Jez toyed with the idea of getting a younger girl guitarist or singer to join the line-up and bring down the average age of the band, but after auditioning three or four we gave up on the idea.

A few months later, although we had stopped auditioning for a female singer, Jez met Lis Murphy, and she came in on violin and, increasingly, vocals.

With Lis, the dynamic changed over night, in a good way. We renamed ourselves The Family Bizarre as we were all putting a fair bit of time into it by now.

Tin Tin, after quitting the group, decided to come back and we began working on tracks for our first album under the new moniker. We were coming up with good tunes - things like 'Hear You're Gonna Sell the World' and first single 'Freeka'.

We got a gig supporting New Order, but that was about as far as it went.

Meanwhile, The Stone Roses had announced a reunion, with three massive gigs in Heaton Park the next year. The city was abuzz with the news.

Ian had spoken to me months before about meeting up with John Squire at the funeral of Mani's mother, and how they got on really well, despite all that water under the bridge.

Still, I was shocked when he told me that the band were going to reform, and the ambitious plans for three nights at Heaton Park. I kept it under my hat.

Once the Roses' reunion press conference had aired on TV news, Ian rang me unexpectedly one teatime and invited me along to a gig that

Mick Jones from The Clash was performing on the *Justice Tonight* tour, in aid of the Hillsborough Justice Campaign for victims of the footballing tragedy. So off we went to the Ritz in Manchester. The Ritz has always been good to me.

Ian and John had been asked to perform 'Bank Robber', the same song Ian and Pete Garner had witnessed being recorded at Pluto Studios on Granby Row when they were teenagers. The backing band, which was made up of members of Liverpool band The Farm, was late, so Mick's bass player, Davo, asked me if I would fill in on drums during the soundcheck.

As I readied myself on the drum kit, I looked up to see a beaming John with a guitar slung round his neck and Ian smiling back at me.

Full circle.

I wondered if they knew just how happy a moment this was for me, bearing in mind I'd not seen John since the breakup of the Roses. I counted the lads in and launched into 'Bank Robber'. It just all seemed to fit together: John, Ian, The Clash. It sounded amazing. I came off the stage shaking with adrenaline. I don't think I'd felt as excited since I played at The Clash soundcheck when Topper Headon was late.

I was hoping the other drummer wasn't going to make the gig in time. I chanced my arm and started asking the monitor guy what time I was on, talking as if it was a done deal.

'I need quite a lot of kick drum in the wedge though mate.'

He looked the other way!

Ah well, it wasn't to be …

The atmosphere was fizzing though. It was the first time Ian and John had shared a stage since 1995. Backstage, I sat next to John who was prodding at the chicken and rice which Ian had laid on.

He leaned over conspiratorially, 'You can't tell if it's chicken or potato, can you?'

I had a chat with Mick in his dressing room about how new bands didn't get any chance to develop these days. I'd exchanged pleasantries with Mick back in the punk days but I'd never had a conversation with him before. He looked dead suave in his pinstripe suit, quaffing champagne. I asked him about recording 'Bank Robber', which he thought was at Strawberry, but I reminded him it was at Pluto. Memory you see. I'm not the only one. Mick was having a great time, laughing his head off he was.

Never meet your heroes they say, well, I found Mick to be an exception to the rule. We went back to the bar in the hotel and things become a bit blurry after that. It was a great night. I just wished someone had taken a photo of the Red Alert reunion.

Ian and I hadn't been this close since school days. Having been through a divorce of his own, I think he sympathised with my plight, now that Sue and I were living separate lives under the same roof. I appreciated his concern and his friendship.

He was really excited about going back on the road with the Roses.

He flew me and Inder, amongst others, to the Amsterdam gig to hang out with him for a couple of days which was really cool of him. This was the night that Ian had a go at Reni on stage, after Reni had walked out, moaning about the sound, before the gig had ended. A couple of people said to me, 'This might be your chance Si', but I knew that people wanted to see that iconic line-up, those four. There was never any chance. I wouldn't have felt comfortable. And deep down I felt there was no one in the drumming game who could fill Reni's shoes.

The big shows at Heaton Park arrived and I went along to all three of them, taking along my sister and niece, Hannah, to the Saturday night show. It was a very impressive production and I really felt proud of Ian stalking around the huge stage and bantering with the crowd. I was really pleased for them all, now they were making some huge money for the first time.

After the divorce, I carried on socialising, more and more, seeing a lot of my old mates and making new ones.

I would go out Thursday nights and play drums on any songs I knew during the Open Mic Night at a place called the Green Room in Altrincham. What first attracted me to the place was a large Mark Kennedy mosaic of Mark E Smith, in a chequered tank top, hanging on the back wall, staring back at you. I thought it was funny because Mark had always taken the piss out of the Cheshire market town with its Range Rovers and brown Labradors. 'You're all soft down there in Cheshire,' he would rant. Steve and I would just go along with the joke - you don't know what you're missing down on the Riviera, Mark.

I met up with different musicians every week to keep sharp. One kid called Corbyn, who was only 17, and a superb guitarist, was as good a player as anyone I've ever come across at that age.

I asked him into the studio to record three tracks for a side project with my mate Stuart called Haus Share. Corbyn had a great voice and was a first-rate programmer too. We used to go to his mum and dad's place up the road where he added harmonies and tweaked his layers of sonic guitar work. He would facilitate any ideas I had. He mixed in an airport passenger announcement and a 737 taking off, which I had recorded for the song 'Jet Plane'. It was good to have top-to-bottom creative input.

When we rang Corbyn a month later to restart the sessions, we couldn't get hold of him. Eventually, he got back in touch and told us that he had been diagnosed with a rare form of lymphoma.

We went to visit him a couple of times and his spirits seemed up as usual, but by November he took a turn for the worse and passed away just before Christmas. He was such a good kid and a phenomenal talent for his age. Corbyn Johnson, RIP.

He had written songs with a view to recording his own album which sadly never came to pass. As the end drew near, his dad said he had asked Corbyn how he felt about it all, and he just said, 'unfulfilled.'

People say to me that I've just missed out on this or that, but when you look at it, I haven't. Far from it. Life can be cruel. With all that could happen in the world, how could I consider myself unlucky in life?

31

Coda

Gazing out the window of my apartment, looking out over Old Trafford into the Stretford End, I cast my mind back to the other night.

Six months ago, my latest hope, The Family Bizarre, ended unexpectedly. Usual thing, internal politics. Etcetera, etcetera.

It can be a lot of effort for very little reward and it would be easy to think *I just can't be arsed with this anymore*. But quitting hasn't crossed my mind recently. I can't give up the drumming yet.

And as one door shuts, another opens.

A few months ago, I got a call from 808 State member Daz Partington. He asked me if I fancied joining his new band, Big Unit, talking it up, saying how they'd recently supported The Fall.

I wasn't bothered about supporting The Fall, but it sounded great - I agreed.

The last time I saw Mark E Smith, outside the Kings Arms in Salford, he'd heard I was working with the band.

'Keep your receipts with that lot, Simon,' he said, quick as a flash.

I had to smile.

Ultimately, I think I'm sanguine by nature. Always thinking there'll be a decent view around the bend.

A few days ago, we played the Ritz in Manchester, opening for Happy Mondays. As I said before, it's always been good to me that place.

I invited my daughter down to the show. Well, I invited her down to all the shows on our mini-tour. She agreed to come to the first one, so I said, oh, you'll have to come to the second one as well.

'I'll be the judge of that,' she replied jokingly. 'Depends whether you're any good or not!'

Fair play.

On the night, the audience is appreciative, but waiting for the main event.

The lights go up and before you can say 'encore' roadies have abandoned my kit at the back of the stage. I scramble, focussed, sweating in the dark, to retrieve my gear, when I hear her voice.

'Dad? Do you want some help?'

My heart stops for a second. Emily packs my kit away swiftly like an old hand. Amidst the chaos, I have an ally.

As fate would have it, the band has finally brought me and Emily together again.

Today, I feel happier than ever and appreciate the life I have led. I'm not proud of the drug abuse or the affairs, but what has happened, has happened. I'm fortunate, in some ways, to be alive, considering some of my earlier lifestyle choices.

Despite the missed opportunities, I feel I've lived the dream.

I have a beautiful daughter, great friends, and a gorgeous girlfriend, Lou Lou.

But most of all, I'm still excited by making music.

Emily returned for the next show.

Acknowledgements

I'd like to thank a number of people who have helped me with the book along the way. I'm sure I'll forget someone, so apologies in advance, but here goes.

Thanks to my co-writer Stuart Bisson-Foster, for helping me get all this down. And also to my girlfriend Louise Antoinette Watson for casting any tie-breaking votes when Stuart and I disagreed. Thanks to Gordon Biggins and Polly Polglase at Strata Books for helping me bring my story to fruition.

Marc 'Tin Tin' Hough, Judith Hey and Rebecca Weaver provided proof-reading, suggestions and enthusiasm, which was much appreciated in what can be a thankless task.

Thanks to the following for any assistance, advice, critiquing, encouragement, memories:

Mike Bennett, Andrew Berry, Chris Bridgett, Ian Brown, Dave Bush, Sarah Champion, Clive Churchward, Steve Devine, Jane Dawson, Tracey Donnelly, Tony Fletcher, Pete Garner, Steve Higginson, Mark Hoyle, Michelle Hussey, Mark Lever, Begona Lopez-Gurtubay, Inder Matharu, Ursula McClean, Colin McGrath, Eileen Mulligan, Joe Pollitt, John Robb, Andy Rourke, Craig Scanlon, Marcia Schofield, Brix Smith Start, Simon Spence, Alex Staszko, Matt Wardle, Gary Wilkinson and, finally, Uncle Eddie.

Thanks also to the people who maintain The Fall fan website, and their discography and gigography, a comprehensive site and a great cross-referencing tool that has saved me a lot of time.

I hope that the pupils at Altrincham Grammar make good use of my old kit.

Any mistakes are my own.